The publisher and the University of California Press
Foundation gratefully acknowledge the generous support of
the Ahmanson Foundation Endowment Fund in Humanities.

Static in the System

CALIFORNIA STUDIES IN MUSIC, SOUND, AND MEDIA

James Buhler and Jean Ma, Series Editors

Static in the System

Noise and the Soundscape of American Cinema Culture

Meredith C. Ward

UNIVERSITY OF CALIFORNIA PRESS

University of California Press, one of the most
distinguished university presses in the United States,
enriches lives around the world by advancing scholarship
in the humanities, social sciences, and natural sciences. Its
activities are supported by the UC Press Foundation and
by philanthropic contributions from individuals and
institutions. For more information, visit www.ucpress.edu.

University of California Press
Oakland, California

Library of Congress Cataloging-in-Publication Data

Names: Ward, Meredith C., 1981– author.
Title: Static in the system : noise and the soundscape of
    American cinema culture / Meredith C. Ward.
Description: Oakland, California : University of
    California Press, [2019] | Series: California studies in
    music, sound, and media ; 1 | Includes bibliographical
    references and index. |
Identifiers: LCCN 2018033917 (print) | LCCN 2018037844
    (ebook) | ISBN 9780520971196 (ebook) |
    ISBN 9780520299474 (cloth : alk. paper) |
    ISBN 9780520299481 (pbk. : alk. paper)
Subjects: LCSH: Motion picture theaters—United States. |
    Noise. | Motion picture audiences—United States.
Classification: LCC PN1993.5.U6 (ebook) |
    LCC PN1993.5.U6 W293 2019 (print) |
    DDC 791.43—dc23
LC record available at https://lccn.loc.gov/2018033917

Manufactured in the United States of America

28 27 26 25 24 23 22 21 20 19
10 9 8 7 6 5 4 3 2 1

Contents

Illustrations

Acknowledgments

I am truly grateful to the following mentors, colleagues, friends, and loved ones for making this book possible. Thank you to my graduate adviser Scott Curtis, who was my steady guide from the beginning of my days of graduate study and my active partner in the process of this project's creation. Its final form is owed in large part to his creativity and insight. Thank you to Jake Smith, who offered a generous and expansive perspective from an expert in sound. Thanks to Lynn Spigel, who served on my committee and whose impressive model of media historiography has always kept my methods clear, my ambition high, and my consideration of objects open. Thanks to Jeff Sconce, who taught me through his teaching and his conversation that what cultural and technological history shows us is rarely interesting without the consideration of why beliefs about technology would be held. Deep thanks to Jean Ma, James Lastra, and Raina Polivka for their feedback on this manuscript. Thanks especially to my talented and remarkable editors Jean Ma, Raina Polivka, and James Buhler for taking this adventure with me.

Thank you to all others who strengthened the project via their own labor, including archivists Barbara Hall and Robert Cushman, whose phenomenal assistance at the Margaret Herrick Library was marked by its generosity and efficacy. Their familiarity with the archives shaped my argument. Thank you to Tom Gunning and James Lastra, who commented on an earlier draft of chapter 1 at the Chicago Film Seminar and who provided me with excellent models of scholarship. Thank you to

Jonathan Sterne, whose model of scholarship offered me a vision of a book like this in the first place. Thank you to the Chicago Film Seminar for the opportunity to present my work and begin to develop these ideas, and to the Alice Kaplan Institute for the Humanities, who funded my research at the Academy of Motion Picture Arts and Sciences through their Mellon Research Grant. Thank you to Elizabeth Nathanson, Bernard Geoghegan, Mike Graziano, Gabriel Dor, Racquel Gates, Hollis Griffin, Catherine Clepper, Dave Gurney, Cary Elza, Jason Roberts, Brendan Kredell, Beth Corzo-Duchardt, and others, with whom I shared ideas while at Northwestern University. Thank you to Linda Delibero, my longtime friend and supervisor at Johns Hopkins University, whose support caused my research to thrive at a new academic home. Thank you to my students, both graduate and undergraduate, whose high level of engagement with material related to my research questions allowed me to think my ideas through during my years of teaching at Johns Hopkins. Some of their words appear here. Particular thanks are due to my mentees, who consistently challenge me with their own impressive brand of scholarship and artistry. Thank you to Eric Dientsfrey, Kyle Stine, and Danny Schwartz, who have developed some of these sound ideas with me since my arrival at JHU. Thank you to my outstanding copy editor Elisabeth Magnus, whose work improved the book.

Thank you on a more personal note to my mother and father, Pamela and Danny Ward. They have both given me so much. My mother's own curiosity as a polymathic academic gave me a model, and she has been a wise and thoughtful adviser as well as a loving mother. My father was the first to praise me for my work ethic and make me realize how important it is to love not only the product of your work but the process. I take pride in my love of this book, thanks to his example. Thank you to my siblings Stan and Susannah, who have supported me at each step of the way. Thank you to my mother-in-law, Ellen Dwyer, who knows what it is like to do historical research and write a book, for her moral and practical support throughout. Thank you to my husband Elliott Huntsman, whose steadfast love, practical support, and willingness to let this project come first in our lives when that was necessary have all made its completion possible. I am deeply thankful for his grounding presence in my life and the beautiful way he conducts our life together, from meals and hand-holding to good advice and real friendship. He has my love as well as my thanks. And last, thank you to my daughter Violet for making me a better writer by providing me with motivation, lighting up each day I have with her, and placing it all in perspective.

Introduction

*Noise and the Concept of the Cinema
Soundscape*

"So, what do you do?" I turn, still grasping the tongs from the cheese platter at a reception, and take a breath as I face the question. Or I bellow the response while waving my pear cider over the nearly tangible sound waves of overly loud music at a dim local bar. I answer it politely over the plate of asparagus at the walnut table at a very nice dinner party hosted by a friend. Sometimes I speak to it quickly while walking from place to place across campus with a new colleague, as we mutually attempt to explain just what it is we *do* before we arrive at a university event. Speaking about my research with friends, family, and new acquaintances, I often find myself having varying levels of conversation about the topic. If I do not believe the conversation will last long, I say that I write about cinema sound. If the conversation continues, I am often asked what I mean when I say this. When most people ask whether I write about the sounds of films, I say that I have done so. I also clarify that it is not really what I do.

All academics, of course, risk boring their listeners when they get too deep into their objects of study in conversation, and I keep an eye out for this. But I also watch for perplexity, which I feel I am more likely to need to combat. So, when I explain what I really study, I monitor where my listeners begin to resist the narrative. As I get deeper into the historical and cultural details of my objects of study, I see their expressions change, moving from a place of understanding and polite interest to a fracture of the social facade. "How is that cinema?" they ask. This story is not what they expected to hear. And then I begin an explanation, with animation and an awareness of the need for what I research and write about. I trace a network with my words and the delicate, excited gestures that I trace in the air with my fingers, often realizing I am doing so only once I have already begun. I am delineating its outlines: sketching the approach I see that we as a culture have taken to film through sound throughout the years. This is unfamiliar territory for most listeners. What I do, I explain, is think about the manner in which we have listened to cinema over time. And this is a necessary precursor to truly understanding film sound in a certain, far-reaching way at all. Film sound is an aspect of a broader culture. I think of the sounds of cinema environments, rather than cinema texts. I think about what we bring with us to the listening environment in terms of sonic predispositions and beliefs, and how that conditions the sounds we hear and the way in which we understand those sounds in cinema culture. I focus on how the history of cinema aligns with the history of American listening culture.

The aim of this book is to make my most profound and best explanation yet, to answer that deep and consistent question clearly: What, exactly, do you do with this research and why do you do it? The answer is that I do it to present readers with a rich alternative to the conventional history of film sound. It is one that focuses on the aural context of film culture in its multiple environments, especially the contexts in which we physically encounter films and hear them. My aim is to articulate how, and why, a broader network of components of American aural culture is necessary for relating the history of noise that occurs within film culture. This history of noise in cinema culture recounts how we have listened to cinema within its varied environments, and what forms that listening has taken. Also, it elucidates what kinds of strictures we have placed upon this understanding and where those originate in our culture. Cinema sound is under these circumstances not the films themselves but the sound culture that surrounds them and allows cinema to be heard in the way it is.

This entails a different method from the mainstream. Interdisciplinary in its focus, broad in its scope of historical and cultural analysis, and clear in its aims of pushing the envelope methodologically, this book looks to move the boundaries on how we explore the topic of film sound. I believe we can expand the scope of cinema's preexisting methodology of sound studies to include projects that help realign the axis along which we construct histories of sound in cinema. Widening the field on which we play and study allows the creation of a new type of history of cinema sound. This is what I do here. In connecting cinema sound in a systematic way to the wider world of sound in the public arts, the history of listening, the study of physics and electrical engineering, the study of acoustics and electro-acoustics, the history of technology, and the history of mobile listening, I map a constellation of forces that intimately connect media's sound historiography with the history of listening within specific moments. These efforts, ultimately, showcase how different forms of sound are connected within a broader culture and how that network of connections then finds a home in cinema culture. This scholarly practice allows us to think of cinema sound differently, as a category: of cinema as a culture in which sound has arrived in particular ways at particular times, emerging out of a meaningful confluence of aural cultural experiences. Cinema sound engages in creating a culture of silence and noise that tells us more than we might have imagined. In a mode of cultural sound studies rather than cinema studies alone, this work attempts to sketch that map, showing us where the fault lines are that mark the boundaries between "good" and "bad" listening.

This method builds upon previous methodologies. Among these are the study of the soundscape as a broader cultural term that allows us to map the sounds of a culture, the history of sound media, the history of listening in America, and cinema sound studies. The work I do here is not entirely new; its important antecedents are evident enough.[1] It draws on the excellent extant studies of the silent film era by scholars such as Rick Altman, the coming of film sound as analyzed by Donald Crafton, and histories of the aural culture of American society. In orientation, however, it is different from these works.

The goal of this work is, by example, to help create a small space for this type of sound work in cinema studies: one that is inspired by work on sound that ventures outside cinema studies. This includes work by sound studies scholar Jonathan Sterne, aural historian Emily Thompson, and film and media sound historian James Lastra, all of whom explore a broad range of sonic texts and contexts. It is similarly inspired by a growing range of texts on noise itself. Specifically, this new approach has to do with the way in which we align our sonic objects of study with the larger cinema culture. In analyzing the nature of noise in cinema and its relationship to what I call the American cinema soundscape, I assert the necessity of an expanded range of sounds that we think of as essential to the writing of film history. Noise, and sound proper, outside the realm of the text, become film sound too. The intervention that I pursue here, then, acknowledges the object of interest to be aural culture, a constellation of forces that constitute and create "cinema sound" in a much broader sense, and investigates a written aural history for cinema that emerges, not in its filmic texts, but in its far-reaching and varied aural-historical *contexts*. In what follows, the cinema soundscape that I analyze focuses on how we encounter motion pictures via the context of multiple forms of creation that bring motion pictures to us. These range from the exercise of creating environments for film exhibition to the industrial cultures of their creation. This book is engaged with how we listen to cinema—and how the construction of a sound culture around cinema creates that mode of listening.

I am also consistently interested in where the boundaries of an ideal culture of listening lie in cinema, and why, for reasons that extend beyond films themselves, they are set there; this is why noise, specifically, is a primary tool for me in my pursuit of the forms of listening that populate this book. I have chosen noise as a focusing device very consciously. Noise allows me to tell the sort of conflicted history that I need to relate to illustrate how the aural culture of cinema manifests its main concerns, and to explicate the issues of aural cultural tension that I have focused on within it. Noise answers many questions within cinema culture when we consider the matter carefully. How is the way we encounter cinema aurally conditioned? How do we know where the boundaries between good and bad sounds are set? The aim is for this book to be a provocative and thoroughgoing study of key moments in the history of two intertwined and neglected objects: noise, that little-understood but much-used term for many types of unwanted sound, and the sounds of cinema's aural contexts that have animated it over the course of its history.

These contexts include a broad range of sites in the history of American aurality in the moments that I study, including the history of modes of listening that, I will argue, turn out to be intermedial across these arts, ranging between and across media; the history of the development of technologies of cinema sound, and sound historiography; the history of acoustics and electro-acoustics; and practices of media use that carry some modes of listening across contexts. While each of these topics has been studied before, this particular mix forms a distinct constellation. My method is also uniquely suited to articulate the need for "soundscape studies" for cinema auditoriums—one that takes the environments of cinematic listening as soundscapes to be explored. Rather than focusing on what is conventionally within the discipline thought to be "cinema sound"—that is, the sound of cinema itself, or of the artworks in which sound appears, or even of film exhibition environments—this work delves into a wide range of disciplines, creating a map of the soundscape of the cinema house itself, the field of acoustical research and development, the rise of architectural acoustics in film culture, and the phenomenon of smartphone listening, as well as the range of sounds that emerge from these contexts. The soundscape of cinema, then, enfolds the entirety of not only purposeful sounds but also incidental forms of noise, the creation of sonic rules for listening, the cultivation of sonic aesthetics, and ways of listening that condition our experience of cinema, on the understanding that each of these affects the way we listen in the auditorium.

The history of noise in cinema culture is not yet generally discussed, but it is consistently present in film history: in the work at hand, it is like an ongoing, flowing river that runs under an inhabited and meticulously mapped city. The city is the established sound culture: this is the basis for our way of understanding our written film history. It maps out the history that we know. We know the structure of the city: its streets, intersections, buildings, and landmarks are familiar to us. We even have a sense of its soundscapes, the sounds that we can expect to hear on any given corner. But we are less familiar with the sounds from underground that trouble the soundscapes above them. The underground river, with its constant sounds, is the history of noise. This book draws the two into a tight relationship, identifying their connectedness: how the familiar map operated in deep conjunction with the underground noise that existed in relationship to it. What was happening under the pavement when a specific series of events was happening on the street? Its sound can be heard between the elements of film history we already know. It becomes audible at the interstices, where the gaps in the official history are clearest: when it echoes through the chinks. Its sound lies underneath the sounds we know, as a sort of white noise that we have often ignored—often because we did not know what to make of it. Though we have been listening to the sounds of films, we have not harkened to the subterranean river, with its sounds. It is the white noise underneath a much more familiar story. When we listen to it carefully, however, we hear what we generally try to filter out: what we did not wish to hear before, and what was considered extraneous to the story. This book thus functions to create a counterpoint to the more familiar history of sound *in* media: one that rounds out the richness and complexity of its entire soundscape, rather than just the sounds.

Throughout this project, I tasked myself, to the best of my ability, to call upon methodologies that lie outside media studies proper in order to analyze noise within that discipline. For that reason, cultural history, the history of the senses, urban history, anthropology, and the history of technology all feature prominently here. As a scholar who works specifically in the relationship between sound technology and cultural history, I find that the relations between sound technologies and our culture's ways of thinking about sound are especially vital to my project. My work, in this vein, relies upon media studies, sound studies, aural history, and aural culture. It draws upon the subfields of the history of electro-acoustics, the nineteenth-century study of the brain and the will, the history of etiquette at artistic performances, and the history of sound technology from transistor to podcast. I analyze how, and when, these factors interact with one another to produce a distinct approach to noise at many moments of cinema history. My mission is always to combine methodologies and produce a history that explicates how the soundscape of American cinema culture came to be. Noise defines where conflict appeared that strained the order. This work is not intended to fill in the gaps; rather, it attempts to identify a history that, despite being previously untouched, illuminates the one we already hear so clearly. It attempts an addition to the dominant threads of film sound history that assume these sonic meanings to be clearly codified as soundtrack, score—and the rest? Just noise.

The conditions that serve as the necessary determinants to how we listen, when, where, and with what understanding become, then, of the utmost importance in the service of the creation of a *different* cinema sound history: one that showcases cinema as *part* of that aural culture, as well as a specific aural field within itself, though it is in constant contact with the whole. This aural field is a site of tension. This culture is determined by listening traditions both within cinema and without it, sonic aesthetics borrowed from other art forms, enormous steps forward in sound technology and the need to adapt to those steps, and the birth and development of acoustical design, as well as changing ways of listening that emerge with cultural shifts.

The cinema soundscape emerges from a host of factors that we haven't often dealt with as cinema scholars and that we tend to see as outside the purview of cinema studies; these include the history of listening, aural culture, and the history of technology, broadly defined. In this, my vision of the soundscape owes a great deal to visions of scholars such as Sterne and Jonathan Crary, both of whom study how modes of art and technology fit into the epistemes of certain sensory formulations.[2] Elements of this soundscape emerge earlier than the birth of movies to inflect the beginning of film culture, and they continue in a modified form even as cinema changes. This book covers multiple moments when the soundscape coalesced into a particularly striking pattern. Each marks a particular turn when the soundscape changed markedly: from noisy to quiet audiences (in chapter 1), from nonsynchronized to synchronized sound (chapter 2), from imperfect to perfected auditorium acoustics (chapter 3), and from movie theater to city streets as our listening venue (chapter 4). Together these instances provide a context in which cinema culture can best be understood not only as the manifestation around an audiovisual art form but as an aural culture. Sounds, and the way they are heard, have a culture and a history. However, cinema culture has less often been considered within the realm of a broad definition of cultural sound studies: as an area of deep and thoroughgoing research into the *cultural* history of sound.

While a cultural study of film sound in the exhibition context has certainly been done before—most notably by Altman, whose *Silent Film Sound* serves as a benchmark for work that powerfully reconsiders cinema to be an *event* and not just a text—it has not yet been done in quite this way. This book finds its home at the intersection of sound media, historiography, and the history of listening. Listening to the soundscape of cinema and its rules, we begin to understand what investment people made in the social meanings of sound and the creation of cinema culture. We can examine how the social, political, cultural, and historical realities of the moment came to affect the manner in which a cinema culture could both sound and be heard by listeners. In short, here the soundscape of cinema culture—and not its sounds—showcases the ways we have invested cinema's sounds with meaning, and then policed that meaning, over time.

Noise has an important role to play in the cultivation of these meanings and in this construction of the soundscape. As a term that is often used in sound discourse, *noise* has had many definitions. Noise's role in my analysis of cinema culture is always to reveal the areas that are believed to be either inside or outside the bounds of the accepted and acceptable sound culture. To do this, I explore how noise has appeared in several different areas that combine to create film's sound culture. These include film exhibition; film technology; auditorium acoustics; and the history of aurality and mobile listening. The first chapter concerns film exhibition: the sounds of the audience. The second concerns the sphere of production—specifically, how noise has been defined, researched, and mediated by technologists. The third concerns the development of architectural acoustics, which determine the sound of films. The fourth considers the sphere of listening to media while we are moving privately, enacting our own rituals of listening within public space.

"Noise" has already been an evocative and provocative concept for cinema studies. But it needs to have this place acknowledged. Art and media historian Douglas Kahn speaks of noise as a site where "productive confusion" can occur, causing us to think carefully about something we cannot immediately grasp.[3] I take that stance to heart here. Noise here will always be the cue to let us know that something more is happening than we had believed within the historical moment under our study; it is an underlying indicator of tension and danger to the status quo.

NOISE

Calling sound "noise" is an act of judgment with sonic, social, and aesthetic ramifications. In making such a differentiation, one acts to classify certain sounds and their makers as undesirable. The etymology of noise itself implies negative responses. Latin roots for the term can be traced back to "nausea," "disgust, annoyance," or "discomfort." Another etymological theory traces it from the Old French *noxia*, meaning, "hurting, injury [or] damage."[4] Philosopher and musician Paul Hegarty writes: "Noise is negative: it is unwanted, other, not something ordered." It is defined by what it is not: "not acceptable sound, not music, not valid, not a message or a meaning."[5] As sound studies scholar Caleb Kelly puts it, "Noise is often heard as excessive and transgressive," or "loud and disruptive."[6] Marxist philosopher Jacques Attali writes: "Noise has always been experienced as destruction, disorder, dirt, pollution, an aggression against the code-structuring messages."[7] However, as philosopher Michel Serres writes, "We must keep the word noise." It is, after all, "the only positive word that we have to describe a state that we always describe negatively."[8] The positive aspects, and generative aspects, of a category that is always thought of in terms of negative and destructive characteristics are key to the study I do within this book. Thinking of noise as positive is a hallmark of certain recent forms of sound scholarship.[9]

Noise is, in this context, bound up with conflicts that occur on the level of the social order. Attali makes this assertion in his work, stating that noise serves as an expression of power relations in a society, connecting sounds heard with struggles being fought. As Hegarty puts it, "Noise is not an objective fact."[10] And as Kelly writes, "The perception of noise occurs in relation to a historical, geographical, and culturally located subject, one whose listening" is grounded in the context of a social order, a power structure, and a historical moment.[11] What constitutes noise, and who is making it, are rooted in the social positions of those involved, their relative power within the social order, and the dynamics that control their interactions. This is true in cinema culture just as it is in our general aural culture. "Noise needs a listener" to make it noise.[12] It cannot exist as a category independent of dynamics of power. As Kahn writes: "Whether noise is happening or not will depend also on the source of what is being called noise—who the producer is, when and where, and how it impinges on the perceiver of noise."[13] Noise is a situated phenomenon. As Attali puts it, noise "does not exist in itself, but only in relation to a system within which it is inscribed"; this is a system of "emitter, transmitter, [and] receiver," and each of these has a part to play in determining whether a specific sound is, indeed, noise.[14] Noise tells us more about its listeners, then, than it does about itself. The category is fluid and may be filled with whatever concerns animate the moment. Noise's presence in each moment analyzed by this book is always an indicator of a conflict larger and more complex than just the immediate sonic scenario. Acoustically, noise is a mess, but the play for power and control that is evident in the ability to assign the category of noise to a sound? That matter is crystal clear and readable through history.

I am consistently engaged with how listening itself was constructed and conceived of. Examples of noise in cinema culture push the boundaries, making the lines that it creates visible. What was considered to be ideal? And what agendas did these ideals serve? The form of listening that has been considered to be ideal at different points in history varies widely; part of what this project does is to draw these moments together and place them in the meaningful and illustrative context of each other. This allows one to see how models of listening have become dominant (and then have passed away into obscurity) in cinema culture. Two of the *most* dominant are musical listening, a public model of listening that encourages transcendent absorptive attentiveness, and listening to cinema as if one were in social space, either on the street or in other forms of public social environments. There are, in short, trends, and they can now be seen, identified, and classified. This too enables a new approach to writing the history of cinema sound as a phenomenon that can be described only as an aural culture.

THE SOUNDSCAPE

This book considers cinema's venues as soundscapes. In 1977, Canadian composer R. Murray Schafer coined the term *soundscape*.[15] An aural analogue to the landscape, the soundscape, Schafer writes, is the sound of a place: the acoustic ecology in which we live and are embedded, whether we realize it or not. The soundscape reflects the geography and natural environment, as well as the effects of the politics, history, and culture of that environment. As sound artist Marina Guzzy writes, "Sound, when understood as an environment, is a *soundscape:* a powerful tool that helps humans relate to their surroundings. They can be consciously designed by an individual or group of individuals, or the byproduct of historical, political, and cultural circumstances."[16] She writes: "Soundscapes define communities—their boundaries, their actors, their geographic intricacies, and industries." The soundscape, Schafer originally argued, went beyond a mere assortment of sounds; it was an ecology of them that created its own ecosystem. The fundamental question asked by Schafer's invention was: "What is the relationship between man and the sounds of his environment, and what happens when those sounds change?"[17] Listening to the sounds of the world around us, Schafer argued, we can tell a great deal about what occurs within it. Sounds, when properly attended to, offer a way to read the space to which we are listening. In identifying the sounds that are characteristic of a space, we are able to tell a great deal about that environment: its sonic priorities and its sound culture.

Of course, Schafer's focus was not that of this work. Schafer was committed to using this understanding of an acoustic environment to determine the relative health of a social space—whether it suffered from sound pollution and whether it was "beautiful" or healthful or not. This book takes the concept of soundscape to quite a different place—one that operates on the level of social analysis. Our society is motion picture culture. When we listen to the soundscape there with the kind of attentive hearing that Schafer suggested with his concept of "ear cleaning," we can begin to make stronger, finer distinctions in our aural analysis of cinema culture. The soundscape is a powerful tool for analyzing. What follows in these chapters, then, is an analysis of how attempts to control noise actually define cinema's soundscape—and how the strains within its aural culture have manifested in motion picture environments.

OUTLINE OF THIS BOOK

This book selects four significant moments in noise within American cinema culture and traces them through historical analysis of the factors that went into constituting the soundscape during that time. Each historical moment comes at a turning point in the history of the American soundscape. The first arrives at the beginning of modern cinema, in the 1910s. The second comes with the widespread adoption and standardization of film sound. The third comes with the midcentury refining of the movie theater's acoustics as a tool for crafting silence. And the last comes at the moment when cinema culture is becoming something else that is much more hybrid with other technologies of listening. For each moment, I explicate how noise presents us with the vital sonic conflicts that were animating film culture. I also explore how noise in each moment provided a keener sense of the tensions in that area of film culture. The chapters of this work trace the evident connections between the cultural scenario in which film culture finds itself at any given moment and the definition of "noise" that arises within cinema culture at that moment. In each instance, cinema negotiates a perceived threat—a threat that takes different forms—to maintain order. In each case, tensions in the soundscape of cinema culture become apparent, complete with their formative conflicts, in the noise discourse.

Often, the story told within each chapter to describe the creation of a soundscape begins *before* this historical moment. This gesture shows that cinema always participates in a genealogy of sound cultures before itself.

In chapter 1, cinema's middle-class reformers create a moviegoing etiquette that mandates quiet in order to quell what they call salacious audience noise. This chapter makes the conflict over the audience's social and sexualized noise in cinema houses in the early period of film exhibition audible. It details the rise of silence among audiences around 1912 and traces where it came from culturally, detailing how a growing culture of public silence came to affect the soundscape of cinema. It explores how cinema manifested, but did not originate, the "aural etiquette" of the silent spectator, which in fact arose as a result of an increasingly normative "constellation of silence" in late nineteenth and early twentieth-century aural culture. It also describes how the maintenance of such a constellation of silence had implications that were classed and gendered: audience noise was categorized as working class and sexualized in the trade press. This chapter, then, takes the now-familiar moment of the rise of feature film and the concretization of audience norms as it has been brilliantly described in the works of Miriam Hansen and Tom Gunning and reads it through the lens of not visual but aural culture.

Chapter 2 explores how noise became a major topic of study in the film industry at the Academy of Motion Picture Arts and Sciences (AMPAS) in the late 1920s and early 1930s, inspired by the concept's life within science and engineering companies. I focus particularly on the significance that Bell Laboratories placed on the subject and how this pet subject became a project of vital importance to AMPAS at the moment of the film sound transition. Tracing the origin of the development of the study of noise at Bell Labs and AT&T, I then follow that phenomenon to Los Angeles along with the sound engineers, where the film studios developed a research strategy very similar to that of their electro-acoustical partners. AMPAS, motivated by a desire to guide their industry during a frightening time of technological change, began to mimic its electro-acoustical partners by developing a specialized study of noise. Creating and then sharing among the studios a "secret" about sound, based in a body of research and in a tradition already started with Bell Labs, AMPAS allowed Hollywood to keep its autonomy during the shift to film sound. Noise, as the focal point of a mission to replicate the labs' structures for innovations, served a purpose true to its role in scientific history: to reveal a secret in sound well worth knowing. This chapter, perhaps most of all, acknowledges that noise does not exist as a category until we quantify it and define it, develop methods to identify it, and at times attempt to eradicate it.

In chapter 3, noise presents itself as a specter that haunts the ideal of absorbed listening we have sought to achieve throughout two centuries, in different architectures designed for different art forms. Noise appears, in this context, as an enemy to listeners attempting to escape it, and also as a motivating factor in the rise of architectural acoustics, which, as I will argue, invites a pure interaction with sounds that comes not merely from film culture but from an earlier culture: that of musical listening. Chapter 3, then, turns to the creation of listening environments designed to perfect a spectator's experience of film. Applying the study of acoustics to the noise problem, this discussion examines how certain movie theaters created environments of silence that encouraged exciting sensations of aural transport. Thinking also of historical models of listening and how they align with modes of spectatorship and understandings of architecture, I work to combine acoustics, noise, and listening into one way of conceiving of the cinema spectator's presence and the dangerous noise that it presents.

In chapter 4, my argument arrives at the noise of our present-day cities and the listening technologies that we use to sonically manage what we do and do not wish to hear. Crafting scenarios in which we listen to our media as we travel along a city street or in other public spaces, we have begun to use audiovisual media in ways that correlate clearly with how we have used mobile listening technologies for decades. This chapter examines how noise, in the twenty-first century, becomes a matter for our personal negotiation. We are armed with personal mobile devices that allow us to engage with films not in conventional, brick-and-mortar contexts, as in the previous chapters, but on small screens of our own, and on the move. We listen now over earbuds, everywhere we like. Rather than having a rarified experience of pure concentration, we employ tactics of negotiation, navigating public space with a device that is used to differentiate sound (our media) from noise (the sounds of the public space). And we do this in a manner that echoes the history of audio technologies more than that of visual ones.

This book outlines the creation and maintenance of the cinema soundscape, as well as its current boundaries. It ends by speculating where this soundscape might be headed in an era in which cinema is changing profoundly. Throughout this work, I address how the cinema soundscape has been inflected by the listening mores of a broader American soundscape, including the life of the other public arts, interactions with the sounds of budding technology, engineering's influence that tends us toward silence in our approach to art, and our current use of cinema media to sift out a desired signal from our noisy experiences of the public realm. Noise becomes our best friend in this often very complex search. It is key to identifying the greater tensions that create the soundscape, tracing where and why they occur, and identifying the ways we have tried to resolve them. Noise can be—and has already been—a rich, challenging, and productive concept in film studies. But it has also been understudied. It deserves to be acknowledged as a real marker of cinema's aural culture's meanings. Finding coherence in the chaos of film sound's history throughout this book, this work aims to make the place of noise clear. Noise is a sign of alterity—of differences in gender, class, modes of listening, and listening cultures within cinema culture. Noise, as the category of undesired sound under which anything may be classified depending on the cultural context, may tell us as much or more about cinema culture than the more properly formed category of the soundtrack. Exploring a soundscape, we discover the subterranean meanings that noise points to in our cinema sound culture of the past century. We explicitly consider the aural culture that surrounds cinema to be the largest component of the history we are telling. We listen to the subterranean undercurrents of the river as they join. In so doing, we begin to consider noise and the cinema soundscape.

CHAPTER I

Songs of the Sonic Body

Noise and the Sounds of Early Motion
Picture Audiences

We may wish we could hear the sounds of an early cinema auditorium. Few, however, would ever have thought to record the sounds of a motion picture's accompaniment, much less those of the motion picture house. The sounds of the audience have never been deemed to have any such significance. But the historian who devotedly wishes for what few have wished for is in luck: what exists are accounts of these sounds. These accounts emerged in the motion picture trade press, to describe and then, later, police noisy behaviors within the nickelodeon. Through them, the soundscape of the early cinema era comes to life. We can form the soundscape that we lack in audio recordings through words. Drawing together specific examples from *Moving Picture World* from 1908 to 1912, we may draw a scene in this way.

The slim teenaged girl moves quietly through the crowded room to reach the old piano that graces the front of the house. She tucks her hair behind her ear, and for a moment she just listens. Her surroundings are overwhelming: the room is hot and overcrowded. Most of all, it is noisy. Everyone has gathered here for the moving picture show. As they wait for the show, they fill the room to the brim with conversation, laughter, and, tonight, the sounds of flirtation. Several girls she knows giggle loudly, performatively, so that people notice, as boys she does not know whisper in their ears. She could be out there among them, but tonight she is working. She sits on the stool and glances over her shoulder. Her boyfriend is there, smiling broadly in the front row. He calls out to her by name; she smiles and gestures quietly but does not respond out loud. It is showtime. The sounds of the environment swirl all about the girl pianist: a tornado that fills her mind and distracts her. She can almost feel the sounds, they are so pervasive. She listens for a moment, with her eyes closed. She attempts to block the sounds out, focusing in on the task at hand. She readies her fingers to play and strikes the keys. The sound of the audience continues around her, and it does not stop for the entire show.[1]

The sounds of the socially engaged cinema audience were part of the soundscape of the movie house from its inception in the United States. This chapter argues that a social conflict over the body played out in the sounds made by spectators in moving picture venues from 1895 through the first decade of the 1900s. The cinema house became a site of a debate over noise, class, gender, and the body. The cinema house, as a result of the presence of what I call the "sonic body"—a body that makes itself heard and felt within social space—had a complex and indeed even corporeal soundscape, full of the sounds of spectators going about their social, embodied, and even sexual business during film screenings. These sounds died down rather quickly in the early 1910s. Media historians have accounted for this mostly by citing the changing class structure of the audience. While this is accurate, the work already done underemphasizes the strong connections between noise and class that were at work in the debate. I will take quite a different tack here, arguing that the change in the cinema soundscape was equally, if not more, linked to a changing understanding of how the body should be heard within public space—and especially the space of entertainments. The quieting that we experienced in film culture in the 1910s was not unique to film culture. Appealing to a broader explanation that goes *beyond* class in cinema as its primary indicator, I arrive at a solution that is connected to a broader aural culture that was manifesting these problems at the same time as, and just before, cinema's great "turn to silence."

By 1912, a shift had definitely occurred. Certain classed and gendered associations with noise had to be excised from the soundscape of the cinema theater. For this change to be enacted, the sounds of certain classes and genders needed to be quieted within the soundscape. These sounds stopped nearly altogether in cinemas in white, middle-class American communities. And with the rise of white, middle-class mores in viewing etiquette, silence began to reign over the picture houses. Understanding why the quieting occurred reveals certain tensions within film culture. It indicates where sounds that were deemed noises began to challenge boundaries, and it reveals cinema culture's relationship to the power dynamics of the culture that gave birth to them. Listening to these sounds, we can see what social distinctions this new aural etiquette of the cinema house sought to reinforce, and what ties it had to a greater aural etiquette that governed the culture at the time.

Several moral panics marked early motion picture culture. One centered on sexuality and the body. It resulted in some notable policing of the nickelodeon environment in which people experienced motion pictures. Another centered on audience noise and its associations with a lower economic class of spectator. It resulted in the imposition of a new form of projection and musical accompaniment, which led to greater audience concentration on the film. We will cover both developments briefly at the top of this chapter in order to ground our sound analysis that follows. Aural culture is rarely discussed as an aspect of these moral panics expressed in the varied *sounds* of moviegoing: the way cinema's sound culture combined concerns about class and sexuality. It was a problem of aural culture, and it was dealt with via aural culture through the cultivation of a sonic etiquette. This soundscape, I argue here, manifested many of the same cultural anxieties regarding gender and sexuality that we are more familiar with in a more conventional film historical context.

With regard to the moral panic centered on the body and sexuality, many film historians have written about the anxiety produced by the presence of spectators' bodies in the dark.[2] This might be expressed in an anxiety over crime, but more often it was expressed in the form of a need to police sexual behaviors at the cinema house, and particularly the desire to protect women moviegoers from sexual threat. The concerns among early twentieth-century reformers that movie theaters were becoming recruiting grounds for "white slavers" provide a clear example of this impulse, as does the discourse on "mashers" who accosted women in the theater. Further, as Jan Olsson has shown, debates over the threats that cinema houses posed to public health and sexual safety focused specifically on the bodies of female spectators.[3] According to cinema reformer Anna S. Richardson, "The principal objection to the dark theater lies in the opportunity afforded for improper acts, verging on immoral, or at least tending in that direction."[4] Film scenario writer W. H. Kitchell similarly asserted, "There is no excuse for a dark house where unimaginable evils may flourish."[5] In response, the Motion Picture Patents Company proposed brighter lighting—what they called "daylight projection"—to "offset illicit activities."[6] Daylight projection made a visual "cleanup" of the movie house possible. Different measures would be necessary for an aural cleanup.

The second moral panic was associated with noise and economic class among cinema audiences. Early cinema audiences were varied in their class identifications, as I will detail later in the chapter, and all classes of audiences tended toward noise. However, cinema's modes of audience address were certainly associated with entertainments of the lower class, and these modes of address encouraged rowdy and raucous audience response. Rick Altman has detailed the "gentrification" of early cinema auditoriums' soundscapes, stating that the standardization of musical accompaniment did a great deal to enforce newly established norms of audience's aesthetic absorption. This was, as he states, in keeping with a growing early 1910s middle-class ideal of absorption in narrative. Altman compares early cinema's soundscape to that of "beer gardens, minstrel shows, Chautauquas, amusement parks, Wild West shows, burlesque, vaudeville, and melodrama," where spectators "were expected to laugh, to sing, to speak."[7] This culture, he argues, was reformed in the early years of the 1910s, when movie houses stopped providing occasions that overtly invited audience participation—for example, banishing "illustrated songs," songs played to accompany slides that represented the actions in the songs and displayed printed lyrics whose choruses the spectators were encouraged to sing.[8] Referring to the early cinema soundscape as "carnivalesque," Altman states that "reformers— of morals and music alike—at first offered simplification as a solution: limit the soundscape to a single sound source, standardize sound practices, gentrify sound choices."[9] "Well-chosen music," they concluded, "would have a desirable silencing effect on the audience."[10] Altman, like many film historians, focuses on the changing nature of cinema audiences with regard to class. Standardization came along with legitimation, and "In a sense, it was the campaign to standardize sound in the early 1910s that first turned cinema into an audiovisual medium, long before Hollywood's conversion to synchronized recorded sound."[11] However, visual tactics of reform and narrative/exhibition tactics of control are just one part of the story.

So while conflicts raged about the necessity of lighting film theaters to keep "mashers" from soliciting women, and while cinema was gentrifying, the two matters of sex and class came together through sound in a way that has never been explored in film studies. The sounds of the cinema house's depravity were dealt with by the trade press. However, these sounds—and the cultural connections that they suggested and held—have mostly faded from memory. In part, this is because they did not last for very long in their original and intense form.

This chapter argues for a new, and significantly more socially and corporally grounded, explanation of what is generally called the "turn to silence" in American white, middle-class cinema audiences in the early 1910s. It is grounded in the body, which the extant literature by cinema historians tends to neglect in favor of the film text and exhibition practices. Film historians are familiar with the turn to silence and have accounted for it in various ways; however, an explanation that links cultural attitudes toward the body with film's aural culture has yet to be made. The complex cultural beliefs the middle class held regarding sound and the body in the 1910s have never been considered a subject in a study of cinema. Stemming from beliefs from turn-of-the-century aural culture regarding the body's associations with class and gender, the new aural etiquette of the cinema house was tied to the culture's symbolic associations with sound. The elaborations of social power that encourage the production of some sounds and discourage others can be heard within the sounds of cinema culture. This showcases what Steve Goodman has called the play of social power as it occurs in sound, or "audiosocial power in the politics of silence and the politics of noise."[12] In returning to these lost sounds, then, I aim to articulate a vital connection between cinema culture's attitude toward spectator sound and the late nineteenth-century middle class's attitude toward the corporal body's sonic behavior in public. In establishing this connection, I show how the soundscape of the cinema house makes audible certain significant broader social tensions regarding class and gender that were present in its historical moment.

Here, specifically, I argue that the aural etiquette of the entertainment culture of the time reflects the sonic concerns of its moment by manifesting a marked tendency toward disciplined silence on the part of the spectator. Drawing upon cultural historical sources that I mine for the sounds of spectators' bodies in the cinema house, I draw together a "constellation of silence" that I identify forming in American culture. Then I place cinema culture's own aural changes within this context. The constellation of silence was composed of a network of relations in mid-nineteenth-century American culture that encouraged means of achieving personal silence in middle-class subjects. Multiple areas of middle-class public culture taught this lesson of personal silence. Cinema was one of a genealogy of entertainments that, as a result of this cultural change, went through a similar transformation. Before audience silence in cinema came audience silence in theater, opera, and symphonic performance contexts. In each case, advisers crafted a sonic etiquette that middle-class subjects were expected to learn and to which they were intended to adapt. This etiquette involved maintaining personal silence in public. It also placed a great deal of emphasis on physical self-control. Etiquette manuals hit a height in popularity during this period, and I argue that they (or texts that we can see as such) were integral to popularizing the etiquette that created silence within the culture in general but within cinema houses specifically.[13]

The silence of the cinema spectator arose not just as a response to a shift in film style, or even in film exhibition (as has often been argued), and not simply as a result of the increasing numbers of middle-class patrons within the cinema audience, who tended to be more quiet (as has also been argued), but significantly, as a response by exhibitors to a specific set of aural beliefs, anxieties, and biases that were popular in American culture. Cinema inherited a set of problems with the body as well as sonic biases against its noise from an entertainment culture of the mid-nineteenth century, whose sonic priorities in turn arose from the aural cultural beliefs of the rising American bourgeoisie. Theirs was an aural culture deeply marked by personal silence, restrained public comportment, and the necessity of downplaying the corporal body in public. This stemmed from a pervasive cultural emphasis on aural "respectability."[14] Traits of self-restraint and corporal self-denial—clearly marked in historical accounts—exemplified the middle class's relationship to sounds of the body. To be silent meant to be properly under one's own self-control. This etiquette filtered through entertainment culture and shaped cinema's own aural rituals that governed its form of spectatorship. The aggression toward the sound of the body can be found in multiple locations within this culture, including discussions of public comportment, texts on acceptable and unacceptable forms of aural manners, antinoise campaigns in the United States and Europe and their attendant activities and rhetorics, and instructions by entertainment exhibitors to their spectators. We must acknowledge a relationship between cinema and this constellation of noiselessness that animated public culture of the mid-1800s if we are to properly understand the cultural motivation behind cinema's "turn to silence" in the 1910s.

Now, this movement did not originate in cinema culture. The discourse on the sonic body as a site of disturbance first appeared in the early 1830s in descriptions of public culture's acceptable modes of comportment, and it appeared soon thereafter in discussions of behavior in entertainment spaces. It was everywhere suggested in each of these contexts that this body was something to be controlled and silenced, and across the board certain specific methods were put forward to encourage such silencing in entertainment culture. The sonic body in the entertainment context was quashed by the creation of an etiquette manual–governed public culture overseen by middle-class cultural arbiters. The turn of the century was marked by two trends that affected this situation significantly: first, the rise of etiquette manuals as a genuine force in popular culture, and second, the creation of a noise etiquette that applied to many areas of daily life.[15]

Historians have generally viewed the question of the rise of silent spectatorship and the "turn to silence" through the lens of film culture, rather than attacking the problem through the techniques offered by the study of aural culture. Rather than focusing on how the aural sense is engaged and controlled, they assert that the shift was created via the means by which visuality was manipulated and visual attention was gained, enacted by the film text or the cinema environment. This leads to different answers—and generally, answers that do not focus on audience silence per se but instead treat it as a by-product of visual attentiveness. Researchers ask, "How did audiences change within the early period? How did the modes of presentation alter over time? What effect did the changes in film presentation have on the modes of audience comportment?" They focus on the period between 1906 and 1913 as a transitional moment during which modes of filmic address altered drastically, along with the types of narrative films being made. This process ended with the codification of modes of narration in the early 1910s and the creation of a modern American cinema that was both narrative and immersive for the spectator. These scholars focus on cinema's own development and the manner in which it predisposes certain modes of attention for spectators. Narrative cinema, they explain, demanded greater audience attention. Tom Gunning has influentially described this period ranging from 1907 to 1913 as the end of the "cinema of attractions" and the beginning of "the true narrativization of the cinema," which culminated with the appearance of feature films.[16] He writes that the cinema of attractions is defined by "its direct address of the audience, in which an attraction is offered to the spectator" in a manner that acknowledges his social and physical presence as a spectator in a social scene. Such early cinema offers a series of exciting displays but shows a "lack of concern with creating a self-sufficient world" by developing characterization and unfolding a story. But during this period cinema became narrativized and turned from a mode directly addressing the spectator to a mode inducing the spectator's "diegetic absorption."[17] Miriam Hansen agrees, stating that early filmmaking is marked by a mode of "display, of demonstration, [and] of showmanship" and that as a result "the viewer is solicited in a more direct manner—as a member of an anticipated social audience and a public, rather than as an invisible, private consumer."[18] For both Gunning and Hansen, the shift from audiences' noisy participation to silent spectatorship is rooted in the "transformation of filmic discourse," and the means by which the spectator is addressed by the text should take primacy in its explanation.[19] Hansen asserts that the spectator was "a fundamental category" of the creation of cinema as an art and a social practice. Although the technology that enabled the creation of cinema was created in the 1890s, it was not until a decade of exhibition had passed that the figure of the modern silent spectator appeared. She argues that the end of first-period cinema (in 1913, with a substantial shift occurring around 1908) was evidenced by "the increasing privatization of viewing behavior and the textual homogenization of positions of subjectivity."[20] This resulted in what Mary Ann Doane has called a "despatialization of subjectivity" that helped make the viewer conscious of the diegesis to the detriment of his awareness of and participation in the social space surrounding him.[21]

The work of the late 1900s and early 1910s, then, was the creation of "a normative process—in the codification of a mode of narration that absorbs empirical viewers into [film's] textually constructed positions of subjectivity."[22] The technical changes that enabled the virtual placement of the viewer's perspective in the film text included "closer framing, centered composition, and directional lighting [and] continuity editing which created a coherent diegetic space unfolding itself to an ubiquitous invisible observer."[23] Classical narration, then, Hansen writes, "crucially expanded the possibilities of placing, or 'positioning,' the spectator in relation to the represented events, in both figurative and literal senses of 'position.'"[24] The spectator's position changed from a physically and socially situated emplacement to "an implicit reference point, functionally comparable to the vanishing point in Renaissance perspective."[25] Such a system suggests, as film's apparatus theorists would later identify, "the illusion of a unified, transcendental subject."[26] Freed from the need to attend to the immediate, social reality of the empirical audience sitting in the theater, the spectator became "part of the film as product, rather than a particular exhibition or show."[27] The spectator, then, was conceived of less as a social subject attending a screening, and more as a means of interacting with the text itself. The abstraction of the category of the spectator entailed a reduction of the focus on the social subject in the cinema auditorium. The virtual—and textual—placement of the spectator as a figure within the text, rather than a figure in the cinema house, created this shift.

As Hansen writes, a "process of negation" that was produced by the rise of narrative cinema "involved representational strategies that aimed at suppressing awareness of the theater space and absorbing the spectator into the illusionist space on screen."[28] Rick Altman has noted how standardizing sound practice when it came to accompaniment, and eliminating the playing of songs that encouraged the audience to laugh at comic or even serious scenes, contributed to the triumph of "a new ideal of spectatorship" by "raising realism above kidding and absorption over attraction."[29] He continues: "The new filmmaking style involves more generalized interpellation, dependent on such broadly defined notions as 'realism' and 'verisimilitude,' and universally appealing situations identified as 'touching' and 'fundamentally human.'"[30] One became, through sound and visual cues alike, a part of an audience rather than an individual participant sitting in the seats. With the introduction of these "storytelling pictures," as one critic wrote in 1909, "the people forgot the film, forgot the screen, and forgot themselves."[31] As film reception was standardized by the use of textual placement, "the moviegoer was effectively invited to assume the position of this ideal spectator created by the film, leaving behind, like Keaton in *Sherlock Jr.*, an awareness of his or her physical self in the theater space, of an everyday existence."[32] Others have also noted a reduction of attentiveness to the theater space as a significant factor in the creation of attentive spectators. Rick Altman writes that by bringing the audience into the filmic diegesis via tricks of perspective and by reducing the opportunities within the show for direct aural audience response, "the film industry succeeded in eclipsing spectators' individuality," fostering a relation to the text that produced audience silence.[33]

A second position lies somewhere between Gunning's more film text–based approach and my own based in the aural cultural context. Jean Chateauvert and Andre Gaudreault have argued that this same period of transition was marked by the "structuration of the sound space" of the cinema house and that this had profound impacts upon the cinema spectator's behavior. The organization of the space and the way it operated in conjunction with the show take primacy in their arguments. "First-period cinema," they write, had a more open and discursive format characterized by "the primacy of a public space allowing for the free participation of spectators in the sound environment of the moving images." They contrast this public space that allowed audience noise "to the private space of institutional cinema (after 1913), where silence in the audience is generally valued." For Chateauvert and Gaudreault, the period between 1908 and 1913 was an "intermediary, buffer period" during which the soundscape of the cinema was being organized. Various "'spectators' noises'" were beginning to be subjected to "constraints forced upon them by different mechanisms structuring the sound space—that is, the space of the screening, which will foster the emergence of an institutional mode of representation."[34] This marks, for them, "the shift from early cinema to institutional cinema."[35] Institutional cinema was marked by a series of choices by exhibitors, including "silent films without lecture, interspersed with titles and accompanied by tailor-made music."[36] Whereas previously there had been an unstructured soundscape with a designated space for the noise of the spectator, institutional cinema allowed for no such opportunities. Only sound intended for the show was permitted within this sphere of the institutional cinema house. Under the new sound regime, audience members were relegated to the role of silent "spectator" rather than aural participant in a social scene, and the "system no longer addresses itself to the multitude but to a singular, individual, and personal spectator isolated in the intimate obscurity of the movie theater." According to Chateauvert and Gaudreault, "This individualized spectator thus consumes images and sounds from the private space of his/her seat, a decidedly intimate space of undisturbed contemplation."[37] Chateauvert and Gaudreault, informed by Gunning and Hansen's arguments about the construction of the spectator by the address of the text, and taking them as a given, extend them by focusing on the concrete devices that are specific to the cinema house. These devices—including the imposition of darkness, the use of intertitles to create an authorized text for the film, thereby increasing attention, and a standardized accompaniment by musicians—assign the onus of the task of quieting the auditorium to the exhibitor. Gunning and Hansen thus turn to the text, while Chateauvert and Gaudreault turn to the machinations enacted by the venue. I highly value both approaches, but rather than subscribing to either type of analysis alone, I focus on the neglected question of what the auditors brought with them into these environments in terms of their beliefs about sound, and how these motivated the shift toward silence. Instead of focusing on how the tactics of cinema exhibitors produced silence within audiences, I focus on how cinema culture was connected to a wider set of sonic beliefs and behaviors that were vital in the greater culture.

This chapter proceeds in three sections. The first addresses how sonic etiquettes came to the fore in American aural culture. The second discusses the popularization of rituals of silence within American entertainment culture. And the third explores how the problem of silence came to prominence in cinema culture specifically. To get at the specificity of the noise problem in cinema, I will be showcasing how certain threads run throughout the discourse on late nineteenth-century personal silence, from the topic of public behavior on the street to the topic of silence while attending entertainments. Then I will show how these culminate with specific force in the cinema context. In a way that is unique to cinema, concerns with audience noise were also concerns about the way that audible behavior interacted with nineteenth-century notions of the erotic, and cinema provided an environment in which many of these same concerns—about public respectability of the working class, the female body, and noise—appearing in entertainment culture got expressed. The noise of the cinema spectator was sexually charged, and this caused discomfort to listeners who attempted to arbitrate the rules of decorum within the changing culture. Spectators' bodies (and their sounds, often heard by contemporary middle-class critics as "carnal") came to be seen as sexually troubling under such sonic systems of belief, and the desire to silence spectators seems to have stemmed from the middle-class fear of a working-class, audible, sexual, and public being.

A GROWING SILENCE: THE RISE OF MANNERS AND "AURAL ETIQUETTES"

The silencing of audiences began when the American middle class began to craft a sonic identity distinct from that of the other classes. The nineteenth century saw what historian Stuart Blumin and others refer to as the ascendancy of the American middle class.[38] "Middle-class identity took shape in both structural and cultural terms," with a "wide diffusion of middle-class lifestyles" on a national scale.[39] An increasingly homogeneous set of cultural guidelines emerged out of the economic ascendancy of the middle class. These were, in the words of Melanie Archer and Judith Blau, "indispensable" for the middle class to exert "social control under rapidly changing conditions."[40] They were part of what John F. Kasson has termed a new and "powerfully influential bourgeois culture" that imposed new rules of polite behavior and standards of conduct governing public interactions—rules that "profoundly affected social relationships of all sorts."[41] The watchwords of this culture were "civility" and "self-discipline." Subjects were encouraged to control their expression of affect in public and to diminish the noisy exuberance of their everyday behaviors.[42] This shift was guided by the popular press, who advised their reading public how to comport itself on the street and in the theater, and, from the 1830s to the 1870s, by etiquette manuals promoting a standard of comportment aligned with popular notions of middle-class respectability.[43] Archer and Blau assert that a new public concern about conforming to "good manners" was evident in the propagation and popularity of literary monthlies, etiquette books, and household manuals.[44] The establishment of a sonic etiquette was, then, part of a larger standardization of etiquette that historians have linked with the assertion of middle-class power.[45] As Zhiwei Xiao argues in a similar study of China, "Good manners and good etiquette are norms of behavior" often instituted by one group for another when the two are of a different social standing.[46] In nineteenth-century America, according to Kasson, appropriate manners became an issue of key interest" as "traditional social divisions and modes of deference came under attack." Through the establishment of etiquette a gendered, classed authority could be promoted within the sonic realm.[47]

Along with this new focus on etiquette came a new focus on the individual's sound. Karin Bijsterveld and Emily Thompson, along with others, have noted that the turn of the century was marked by the creation of a "sonic etiquette" in the United States as well as Europe.[48] Focused on public streets and on entertainment venues, this etiquette promoted a new watchful monitoring of and control over one's own and others' sound making in public. The numerous "anti-noise conferences, anti-noise campaigns, anti-noise exhibitions and 'silence weeks'" that were organized in cities in the United States and western Europe during the early cinema period clearly showed these virtues being taught.[49] These efforts, coordinated by such groups as the Society for the Suppression of Unnecessary Noise (founded in New York in 1906), the Anti-Noise Society (founded in Germany in 1908), and the Street-Noise-Abatement Committee (founded in London in 1908), attempted to instill a sense of personal responsibility regarding noisemaking as a way of controlling the din of public space and public life.[50] Middle-class advisers of various sorts, including public health activists and reformers, led these groups. Noise, they believed, was a danger to both contemplation and productivity. The solution they proposed was to educate the public: instructing them in the art of silencing oneself and the reasons for doing so. These arbiters sought to make noise an undesirable activity. In their publications they drew on the idea of the philosopher Arthur Schopenhauer that noise "murders thought."[51] Theodor Lessing, the German founder of the Anti-Noise Society, similarly stated that noise "raised and exaggerated deeply-rooted instincts and emotions—the 'subjective' functions of man's soul—and narrowed and dimmed the intellectual and rational—'objective'—functions of the soul."[52] Lessing and his colleagues believed that people needed to be educated to show sonic self-restraint for the good of society, out of feelings of "societal conscience."[53] Antinoise campaigns succeeded in changing the symbolism of sound in the culture. Noise became transgressive, and keeping silent became a mark of propriety.[54] The Anti-Noise Society boasted, "Tranquility is distinguished" *(Ruhe ist Vornehm)* as its slogan.[55] "Culture," Lessing stressed, "embodied the genesis of keeping silent."[56] Proposed ordinances to curb the noise of individuals and crowds were even more obvious attempts to control the bodies of the public.[57]

Sociologist Richard Sennett, in *The Fall of Public Man,* also identifies a significant trend toward silence in public culture of this era. He argues that the mid- to late nineteenth century marked the fall of what he terms the "public man"—the interactive, social figure who considered public space to be social space.[58] The public man was giving way to a man more focused internally, and more intent on keeping his thoughts to himself. He traveled in a form of modular self-involvement, eyes straight ahead, silent and reserved.[59] This "new ideal" of public comportment was aligned with the new middle-class ideal of "respectable noiselessness in public."[60]

Strictures on noise in etiquette texts were associated with a broader stress on self-mastery and corporal discipline. Burton Bledstein has written that the middle class of the period showed "an unprecedented enthusiasm for . . . forms of self-discipline" over the body.[61] Crary has likewise noted that there was a vogue in the nineteenth century for "learned behavior" that affected the body and that this trend paralleled the introduction of "many other new social forms of self-regulation and self-control."[62] Thomas Hamilton, in *Men and Manners in America* (1833), noted the success of such a program of self-containment when he remarked, about gentlemen in the New York social scene, that there was "a certain uncontrollable rigidity of muscle about an American"—a lack of grace that indicated the constant exercise of effortful self-control.[63] The expectation of such control as a marker of "civilized" status is described by Gwendolyn Audrey Foster in her discussion of etiquette manuals. The reader of such texts, says Foster, and most notably the female reader, was encouraged to "transcend the experience of the body in its Rousseauian state" through a constant preoccupation with her body's appearance to others and "constant supervision" over her own posture, stance, and gestures.[64] Etiquette books provided detailed guides for this kind of constrained comportment, over which, as Kasson describes, respectable middle-class people were expected to exert "a strength of self-discipline so practiced as to be 'natural.'"[65] One 1841 manual, *Etiquette for Ladies*, actually features the heading "Outward Control of the Body" in its table of contents.[66]

The aim of this "strategy of self-discipline," according to Kasson, was "self-effacement." On urban streets it involved "pretend[ing] to be private" in order "to shield against the public gaze and guard against . . . intruders and deceivers."[67] For example, an 1892 etiquette manual instructed readers that "a lady or gentleman should conduct herself or himself on the street so as to escape all observation."[68] An essential part of this self-effacement was silence, which for women was closely linked to modesty. An 1860 etiquette manual directed specifically to women tells readers that a lady should "let [her] conduct be modest and quiet": "loud talking and laughing in the street" are "excessively vulgar" and can "expose a lady to the most severe misconstruction."[69] According to what the anthropologist Mary Douglas described as a "purity rule" characterizing societies, "The more the social situation exerts pressure on persons involved in it, the more the social demand for conformity tends to be expressed by a demand for physical control."[70] Social control is symbolized by a bodily control that is expressed by an aloofness and personal purity unsullied by physical rituals, and it is marked by a refusal to engage in activities that draw attention to the body, such as eating, drinking, or self-maintenance—and, we may add, noise.[71] Kasson notes the application to nineteenth-century urban America, adding that "through attentive and disciplined body management, an individual paid deference to the social situation of which one was a part and guarded against any weakening of controls, either one's own or another's."[72] One way of doing this was keeping silent. And the control one exercised over impulses helped defuse an increasingly culturally "inappropriate" awareness of the corporal self in public life. What Norbert Elias describes for the post–World War I period as "habitual, technically and institutionally consolidated self control" in the "respectable" citizen that "takes on the form of a more or less total and automatic self-restraint" was already beginning to take hold, inculcated very early in children as bodily techniques.[73] The body was a site that needed to be controlled. Etiquette took on the task of doing so and began to silence the body.[74]

The model of silentious behavior was, significantly, always male. This ideal came from sources as far back as the ancient Greeks. As Anne Carson points out, in antiquity self-control and noiselessness were often bound up with virtues of masculinity. Women, on the other hand, were seen as undisciplined creators of noise. Femininity, according to Aristotle, was marked by an inability to keep one's peace. Masculinity was marked as "self-contained and firmly bounded."[75] Masculine virtue was grounded in the notion of what the Greeks termed *sophrosyne,* the ability to exercise "moderation, temperance, [and] self-control." Carson notes that "verbal continence is an essential feature of *sophrosyne*" and adds that "woman as a species is frequently said to lack the ordering principle of *sophrosyne.*" This distinction, she argues, "divides humanity into two species: those who can censor themselves and those who cannot."[76] Carson writes: "It is a fundamental assumption . . . that a man in his proper condition of *sophrosyne* should be able to dissociate himself from his own emotions and so control their sound." The Greeks, then, had a gendered society whose binary was a sonic one. Women, writers such as Plutarch asserted, blurted out "a direct translation of what should be formulated indirectly." So if a woman lacked the ability to keep her peace, she needed to be controlled by the men who could. If a woman could not hold her tongue, it was the responsibility of her man to ensure that it was held.[77]

In the nineteenth century, cultural critics have noted, such long-held cultural assumptions about noise and gender became reanimated within the noise debates in public culture. John Kasson and others have argued that a Greek sonic aesthetic of self-control and "virtue" reemerged in the nineteenth century as an ethic of silent "respectability" and public presentability in middle-class manners.[78] Men were expected to change themselves into silent subjects and spectators at entertainments. They were expected to exercise self-control in terms of their sonic expressions. Women's sound production was policed, as it was seen as excessive and dangerous.

NOISE IN NINETEENTH-CENTURY ENTERTAINMENTS

In venues from theater and opera to symphonic performance and film, we find the same pattern emerging in the nineteenth century: a new culture of silence. After a fifty-year period from the time of the American colonies up through the 1830s, in which public auditoriums were full of audience noise, silence descended over these spaces. In the discourse on these entertainments, noise became associated with social disruptiveness and silence with respectable comportment that was coded as virtuous, middle class, and masculine.[79] Prior to the nineteenth century, the space in which a performance took place was also a sphere of social interaction, and producers "acknowledged and sanctioned the active" participation of the audience.[80] Making noise was an extremely common and accepted way for audiences to express their feelings about the show being performed. Indeed, the tradition of the noisy audience allowed them to shape the program, calling for the curtailment of an element they did not like or the repetition of one they did. For many years, from the Middle Ages to the mid-nineteenth century, the audience's audible expression of approbation or disapprobation was considered to be a vital part of the performance.[81] Audience members catcalled, booed, hissed, and stamped their feet. They pounded the floor with walking sticks to call for a change in program, and more often than not, the exhibitors in charge met with their demands.[82] They heckled the actors and made themselves a part of the show through such vocal antics. Audience members called for their favorite songs. Men and women together called out their approval when they saw a particularly pleasing scene depicted onstage and pelted the performers when they did not comply with their demands.[83] This noisy role solidified into the concept of "audience sovereignty."[84] It was such an expected component of a show that theater managers commonly used spectator noise as a barometer of the performance's success.[85] As the *Times* printed in 1846: "There are two legitimate modes of evincing approbation and disapprobation in the theatre—one expressive of approval, by the clapping of hands, and the other by hisses to mark dissent."[86]

In the United States in the 1830s the understanding of the sonic role of the spectator began to change.[87] The model of audience sovereignty that had been operative for centuries began to decline.[88] Though up until the 1840s elites had participated in such audible outbursts themselves, they now condemned the expression of audible communal opinion at entertainments.[89] Such behavior was rewritten by the press as "rowdyism,"[90] and noisy audience sovereignty, now associated with the mores of the working class, was termed "poor manners rather than an exercise of audience rights."[91] To be noisy was to be out of step with the norms of society. For the first time, noise took on a genuinely negative dimension in performing arts culture—a marked change in the symbolism of sound.

Noisemaking among spectators, rather than being simply accepted and expected by theater managers, audiences, and even the actors themselves, became shameful, even punishable behavior.[92] The middle class became increasingly consumed with the idea of suppressing the tendency of working-class audience members to express their opinions about entertainments through noise.[93] Throughout the nineteenth century and into the twentieth, social reformers and entrepreneurs alike would try to "contain or eliminate rowdiness in audiences."[94]

Audiences were silenced, first, by the segmentation of public entertainments into discrete arts. The division of the arts created a space in which cultural authorities of the middle classes could craft etiquettes for more specialized audiences.[95] The idea of such a separation was not merely to isolate an event as distinct from all of its fellow arts—it was to create a distinctive social experience associated with that event and to elaborate a set of social rules that would be active among the spectators. This was the moment of the creation of many of the social etiquettes that we now associate with the separate cultures of theater, opera, and symphonic performance.[96] This new conception of the performing arts, as Kasson puts it, "had profound implications for the intended audiences."[97] Multiple institutions attempted to change the behaviors of their audiences—in the words of George Templeton Strong, to teach the boisterous masses "good manners" through new rituals of silence.[98]

From the 1850s to the early 1910s, specific changes also occurred in cultural authorities' ways of describing the people attending a performance. These changes of wording were by no means coincidental; if audiences were to be shepherded to new behavior, one had to promote new terms. First, the "audience" became a "spectator." The root words for both *audience* and *spectator* are revealing.[99] *Audience* is rooted in the Latin verb *audire,* to listen, and is related to speech, produced for the audience or even, perhaps, produced by it. *Spectator*, on the other hand, comes from the Latin verb *spectare,* to see. The modern spectator, then, was rooted in a mode of silent viewing rather than noise production. Second, *spectator* was a singular noun, whereas *audience* had been a collective one. Wolfgang Schivelbusch states that by the end of the nineteenth century a group of viewers attending a public entertainment "was no longer 'an audience,' but a large number of individuals, each of whom followed the drama for him or herself."[100] In the words of Lawrence Levine, "Audiences in America became less active" during this period, "less of a public and more of a group of mute receptors."[101] As Levine writes, "The desire of promoters of the new high culture to convert audiences into a collection of people reacting *individually* rather than collectively, was increasingly realized by the twentieth century."[102] Rather than being a social milieu, "Art was becoming a one-way process: the artist communicating and the audience receiving."[103] Indeed, "'Silence in the face of art' was becoming the norm."[104]

The legitimate theater crafted several means of defense against the noisemakers who beset it on all sides. Etiquette instruction was vital to its success. "Written admonitions to the audience" in the form of mini-etiquette manuals were distributed as early as the mid-1850s in America, and they struck a decisive blow against patrons who, as Washington Irving put it, "indulge in loud conversation, without any regard for the pain it inflicts on their more attentive neighbors."[105] The New York Philharmonic Society subscribed to this approach of overt instruction and scolded its patrons in its annual report of 1857: "The inattention and heedless talking and disturbance of but a limited number of our audience are providing a serious annoyance."[106] There was a card that ushers passed to offending patrons who laughed too loudly.[107] A 1913 tutorial taught spectators how to deal with noise among their fellow audience members and detailed the process by which one could discipline a noisy neighbor. The first step, the tutorial instructed, was to hush the offender. Then the victim could "lean toward the offender and say in a polite tone: 'My attention is very easily distracted by little noises.'" The aggrieved party should add: "I am going to ask you as a favor not to talk (or beat time, or rustle your programme) while the orchestra is playing."[108] The management of Keith's New Boston Theater said in its handbill: "Please don't talk during acts, as it annoys those about you, and prevents a perfect hearing of the entertainment."[109] These instructional handbills made the expectations of the house explicit. They taught spectators how to discipline their behavior while enjoying the entertainment, and even how to discipline their peers who failed to do so of their own accord.

Contemporary with these handbills, mentions of audience misbehavior became a regular part of the popular and trade press coverage of events, and the press played a major part in popularizing a new etiquette. In fact, many of these journalists predicted behaviors they wished to see, rather than describing the current behaviors of the audience. Their work was thus prescriptive rather than descriptive, although it was almost always presented as the latter.[110] The press described a fantasy of spectator behavior and, in describing it, hoped to help create it as a reality. Later, press coverage of the cinema would do the same thing. Journalists also scolded those they identified as badly behaved. English novelist

Frances Trollope's account of her travels in the United States appeared as regular reports in the arts and culture weekly the *New York Mirror.* In the press, Trollope criticized American spectators for their noisy public behaviors. As Kasson writes, her observations were "supported by a catalogue of theater 'indecencies'" listed by multiple writers in the *New York Mirror.*[111] The press served as a forum in which a new etiquette could be disseminated and as a form of etiquette manual itself.[112] This work of changing expectations on comportment in entertainment venues was continued through etiquette manuals.[113] *The Illustrated Manners Book* advised, "In listening to music, *never* beat time with your feet and cane upon the floor," adding that "any one who speaks should be hushed into silence, or compelled to leave the house."[114] Likewise, *The Ladies' Book of Etiquette* advised female operagoers: "Never converse during the performance. Even the lowest toned remark will disturb a real lover of music, and these will be near you on all sides." Instead, they were told, "Show your appreciation by quiet attention to every note, and avoid any exclamation or gesture."[115] Repeatedly in the literature on spectatorship, noisy spectators were denounced as criminals and thieves for robbing others of their natural right to listen.[116] In an article entitled "Jackass Music" in *Moving Picture World*, Louis Reeves Harrison wrote that in the cinema house "ten millions of people pay their nickels and dimes to see the moving pictures, and these shock-headed kleptomaniacs steal their pleasure away."[117] *The Illustrated Manners Book* asserted that, at the symphony, "a man has just as good a right to throw dirt in your soup, as noise in your music."[118] By the end of the century, Kasson writes, etiquette advisers became "emphatic on the subject" of auditors' right to silence, denouncing disrupters as "'thieves and robbers' who cheated performers and spectators alike.

At the opera, too, what opera historian Bruce McConachie refers to as the "formalizing" of audience response occurred through "advice from etiquette books, opera critics, and elite visitors from abroad, coupled with self-education and 'policing.'"[119] The press was instrumental in creating this response. George William Curtis, writer of "The Easy Chair," a regular column in *Harper's Monthly*, reproved noisy operagoers in his column, making their offenses public and suggesting that spectators who were behaving themselves should "fix their gaze upon the vulgar disturbers!"[120] Curtis wielded his position as a means to educate. So did a number of other critics of the time.[121] A disciplining was under way. "Socially sanctioned arbiters of taste" such as *Harper's*, the *New York Mirror*, and the *New York Times* "helped readers to distinguish proper and improper behavior by . . . featuring articles that poked fun at bad examples."[122] As McConachie writes, "Opera critics were especially important in educating the elite." By 1850, such forms of chastisement were common in the press.[123] Critics rewarded theatergoers who obeyed their advice with lavish praise. Writers such as Matilda Despard in *Harper's* "congratulated theater-goers on their improving tastes and urged them to keep progressing along the neat evolutionary path she laid out."[124] This path led them from the noisy audience practices associated with the first half of the century to the new middle-class conventions of silence. Concertgoers, Levine writes, "were increasingly lectured on the elements of proper behavior."[125] Edward Baxter Perry, for example, explicitly told his readers that "attention is the rigid rule of concert-room."[126]Such conventions suggested by the press "became an integral part of the rules and mores governing audience behavior."[127]

At the symphony, a few key figures created silence: the conductors of the major philharmonic societies across the country. During the 1830s and 1840s several conductors tried to "raise standards of disciplined attention to new heights."[128] Theodore Thomas, conductor of the Chicago Symphony Orchestra, explicitly enforced an aural etiquette on his spectators. The diminutive man boldly scolded audiences, frequently stopping his orchestra in the middle of a performance to address the miscreants. At a Central Park Garden Concert, he interrupted the performance in order to chastise a young man who was repeatedly trying to strike a match so that he could light a cigar. The repeated noise so troubled Thomas that the pause was obvious and his rebuke was biting: "Go on, sir! Don't mind us! We can all wait until you light your cigar!"[129] In another instance, Thomas instructed his musicians to play a spontaneous drum roll during their performance of Mendelssohn's *A Midsummer Night's Dream* while he stared at a couple who was chatting and disturbing other patrons.[130] Echoes of these earlier incidents appeared during an 1867 performance of *Mephisto's Waltz* that was poorly received. The audience exercised their sovereignty by disagreeing with the conductor's choice of such a difficult piece. Thomas stopped the orchestra, but he made it clear that audience sovereignty would be no match for the new authority of the program over the audience. He began the piece afresh. After a third outburst of "hisses, howls and whistles" from the audience, he turned and addressed the audience.[131] Whatever their feelings, he announced, the piece would be played in its entirety, and he added: "I will give you five minutes to leave the hall. Then we shall play this waltz from the beginning to the end. Whoever wishes to listen without making a noise may do so. I ask all others to go out." Thomas instituted a new discipline on audiences, clearly asserting his authority and the performance's newfound sanctity, and stating his expectations regarding their participation. His tactics worked.[132] Thomas was not alone in these behaviors. Arturo Toscanini, conductor of the Metropolitan Opera, interrupted performances to rap upon his podium until all whispering stopped.[133] Frederick Stock, who succeeded Thomas at the Chicago Symphony, waved his handkerchief in the air to signal that a member of the audience was disturbing the performance with his coughing. Similarly, Stock once interrupted a performance to reprimand those who rose early to don their coats. Serge Koussevitzky, of the Boston Symphony, simply stood with his arms folded and waited for silence to return.[134] Walter Damrosch at the New York Symphony and Leopold Stokowski at the Philadelphia Orchestra took things one step further: they would "stop the music, turn to the audience, and lecture them on their various faults."[135] As Levine writes, "Such tactics became commonplace" and were quite effective in producing silent, "passive audiences."[136]

BODIES, NOISE, AND THE SOUNDS OF CINEMA THEATERS

Cinema's noise debate emerged from the context of the discussion of noise in these other entertainments. And cinema had its form of audience sovereignty too: its audiences were "anything but passive" or quiet.[137] Cinema was slow to adopt the methods of enforcement used in other venues, however.[138] Theater owners in the early days of cinema knew that "their livelihood . . . depended upon pleasing an opinionated audience," and moviegoers knew that their ability to see what they wanted "rested on their ability to communicate" directly with the managers through riotous audience displays of approval and disapproval.[139] By working with their clienteles to adapt their programs to audience taste, cinema house exhibitors regularly took part in this ritual of compromise, which hung on particularly late in cinema houses in some of the poorer neighborhoods in cities like New York.[140] The atmosphere during the performance was informal, with "much neighbourly stepping to and fro" among audience members and "a hum of conversation" that animated the space.[141] Moviegoers "yelled and joked with each other. . . and hooted" while exhibitors tried to put on the show.[142] During chase scenes they often yelled "Get 'em!" or "Catch 'em!" at the screen. Early audiences "ate meals. . . and even made love in the darkened theatre."[143]

Movie theaters, then, provided not only the shared cultural experience of a show but also a venue in which local community members could regularly meet, converse, and flirt.[144]

Altman notes that, as we have seen with theater and opera, the press deemed it necessary to describe the audience at these moments: "At the turn of the nineteenth century, audience activity was so important that newspapers often reviewed the audiences as well as the performers."[145] But over time, these descriptions changed. In 1909, for example, one observer wrote: "Stand among the audience and what do you observe? As the story progresses, and even at its very beginning, those gifted with a little imagination and the power of speech will begin to comment. . . . This current of mental electricity will run up and down, wild, irregular, uncontrollable."[146] The conduct of later audiences, in contrast, was described as being in keeping with the sonic aesthetic of the middle class. For this change to occur, there needed to be a transformation of both behavior and expectations for behavior.

One of the very earliest accounts of the act of moviegoing indicates an unruly sonic body among the spectators, and the lesson we may take from this screening animates the rest of this chapter. In a dimly lit crowd of spectators at the All-Russian Fair of Industry at Nizhny-Novgorod, Russian novelist Maxim Gorky sat waiting in anticipation. The man from the Lumière Company started the Cinematograph, and ghostly black-and-white images began to spool out against the wall. Gorky watched in fascination as the flickering images played across the screen, and he waited for the sounds of the depicted world that he instinctively felt would accompany them. The images that Louis and August Lumière's cameramen had captured—mute card players throwing down silent cards, a gray train pulling into a station without the clatter of wheels along the rails, a laughing face whose muscles contracted visibly but without any mirthful gurgle issuing from its mute throat—took place in silence, without, as the author notes, "a single note of the intricate symphony that always accompanies the movements of people."[147] When you see the "mute, grey life" onscreen, Gorky wrote, "you feel as though Merlin's vicious trick is being enacted before you" and as if the people shown are bewitched and diminished to a strange half-life.[148] Noise, he implied in his account, was the natural right of all living things to create: to make's one's presence in the world heard was a right of living within it. The cinema, strangely, robbed the people it depicted of that right—something that Gorky found profoundly unsettling. The scene, unfolding so silently "begins to disturb and depress you." Under the influence of such silence, "You are forgetting where you are," and "Your consciousness begins to wane and grow dim."[149] The silently pulsing visual world onscreen, with its flickering phantoms, seemed to pull Gorky out of the space where he sat watching.

The account of this early cinema viewing is from Gorky's musings after he attended the first Russian exhibition of moving pictures.[150] Gorky was repulsed by the silence of what he termed the spectral images onscreen, calling them the "Kingdom of Shadows." And indeed his account plays out like the description of a nightmare remembered at the moment of waking. Something, however, interrupted Gorky's dream and caused his waking. It was, indeed, a sound but not from the film. "Suddenly, alongside of you, a gay chatter and a provoking laughter of a woman is heard . . . and you remember that you are at Aumont's, Charles Aumont's."[151] The Moscow establishment of French-Algerian entrepreneur Charles Aumont played two different roles in Russian culture at the time: theater house and assignation place for prostitutes. It was the practice of working girls to meet patrons in the theater by pre-arrangement.[152] The woman sitting at Gorky's elbow, whose laughter jarred him from his nightmare, was, very likely, a prostitute there to offer her services. Gorky, then, saw silent moving pictures in the sonic context of a brothel. The sounds associated with the images spilling out of the Cinematograph were not the sounds of the world depicted onscreen but the sounds of the commerce of the body; and the sounds of the cinema house were not the sounds of the depicted diegesis but the sounds of the bodies in the audience. The prostitute's presence in Gorky's 1896 account gives us a very early connection between cinema, noise, and sexuality.

Speaking in the somewhat different context of twentieth-century phonograph culture, Jacob Smith has noted the erotic potential of just hearing the female voice without being able to see a body. He also notes, separately, and in keeping with the work of Erving Goffman, that laughter is often considered to be a "flooding out" on the part of the subject— an act marked by its lack of self-control.[153] The sounds of female laughter in Gorky's account, I believe, tap into both of these assertions, combining the "inherent erotic potential" of laughter with that of the disembodied female voice, which, as Smith puts it, tends to conjure up the image of a corporal body.[154] This was especially relevant considering the associations between eros and sound that animated the soundscape of the historical moment.

The connection between cinema, noise, and prostitution is, in Gorky's account, explicit. In Russia, as Yuri Tsivian notes in *Early Cinema in*

Russia and Its Cultural Reception, "The image of the prostitute seems to be as immanently connected with film reception as that of Lumière's train."[155] Of course, the two are literally connected in Gorky's tale. As Tsivian writes, early visitors to both Aumont's café chantant and the moving picture screenings closely associated the cinema with prostitution. The prostitute stood in as a metonym for the moviegoing audience, and she was always mentioned when early accounts of moviegoing described who, precisely, was sitting in the theater. She appeared in most accounts, sitting up front with her "rouged cheeks."[156] Charles Aumont's carnal approach to entertainment entailed the girls' presence in the auditorium, circulating through the audience with a slight audible hum during motion picture screenings. The girls, then, were undeniably a part of the cinema scene, an attraction of their own among the cinematic attractions.[157] The cinema grew, naturally, out of the brothel. And with this came an aural association. The silence of the images was backed by a carnal discourse, the call-and-response of the commerce of the body.

In what follows, I elucidate a connection between spectator noise and the sonic body that was reinforced by the trade journal *Moving Picture World*. I suggest that *Moving Picture World* functioned as an industry etiquette manual. It identified a popular middle-class connection between working-class eroticism and the female body. Two connections were made by the trade press: first, that of the noise of the body with multiple kinds of promiscuity, and second, that of its control with "harmony."[158]

Noise took two forms in the debates I outline here: first, the musical accompaniment to moving pictures offered by young women was labeled "noise" by *Moving Picture World* when it was considered inappropriate to the film content. Second, the audience itself was a site of disturbing noise. The struggle during these transitional years to quiet these "promiscuous" noises played out in moving picture culture. Both kinds of noise had to be quashed, the first in the name of a "harmony" between accompaniment and film and the second in the name of attentiveness to the film, or a social kind of "harmony." Jacques Attali writes that because "noise is the source of power," "power has always listened to it with fascination."[159] *Moving Picture World*'s writers attended to noise, as a form of social and erotic distraction, with great fascination. Noise was attended to so that it could be controlled. Moving picture culture was, I argue, dealing with a crisis of promiscuity, both musical and social, that was embodied in sound, and it was addressing that crisis by quieting audiences.

In the United States, the connection between early cinema and sexuality was not as apparent as in Gorky's narrative: the cinema did not start literally in the brothel, as in Russia. However, the connections at the heart of Gorky's anecdote still applied: there was a potent connection between cinema, noise, and eroticism at the turn of the century. The sounds made in darkened movie theaters were, from the first, affiliated with the erotic. The prostitute's laughter, when it enters Gorky's account, utterly changes its direction. When he hears this sound, he begins to detail a future for cinema as an art. He envisions that the infant art midwifed by Aumont's, where "the victims of social needs" meet with "the loafers who here buy their kisses," will be true to its birthplace. He imagines that, from that night on, a "blue" cinema will be created in which patrons will pay for the privilege of seeing women do burlesque in films with titles such as *As She Undresses*. In his account after the prostitute's giggle, the cinema itself takes on the character of a harlot, or to quote another one of his imagined film titles, "a woman in stockings."[160] He imagines it to be a whore that, contrary to the scientific value of the Lumière brothers' discovery, has decided to sell herself. Beginning with the account of the laughter of the prostitute, we can trace a crisis that lasted some years in early American motion picture culture. We can also discuss how a social concern with sexuality and embodiment was expressed via noise.

Two "promiscuities" were effectively brought together in the press's discourse on early American motion picture venues. First, the sounds of early cinema were "promiscuous" in their variety, as Rick Altman's detailed work in *Silent Film Sound* has made clear.[161] They were promiscuous in the sense of *promiscuity*'s definition of heterogeneity, being "grouped or massed together without order; of mixed and disorderly composition or character."[162] They could hardly be classified under the single category of "music." First there was the noise that beckoned to passersby out on the streets, the "ballyhoo" horn. Borrowed from a carnival tradition by motion picture exhibitors who sought to get bodies in the seats, the fluted horn already had a history at Coney Island; it was designed to lure patrons from long distances, rather like a musical barker. It enticed them like a siren song into the commercial entertainments.[163] Noise became a major attraction in moving picture theaters themselves as well and constituted a distracting spectacle. *Moving Picture World* printed full-page ads for a myriad of sound devices, or professional "playthings," including "bells, chimes, forks, and traps."[164] They made everything from the sound of a squalling baby or the quacking of a duck to a pipe with a "noise like a rotten egg for punky films."[165]

Within this sonic "carnival of attractions," sound technicians were charged with a significant task: making appropriate sonic choices, from the promiscuity of options, to match their sound performances to the images presented by any given film. The sound effects men and the girl pianists, however, often chose to exercise their own standards of appropriateness, which could show a surprising lack of discretion and could undermine the intended effect of the film.[166] The sounds were also "promiscuous" in its second listed definition of being indiscriminate: "without discrimination or method; done or applied without respect for kind [or] order."[167] Writers for *Moving Picture World* often objected to extremely inappropriate sound-image matches. One of them tells how "at Coney Island while the poverty scene of 'Tim Mahoney, the Scab' (Vitagraph) was upon the screen, the band was vigorously playing up the 'Star Spangled Banner,'" and another describes how "a wretched picture depicted the beheading of Charles II of England to the tune of a lively dance." The writer, despite his disgust, does not seem surprised by the unholy sound-image match-ups. They happened, he every-where implies, because the movies were being shown at Coney Island, a place marked by its promiscuity. He writes that, at Coney Island "it is only to be expected that dance music should accompany a murder."[168] The writer thus creates a surprising and highly significant connection between vice, an amusement venue, and promiscuous sonic practice. At Coney Island, promiscuous sonic practice reflects social promiscuity and misbehavior.

Another *Moving Picture World* writer fills in this picture of Coney Island as immoral and sonically discordant in a July 1911 review called "At Coney Island." He begins, "In the Economopoly picture resort, discord was rampant," adding significantly, "Everyone knows that the ethics of Coney Island will not permit the blending of harmonies; it is the one place of all others where extremes must meet; in this respect, they are masters unto perfection."[169] He ends the review with "Grand Coney Island! Anything goes there—but the good." The writer connects a failure of ethics and sonic dissonance all in one assertion here. What goes wrong at Coney Island is twofold: first, a failure to achieve musical harmony, and second, a failure to achieve "harmonic" or satisfactory ethics. Discord is "rampant" at Coney Island. The sound-image matches seem arbitrary, with one image as likely to be paired with a sound as another—forming an essentially promiscuous soundscape in which any visual can pair with any sound, a soundscape without discretion or restraint. Sonic practice and different forms of vice were repeatedly linked in the pages of *Moving Picture World*. The ideal of "harmony," then, had both a sonic and a moral valence.

In contrast to such sonic promiscuity, *Moving Picture World* suggested a more coherent pairing system for sound and image. Its 1911 article "Chicago Houses in Review" recommended that sound accompaniment "express, lyrically, the same feeling that the photoplay, dramatically, tries to suggest."[170] The joining of a logical sound-image pairing, they stated, would be beneficial to moving pictures and their improvement. The discourse on sound accompaniment was not, however, simply an internal debate that pertained to the development of cinema exhibition. It tied in to broader cultural and sonic beliefs. The multiplicity of sound-image pairings at Coney Island, I believe, mirrored another kind of multiplicity of couplings possible at the entertainment site. In this, it tied in to certain middle-class anxieties in the culture of the time, as well as certain beliefs about the connection between noise and gender. Coney Island, as a turn-of-the-century popular amusement, had well-advertised and literal ties with working-class promiscuity. Here I refer to the word's most common, and most charged, definition, as a lack of sexual discrimination.[171] Heterosocial entertainment environments challenged conventional sexual norms. This was one of these amusements' primary characteristics that drew both comment and concern from middle-class reformers. Kathy Peiss asserts: "Leisure entrepreneurs consciously encouraged the participation of women in mixed-sex amusements, altering traditional patterns of sociability."[172] Commercial entertainments that thrived in urban centers at the turn of the century opened up a new social arena, particularly for single female city dwellers. These venues enabled the free and easy heterosocial mixing that, occurring outside the domestic sphere and traditional courtship practices, held the seeds for a new culture of dating. Commercial culture was, as Peiss asserts, definitively heterosocial culture.[173] Shelley Stamp also persuasively links middle-class reformers' anxieties about turn-of-the-century amusements to the role these sites played as hotbeds for the new dating culture. According to Stamp, social critics such as Richard Henry Edwards conclusively linked "the amusement problem" and the "vice problem," writing that the "easygoing familiarity" of these environments allowed a "promiscuous sociability" in which "a more or less general promiscuity of relationships may emerge."[174]

This heterosocial environment had several new social practices associated with it.[175] Social conditions contributed to creating a common arrangement that was generally termed "treating" in which, as social worker Belle Linder noted in her 1909 study, a young single woman's date for the evening could "exact tribute for a standing treat."[176] Or as Stamp says more explicitly, "Within this turn-of-the-century dating culture it became acceptable for working-class women to offer sexual 'favors' of one degree or another in exchange for being treated at amusement sites."[177] Connecting the sounds of the Coney Island nickelodeon with prostitution is, then, quite easy. Willing exchange was a concern when, as *Collier's* magazine wrote, a girl's "chastity" was "entrusted to her young eager self for safe-keeping or for bartering."[178] Entering into commercial culture, then, for young working-class women, meant entering into a sexual barter system in entertainment culture that was akin to, if not the same thing as, prostitution. The siren song of the ballyhoo horn, calling spectators in from the street, invited them into an erotic milieu. The noise of the nickelodeon was, then, associated with two kinds of commerce: that of the cheap commercial attractions, and the illicit commerce of the female body. *Moving Picture World* ran a "Chicago Letter" in March 1912 in which Ellen Peterson, a social worker, described such associations. She said of the young women of her acquaintance: "An invitation to a nickelodeon [offered upon a chance meeting on the train] . . . and you hear no more of them."[179] Further damning the nickelodeons, she stated, "I look upon the nickelodeons as cesspools of iniquity" and added, "The auditoriums are dark and there is always some noise or conversation, and many things happen there"—implying that these things were not good.[180] In contrast, the legitimate theater usually featured "absolute silence."[181] Here noise served as a sure-fire marker of social misbehavior.

In a period in which "familiarity" was quite explicitly linked to flirting and to overtly familiar relations between the sexes, some feared "the likelihood that the much more easy conversational relations among spectators will lead to improvised and clandestine acquaintance with men."[182] Miriam Hansen writes that the cinema attracted "support from Progressive crusaders and reformers" who were concerned about the "unprecedented hazards that lurked between the flickering screen and the darkness of the theater space."[183] And while *Moving Picture World* asserted that, "like a false report of Mark Twain's death, this sort of thing is of course 'greatly exaggerated,'" even they took pains to advise how to make cinema culture more respectable.[184]

Cinema's erotic associations could also be those provided by the accompanists, who very often played a game with the auditors by making salacious sounds. *Moving Picture World* writer Frank H. Madison complained that at the "Springfield, Ill. Picture Shows," one show featured "an exchange of kisses blown from the finger-tips" with which "the inter-

FIGURE 1.1. Scott and Van Altena, "If Annoyed When Here Please Tell the Management," 1912. Etiquette slide. Library of Congress, Washington, D.C., Prints and Photographs Division. www.loc.gov.

preter of martial music kept tally with the tom-tom."[185] Further, as Stephen Bottomore has noted about sound effects in early cinema, viewers in the auditorium were often encouraged to make their own smacking, wet kissing noises for onscreen kisses.[186] One young female accompanist even wrote disgustedly to *Moving Picture World*'s "Letters" section that "the manager wanted me to imitate the kiss."[187] Despite her disgust, she apparently did so. In each situation, the noises of the commercial amusement evoked the promiscuous exchange of erotic favors.

In his 1911 article entitled "Jackass Music," Louis Reeves Harrison of *Moving Picture World* refers to two promiscuous practices (the first musical and the second corporal) and incorporates them into one female caricature. Writing about the nickelodeon girl pianist "Lily Limpwrist," Harrison first attacks her amateur musicianship by noting her Coney Island tendency to mismatch sound and image. He writes, "Lily is all right at home, when her mother importunes her to 'play something and don't wait to be teased,' or still better as a summer-eve girl on a Coney Island boat." He continues, connecting her poor musicianship to Coney Island's bad reputation in moral terms: "But no man will ever marry a girl who plays a dance while the pictured man is in a death struggle"; and he significantly adds, "She would probably be *at* one when the real one was in trouble." The girl, he implies, is promiscuous sonically, with her inability to match sound and image, and socially, in that she blithely jumps from man to man in the new working-class dating culture that enables such behavior. What he calls Lily's "I-seen-you-glances" directed at the "box of candy young man in the first row" also marks her participation in the sexual exchange associated with working-class women in commercial entertainment venues.[188] His concerns illustrate an observation by Karin Bijsterveld:

> The historiography and anthropology of sound make clear that noise and silence refer to deeply rooted cultural hierarchies. The right to make noise as well as the right to decide which sounds are allowed or forbidden has long been the privilege of the powerful, whereas those lower in rank (women, children, servants) were supposed to keep silent, or were under suspicion of intentionally disturbing societal order by making noise. Positively evaluated loud and rhythmic sounds have had connotations of strength, significance, and being in control, whereas noise as unwanted sound has often been associated with social disruption.[189]

So it was with cinema. The middle class worried about the noise of the working class as a sign of social disorder, and men concerned themselves with the noise of women as a sign of their potential unruliness.

The ideal of pure focus and attentive silence denies certain social and sexual realities of motion picture exhibition at the time. Nowhere is this clearer than in one specific legacy of the theater spectator to the motion picture spectator. Nineteenth-century American theaters had already experienced a significant mixture working-class misbehavior and eroticism that was manifested in noise. In 1831, the *New York Mirror* characterized the theater as "the morsel of voluptuousness, sweetened with music and poetry, and the undisguised disgusting dash of ribaldry, from which good taste and common decency recoil."[190] The *New York Evening Post* expressed concern that the theater would "degenerate into licentiousness by seeking its patronage from corrupt taste and vitiated indulgences."[191] One real site of this indecency was to be found in the noisy audience, who seemed unwilling to keep their propriety in hand. In cities all over the United States, major and minor theaters were equipped with a "gallery" where noise and sex were utterly coincident. This was the "guilty third tier" balcony that held the cheapest seats in the house.[192] It was the home of the theater's prostitutes. As theater historian Claudia Johnson writes in "That Guilty Third Tier: Prostitution in Nineteenth-Century American Theaters," the third tier was an established tradition in major American cities such as New York, Boston, Philadelphia, Chicago, and New Orleans, as well as smaller ones such as Cincinnati, Mobile, and others by the 1830s and 1840s.[193] The theater and houses of prostitution were symbiotic entities; brothels were often situated within an easy walk from the theater for the two industries' mutual benefit. This siting was extraordinarily common, even simply according to statistics. In the 1850s, more than half (53 percent) of all brothels were conveniently located within 2.5 blocks of a theater.[194] Many theaters consciously appealed to this trade, offering prostitutes discounted tickets.[195] Indeed, when theater attendance lagged, the prostitutes were often appealed to in hopes of raising revenue with this added attraction.[196] Higher-class prostitutes sat down among the theatergoers, and the low-class, more "boisterous" prostitutes of the gallery interacted with their johns, the "gallery gods."[197] The gallery gods earned their nickname both because of their elevation in the third tier and because of "their propensity for making sudden interventions on the world below," rather like the gods of the house.[198] The gallery was where noise met with vice. "The house of the harlot," where she "holds her court" was charged with the boisterous noise of sexual misbehavior, and the antics of the third tier often rang out and disrupted the rest of the relatively well-behaved house.[199] The top gallery was, according to nineteenth-century preacher and social reformer Thomas DeWitt Talmage, home to the "hard-visaged, the ill-behaved, the boisterous, [and] the indecent."[200] Contemporary accounts describe "the yells and screams, the shuddering oaths and obscene songs, tumbling down from the third tier" to disrupt the rest of the space.[201] Because of the antics of this tier, the entire theater was, in some accounts, called "a temple devoted to the harlot."[202] Far from being a sacral space, it was boisterous: a home to "howling roughs" and their prostitutes.[203]

The gallery was also, in most instances where it existed, the most lucrative aspect of a theater's business.[204] In 1833 the *Commercial Adviser* called it "the most valuable part of the house."[205] As the *Hopkinsian* religious magazine put it in 1829: "It is a fact not to be concealed that the company of lewd women is expected and desired at the theatre."[206] Prostitution was banned in the legitimate theater only at the end of the nineteenth century, when theater sought legitimization by courting middle-class, family audiences.[207] When the gallery did close at the turn of the century, it was with great trepidation that exhibitors allowed it; they were convinced these actions would damage business, since, as one critic wrote, "That class of persons know that [the theater] is a favorite amusement of those who are most easily tempted to sin."[208] Indeed, historians note that many "gallery gods" did abandon the theater at this point in time.[209]

The movement of the gallery gods away from the legitimate theater was concurrent with the arrival of the commercial amusements of the turn of the century, including the fairground and the cinema. And the cinema, according to *Moving Picture World*'s own accounts, was absolutely where the gallery gods migrated. In 1911, an editorial in *Moving Picture World*, "The Theater 'Gods,'," stated: "Theaters are now bewailing the fact that the moving pictures are depleting the ranks of their lower-priced patrons" and added that "the much abused 'gods' suddenly appear as possessing both a financial value and discriminating critical judgment." Upon that judgment turned "the success of the actor and the profit of the manager." "It is an old truth," the writer asserted, "that the value of some things are not known until they are lost; also, what is a loss in one place is a gain in another."[210] Another *Moving Picture World* article, "The Lost Gallery," similarly exults that the "'gallery god' has been lured from his accustomed haunts in the top balcony of the legitimate theater by the motion picture." These new patrons, according to the article, are a windfall comparable to "the fabulous treasures of the 'Lost Galleons of the Spanish Main.'" The author explains that "the gallery god . . . has been enticed from the 'legit'" because all patrons go "wherever suitable arrangements for their comfort are provided." One can only assume that he does not know precisely what the gallery gods would expect. He ends with the assertion that cinema has earned the "allegiance of the 'gallery god' by giving him the sort of entertainment his discriminating soul craved at a price that suited his purse."[211] Here, this writer rather accidentally asserts that cinema as an artistic medium, and the cinema as a social milieu, perfectly served the gallery gods' needs at only a nickel a pop. Entertainment, noise, and sexuality, it is implied, were all available at the cinema, and indeed, *only* at the cinema, as the gods were being driven from their accustomed haunts by the sweep of the middle-class reformer's movement. Either the *Moving Picture World* writer was naive or the article was a subtle wink at his readership. Regardless, the connection between cinema and the perpetrators of sexual misbehavior is explicit. The gallery god hooting and leering and the young single working woman are two figures of erotic promiscuity and audible misbehavior that animated the cinema house. Cinema had inherited the problem of noise, sexual antics, and the unacceptable norms of working-class spectatorship from other entertainments that were in the process of clearing such offenders from their own houses. The "turn to silence" can be seen as a response to that very concern: a solution to the problem that this combination of noise and sexuality posed.

When *Moving Picture World* introduced a new sonic etiquette and sought to redefine what made a good spectator, it was fighting against the traditional model of raucous spectatorship. Moving picture critics would have become increasingly aware of the migration of the "gallery gods" from the third tier of the legitimate theater. *Moving Picture World's* presentation, in the 1910s, of the ideal of the self-controlled, middle-class spectator was thus an attempt to counter the mores of the working-class "gods of Paradise" who were then entering the cinema in large numbers.

Moving Picture World promoted its new etiquette as a means by which moral harmony could result from sonic harmony. If the theme of promiscuity was threaded through *Moving Picture World's* diagnosed problems within cinema culture, then the ideal of "harmony" was woven through their solutions. It was at the core of the middle-class approach to silence in the cinema.

In an article titled "Reforming 'Jackass Music,'" Tim Anderson points to this shift toward evoking "harmony" as a new ideal for standardizing the sound-image relationship in moving picture accompaniment.[212] Sound began to serve the story and the themes present in any given film, in large part because *Moving Picture World* published scene-by-scene outlines complete with suitable musical selections for all pictures currently in distribution.[213] Clarence E. Sinn's regular column "Music for the Pictures," which instructed accompanists how to "play to the pictures" and create musical accompaniment that supported their basic themes, and Clyde Martin's column "Working the Sound Effects" made the publication a voice of authority standardizing practices of sound-image pairing as a new field starting around 1910.[214] Thus the journal became "a de facto clearinghouse for the matching of musical selection with features, scenarios, and narrative types," all to supply answers regarding what constituted "correct" music for the picture as opposed to the haphazard quality of previous sound-image matches.[215] *Moving Picture World* thus provided an aural analogue to the middle-class moral code. It sanctioned suitable marriages between sounds and images to create a union that was blessed by "harmony." One of its articles stated: "Whenever a good song can be wedded to a photoplay, the marriage will be a happy one."[216] Just as with audiences, with accompaniment the standard pairing practices needed to be reformed, and the scenarios in which they happened had to be controlled by the creation of defined rules. The sonic aesthetic that was being promoted reproduced the socially sanctioned relationships of the moral code that arose with the middle class. The *MPW* did the work of reformers in policing both sound and morals.[217]

The aesthetics of shows' accompaniment was just one aspect of cinema culture that needed reforming. The new method of exhibition would "harmonize" only with a very different sort of audience from the one that had populated the nickelodeon. As in theater, the opera, and symphonic performance, the cinema's shift to a silent form of spectatorship was shepherded by its own "etiquette manual." Here *Moving Picture World* led the way. It noted in 1909 that moving picture audiences "constitute an interesting study in themselves," and from 1907 to 1912 it conducted that study.[218] As Hansen has noted, "Beginning in 1907, the nickelodeon and its audiences became an object of attention by journalists," who generated new models of spectatorship that promoted "middle-class standards of silence and passivity."[219] The writers at *Moving Picture World*, like their predecessors at *Harper's*, the *New York Mirror*, and the *New York Times*, played an integral role in cultivating the shift toward silence in the cinema spectator by disseminating the rules of a new sonic cinematic etiquette. The publication, in many ways, self-consciously cultivated this role for itself.

Reporters for *Moving Picture World* described nickelodeon audiences as very different from the type of patron they sought to cultivate. Their descriptions of silent audiences were, largely, fantasies about ideal rather than actual audiences.[220] But this method of producing expected results by clearly describing them as if they already existed seems to have been highly effective.

The descriptions of the desired audience could not have been more different from earlier accounts that emphasized noise, embodiment, and sexuality. The audience in the new accounts seemed restrained, even slightly detached. In 1911, *Moving Picture World* published "The Picture the Audience Likes." Here we have our first introduction to the kind of "well behaved" silent and attentive spectator that the journal desired.[221] The audience depicted was much less interactive and a great deal more focused on the film. According to the "World Reviewer," "The attitude of the audience is much like that of most persons after finishing a book or looking at some picture. They do not lay down the book, or turn away from the picture with vigorous hand-clapping. They are in a more thoughtful mood, and their enjoyment and appreciation cannot be translated into applause. It goes deeper than that, and is more pleasurable than that which causes a noisy demonstration of applause."[222] Another article similarly asserts that "the silence [of the audience] is, in itself, applause of the most sincere sort. The audience has been too deeply moved to resort to the conventional expression of appreciation."[223]

Moving Picture World writer W. Stephen Bush, whose position as a cinema lecturer gave him a unique viewpoint on the audience, claimed that even though "audiences of this kind are by no means demonstrative" they could be deeply engaged.[224] They were paying rapt attention but exerting self-control to maintain their silence and keep their affect to themselves. "When the lights are turned up you may see that they are thinking about what they have just seen, for the intensity of expression, so plainly visible in their faces, relaxes but slowly, showing how deeply they have been impressed with what their eyes have seen."[225]

A priority on internal thought and mental processing replaced external expression in these accounts. Michael Fried has articulated a similar mode of aesthetic absorption in his work on eighteenth-century painting. Critics then, as well, valued "the persuasive representation of absorption[, which] characteristically entailed evoking the obliviousness or unconsciousness of the figure or figures in question to everything other than the specific objects of their absorption."[226] Diderot, the primary critic he discusses, used "notions like harmony, peace, and silence to evoke the distinctive effects of absorptive paintings":[227] with regard to one painting, Diderot stated, "One forgets oneself in front of this work; that is the strongest magic of art," and added, "A calm, a silence that touches, a delicious coolness reign there."[228]

By supporting this deep-feeling but outwardly restrained mode of spectatorship and criticizing other modes, critics at the paper helped craft new expectations. In a *Moving Picture World* article titled "Managerial Stupidity," the exhibitor was explicitly cast as "stupid" for not understanding that "those who go [to the cinema] seldom are easiest amused, while the great solid patronage, those who go often, escape notice because they enjoy in an inconspicuous way."[229] The description was a fantasy that exaggerated the salience of an audience preference for quiet in the hope of creating a new reality and thereby justified the shift in spectatorial etiquette that it was helping to create. There was a "New Patron" that *Moving Picture World* prized and held up for emulation. The article stated, "The boisterous element of the audience," as "anyone but a theatrical bonehead knows," was not the audience that exhibitors wanted. Simply by stating this, writers helped shift standards by expressing the exhibitors' preference. The "boisterous element" was déclassé. *Moving Picture World* then attempted to rewrite history to justify the change in standards that it promoted. "The noise boxes," according to the article, "do not furnish enough support to pay the rent" for the exhibitor. Of course, this was a bold assertion since, up to this point, they always had.[230]

Moving Picture World, then, displayed a spectator who "kept his peace." Self-control and restraint were the order of the day. The new mode took the energy that had previously been dispersed across the auditorium through the social scene and funneled it toward a concentration on one object: the film itself.

Once audiences were gathered in the cinema, exhibitors had their own special methods to promote audience silence. Spectator slides were one way of establishing a sonic etiquette for the cinema.[231] Each storefront theater kept a stock of announcement slides instructing patrons in the aural etiquette of that cinema.[232] Samantha Barbas notes that slides "urged viewers to refrain from eating, talking and rowdy behaviour," and cites the slide "Please do not stamp—the floor may cave in."[233] Between films, spectators would see a slide stating: "Loud talking, whistling or boisterous conduct not allowed!"[234] Other slides in the Library of Congress's collection include "Please applaud with hands only!" a reference back to the days when stamping, pounding, hooting, and catcalling were still permissible.[235] Another slide, showing two women chatting as a man whistles above their heads, reads, "Loud talking or whistling not allowed."[236] As the Library of Congress states, exhibitors used slides to "control their audiences," urging moviegoers to "behave quietly" and to "report disrupters."[237] In most storefront theaters, these "announcement slides were regularly used," making them one more part of the uplift of cinema conduct in the late 19-aughts and early 1910s.[238] As Rick Altman notes, they disappeared in 1913 with the rise of classical cinema and its spectators.[239] Such tactics, then, encouraged the adoption of a more "middle-class" etiquette of silence among patrons.[240]

Silencing the audience was one aspect of a middle-class culture that took pride in physical self-control and self-effacement. With the earlier *embourgeoisement* of other forms of entertainment culture, the gallery gods had become a major source of the cinema audience, and the cinema, in response, was pushed to find its own form of sonic *embourgeoisement.* Male spectators became marked by their self-control. Female spectators were controlled and disciplined via the press. The working class was also seen as a dangerous site of noise and was controlled by these same means. Cinema culture followed the earlier cultures of theater, opera, and symphonic performance and aligned itself with middle-class standards of decorum. Cinema's own organs of opinion, like those before them in the context of other public arts, churned out advice suggesting that spectators accept the necessity of silence and police their own bodies and those of others. Through this means, silence was eventually achieved and the

FIGURE 1.2. Scott and Van Altena, "Please Applaud with Hands Only," 1912. Etiquette slide. Library of Congress, Washington, D.C., Prints and Photographs Division. www.loc.gov.

FIGURE 1.3. Scott and Van Altena, "Loud Talking or Whistling Not Allowed," 1912. Etiquette slide. Library of Congress, Washington, D.C., Prints and Photographs Division. www.loc.gov.

dangerous noise of the body was quashed. The internalization of these rules eventually led to a silent cinema auditorium filled with silent spectators. But it also led to an alignment of cinema's own small culture with the larger culture that was, increasingly, valuing silence as a dominant mode in public. Silence was on the rise. Cinema, noisy as it once was, could not avoid the silence that came along with the rise of the middle class, nor could it escape the disappearance of the body's sounds that came along with it. In Chapter 3, we will return to the cinema auditorium to discuss how acoustical design suggested new ways of listening in cinema venues and how this also helped create a silent, attentive spectator. But first, in chapter 2, I consider a major shift, not in films' exhibition, but in the industrial processes that enabled their production. Here I discuss how the concept of "noise" took on potent new life in the context of film's sound shift in the 1920s and '30s. I look at how the electro-acoustical companies' model of research into noise inspired Hollywood to conduct its own research, resulting in an ongoing study of noise that flourished in the new sound era in Los Angeles.

CHAPTER 2

The Film Industry Lays the Golden Egg

Noise, Electro-Acoustics, and the Academy's Adjustment to Film Sound

The Technicians Branch of the Academy of Motion Picture Arts and Sciences (AMPAS) was assembled for a meeting on the night of October 9, 1928. The previous year, the Five Cornered Agreement had committed the "big five"—Loew's (MGM), First National, Famous Players-Lasky, Universal, and the Producers Distributing Corporation—to working together in an all-for-one partnership determining the "system or systems best adapted for standardization in the motion picture industry."[1] That decision had produced a new model of cooperation in an attempt to standardize sound practice. Now, however, was the time to address the crisis, and all the studios had selected one member of each of their ranks to form a new producers' committee within AMPAS to deal with the problems arising with the industry-wide application of film sound. One member of the gathered audience at the meeting asked a sound technician who was speaking: "[Has] any progress been made on filtering out noises?" The technician replied "no." Fred Pelton, chair of the session, followed up: "No physical way?" The response came back. No. "Noise is noise."[2] Noise was disruptive to the industry, but the film industry's people were still unqualified to understand it. They were hoping that the technical men could offer an answer to the mystery. An internal memo from AMPAS during that same year read: "The arrival in Hollywood of the talking picture idea in the tangible form of recording equipment and a handful of experts who understood the operation of this equipment stirred the studios and noticeably disturbed the studio personnel. Their concern showed itself in an intense curiosity of the magical equipment and its mysterious operators. The sound stage became a sacred room and the sound engineer the studio high priest. He alone held the key to the future."[3]

Noise presented a serious problem at the time of the standardized adoption of film sound within the film industry in the late 1920s; its interference made the recording of clear and articulate sounds difficult. However, it was also beneficial in that it presented certain opportunities for the film industry. During early standardization processes with the adoption of film sound, noise shifted from being considered a mere technical problem to becoming a tactical tool for the film industry to use against the very industry that had crafted it.

This chapter discusses how the problem of noise actually facilitated the creation of an influential though small-scale culture of industrial research within the film industry during the film sound transition. Noise, supposedly nothing more than an obstacle, became a generative, unifying force as the film industry made the transition to full cinema sound between 1929 and 1931. During this period, AMPAS modeled itself on its competitors—the electro-acoustics companies—in promoting a tripartite program of industrial research, dissemination of technical findings, and education in basic sound principles that was designed to locate the sources of noise, eliminate it on film sets and in film recordings, and educate employees so that they understood its complexities fully. In so doing, AMPAS worked to standardize sound recording practice.[4] The now-little-discussed research program on noise that the Academy instituted played a vital role in enabling the success of film's transition to synchronized sound.

Standardization regarding sound contributed to the success of that transition by clarifying how the film industry would use and implement new technologies across the board. The form of industrial research that AMPAS used to standardize sound practice helped create a new era of the sound film industry: AMPAS adopted and extended the research methods of the electro-acoustics companies to mobilize those companies' research on noise toward its own ends. It also trained its own members for a time when the electro-acoustical engineers would be sent back east and the film industry's own personnel could lead in all matters sonic. AMPAS had recently claimed the mission of forming unifying ties among competing film studios, and noise presented it with the opportunity to make a technological problem the focus of the film studios' collaborative pursuit. Certainly it seized that opportunity both to expand

FIGURE 2.1. The founders of the Academy of Motion Picture Arts and Sciences at their inaugural meeting in 1927. Courtesy of the Academy of Motion Picture Arts and Sciences, Academy History Collection. The photograph shows (*standing, left to right*) Cedric Gibbons, J. A. Ball, Carey Wilson, George Cohen, Edwin Loeb, Fred Beetson, Frank Lloyd, Roy Pomeroy, John Stall, and Harry Rapf; (*seated*) Louis B. Mayer, Conrad Nagel, Mary Pickford, Douglas Fairbanks, Frank Woods, M. C. Levee, Joseph M. Schenck, and Fred Niblo.

its own role and to control its own industry. Consequently the research had both practical and political goals. As AMPAS secretary Frank Woods put it at a 1932 AMPAS meeting, "This is an Academy but don't make this purely an academic meeting. Action must follow."[5]

The research and development wings of the electro-acoustical laboratories Bell Labs/AT&T/Western Electric and RCA/Westinghouse/General Electric developed the technologies that made possible the shift to synchronized film sound in Los Angeles film studios. This chapter outlines how the model of research that the labs provided influenced certain necessary finer points of the film industry's approach to listening and noise during the film sound transition. AT&T and Bell Laboratories gave the Academy a model on which to base its activities. The labs provided the necessary infrastructural framework, agenda, and research methodology to sustain AMPAS. They also showed AMPAS how to do research and demonstrated the value of that research for guiding the film industry over a significant obstacle in its history. By extending AT&T's research model, the Academy became an umbrella organization for the dissemination of technical knowledge, a sponsor for technological research, and an educator in sound technologies. Research on noise enabled AMPAS to find its place in the film industry of Los Angeles. The problem of noise thus became a godsend to the troubled film industry under AMPAS leadership.

The archives of AMPAS's Research Council on the sound shift illuminate how the meeting of the film industry and the sound industry affected early film sound aesthetics and education and, eventually, had ramifications that extended beyond the sound transition itself. As an AMPAS memo from the transition states, full film sound was made possible through preexisting technology developed by another industry. "Born in the Bell Laboratories the idea of talking pictures traveled to Hollywood and nestled in the brains of the Warner Brothers. Nourished by the rich imaginations of these pioneers the brainchild grew sturdy from early trials and tribulations and finally came forth to startle the world with 'The Jazz Singer.' The arrival in Hollywood of the talking picture idea happened in the tangible form of recording equipment and a handful of experts who understood the operation of this equipment."[6]

The uncomfortable meeting of two industries with different working models and understandings of sound destabilized the film industry and noticeably affected the sets on which these men worked.[7] The presence of the Bell Labs personnel and their technologies bred discomfort among studio workers. Antagonistic feelings evidently ran high, with disrupted working conditions manifesting themselves as squabbles on the set, tense conversations between higher-ups in back rooms, and, it was repeatedly said, "secrets" being whispered about by the sound engineers. Hollywood filmmaking, such buzz implied, was under threat from a wave of outside technical influence, brought into its sphere by the acoustical experts.[8]

Since the production of sound motion pictures required cooperation between two groups that felt ill at ease together, the focus on noise research during this three-year period seems to have played a key tactical role for AMPAS. Scientific research became a prized common mode of encounter with sound that would uncover the "secrets" of noise's fundamental principles, the purview of the electro-acoustics labs, for the film industry. By aligning itself with the practices of technological culture, AMPAS created a research program that resulted in the reduction of noise and then created an education program in the technological components of sound. This, as James Lastra has observed, enabled the eventual adoption of the technological sector's methods and areas of knowledge so the film studios could minimize the involvement of the laboratories later and prevent them from destabilizing the film industry.[9] And the threefold program not only allowed AMPAS a measure of control over the transition but created a common dialogue and a common language within the otherwise divided film industry. The major and minor studios could get behind AMPAS's plan of industrial research because it was noncompetitive. No studio had a "lock" on noise or an exclusive problem with it. It was common to them all. Noise was, then, ideally suited to the project of creating a new unifying organization. AMPAS, founded in 1927, was still a newly formed agency in 1929, seeking to cement itself in Hollywood's culture of work, and it did so via the execution of these programs, which, from 1929 to 1931, pushed Hollywood, along with AMPAS, into a new relationship to sound, noise, and industrial research. Its actions enabled the industry to move forward by better understanding sound and gaining mastery over noise.

AMPAS identified the opportunity to extend its mission and prolong its early influence on the film industry.[10] Coming off of a successful effort to gather information on the benefits and drawbacks of incandescent lighting, which was beginning to replace arc lamps in film studios, the Academy needed to sustain its run to ensure a lasting place in Hollywood's film culture. Sound culture was becoming vital to Hollywood, so AMPAS adopted it as a new stock in trade. But AMPAS was also seeking to break the engineers' monopoly on new and valuable knowledge by adopting the methods and habits necessary to study it. AMPAS often referred to the process of learning about sound and noise as a process of uncovering a "secret," a hidden truth that was otherwise inaccessible. This secret was, as Lastra has noted, the knowledge that the engineers held and Hollywood wanted, but I argue here that the learning of research methods proved to be equally important; it was about the mastery of a new set of survival skills. Bell had become a research giant when it was faced with a major crisis in its own industry, the need to quell noise in coast-to-coast telephone service. The film industry began to do the same as it turned to sound. Revealing the "secret" was AMPAS's gift to the industry, thereby ensuring its own relevance but also securing the industry's future. The techniques of sound recording and the manipulation of noise allowed the film industry to move forward into a new era of productivity.[11] And while AMPAS did not succeed in producing a culture of research quite like that of Bell or RCA, its culture of research still exists in a limited form in Hollywood today.

The incorporation of sound technology from these laboratories into the film industry is not a new topic for film scholarship. However, it remains understudied when it comes to the precise forms of influence that the two groups had upon each other. Any research done on it now is tinkering with the pieces of a framework already crafted by historians. However, the archive of documents I work with here has rarely been seen, and my approach is markedly new. Donald Crafton focuses on how the studios, enabled by a larger network of economic, technological, and cultural factors, navigated the sound transition in order to produce a fully functional sound aesthetic. Detailing the forms of technology the industry used during the sound transition, he deals also, incidentally, with the problem of noise. Crafton accounts for noise in various practical contexts: the design of sets and microphones, the "surface noise" and "needle scratch" of Photophone recording methods, and the buzzing of arc lamps. Though Crafton does engage with how AMPAS worked with the engineering laboratories, he does not account for how AMPAS became like them in its work. Nor does he discuss noise's evident role in this event.

The incorporation of outside engineering talent into Hollywood filmmaking practice has been addressed by Lastra in *Sound Technology and the American Cinema,* a work that has been directly formative for this project, and more recently by Emily Thompson in her newest work that is currently still in progress. It is also the subject of a project by Luci Marzola, currently in progress, on the history of the Academy. Lastra and Thompson are among the few scholars who have consulted the archive of the Academy's Research Council that oversaw the shift to film sound. Lastra focuses on personnel conflicts between Hollywood studio staff and sound engineers and points out how the creation of AMPAS's School of Sound Fundamentals achieved the desired end of resolving those conflicts. But Lastra does not elect to discuss the school as part of a much larger research campaign by AMPAS.[12] AMPAS did more than just adopt knowledge about sound through this model; it adopted the model itself.

As Emily Thompson notes, the birth of the acoustics industry was concurrent with the rise of corporate research, and "Some of the earliest and most innovative industrial research libraries were established by companies committed to the design and delivery of acoustical products."[13] Thompson describes the rise of noise as a category defined by and in use among technicians and discusses electro-acoustic methods of noise measurement and control, citing the history of the condenser transmitter and its role in creating a culture of technological development and inquiry. The development of this device, she writes, made noise measurable and hence technologically manageable. It also catapulted the sound engineer into public life, bestowing on him the role of protector of a city's soundscape. With such a focus on noise came a movement toward noise management in spaces as diverse as city streets, office buildings, and concert halls. Thompson's history is absolutely integral here in showing how a technological definition of noise, created by the new science of electro-acoustics, gave sound engineers in the United States a new prominence in public life.

The electro-acoustical companies' approach to noise also reflected a wide-scale investment in industrial research that marked the decade of the 1920s. The culture of industrial research in the 1920s provides a necessary context for any study of noise. The twenty years before the full-scale introduction of synchronized sound films in Los Angeles were marked by a boom in the field of scientific culture, and the ten years before it were marked by a surge in the growth and development of industrial research. As Marzola has detailed, "In the early twentieth century, major companies began building research and development departments, attempting to transform 'what heretofore had been the result of random discovery and ingenious invention into the routine product of a carefully managed process.'"[14] Multiple research firms began their operations in this short window of time: chemical plants, energy plants, and, of course, communications companies, including those that would make possible the shift to sound film—among them DuPont, Kodak, General Electric, and American Telephone and Telegraph.[15] General Electric established the first formal research laboratory in 1900, followed by DuPont in 1902, Westinghouse in 1903, and Eastman Kodak and Bell Telephone Labs in 1912.[16] These industrial giants grew fast over the course of the 1920s, producing new data from research that was applied to improving their products. They also added new data to the existing store of knowledge in their respective fields. With this new mode of research came the rise of industrial organizations that attempted to standardize and apply knowledge gained in these companies. In all sorts of technological industries in the 1920s, professional organizations grew out of this fertile ground, designed to manage the entirety of the industry, especially to arbitrate between conflicting or competing parties and to mobilize and standardize research.[17] They cultivated cooperation between parties within their industries.

AMPAS has been underrecognized in its role as a technical forum that ran precisely in this way in 1929–31.

In an article entitled "A Society Apart: The Early Years of the Society of Motion Picture Engineers," Marzola traces how one of these professional organizations, the Society for Motion Picture Engineers (SMPE), cultivated its relationship with the film industry in an attempt to gain a foothold there. She writes that "throughout the late 1910s and the 1920s, the activities of the SMPE both facilitated collaborative efforts toward standardization" and "provided a forum for competitive innovation," reflecting "larger trends in American industry at the time toward an engineering ethos that emphasized scientific progressivism."[18] But in the conversations she details as happening between the members of the SMPE and those of the film industry, the topic of sound is notably absent even as late as the end of the 1920s.[19] The SMPE was slow to act when it came to standardizing the industry in matters of sound. In the meantime the Academy was able to seize the initiative. My own research shows that the SMPE was not the only organization "seeking to define its place in a new kind of business":[20] AMPAS actively campaigned for the position of dominant researcher and standardizer in the film industry during this time and in fact seized it before the SMPE could claim it. As Marzola notes, when in 1928the SMPE reached out to establish an ongoing dialogue with Hollywood, it was already too late.[21] A speech from 1929 by AMPAS's Lester Cowan declares that in the supposed absence of the SMPE's ability to take leadership in this area, the Academy will step in and take it instead: "Unfortunately, the Society [SMPE] does not have a notable reputation, due to commercial influence and other factors, with the result that at the present time, I do not hesitate to say that the entire motion picture industry looks to the Academy for achievement in co-ordinating and guiding technical progress in the motion picture industry."[22]

In exploring AMPAS's involvement in investigating and disseminating sound technology, conducting research, and tackling the problem of noise, I have drawn heavily on archives of the Research Council, which oversaw AMPAS's own initiatives during the shift to sound; the Technical Bureau, which launched a series of noise tests and published an informational series on the sound shift; and the Art and Technique Committee, which fine-tuned such initiatives and encouraged further dialogue. These underutilized documents make the broader claims of preexisting texts in film history more specific, fleshing them out in greater historical detail. My perspective is also informed by the technical approach that engineering brought to the table during the sound transition.[23] Here it draws on a technical literature that includes histories of research and development at the electro-acoustics labs, both from their own perspectives and from outside historians', and the journal published by Bell Labs. This understanding of an engineer's point of view is particularly important because the perspective the engineers brought to their work in the film industry was alien to the studio staff they worked with, causing friction between the groups, and leading to the adoption of AMPAS's programs. The engineering perspective is also almost as alien to most film scholars as it is grounded firmly in the technological discourse of electro-acoustics. But the details of Bell's culture of research are of vital importance if we are to understand how they affected the culture of filmmaking. Focusing not on the results of these efforts themselves but on the industrial model that generated them, I analyze the two industrial histories of electro-acoustics and film to see their meaningful structural and tactical similarities. As Dana Polan has noted, AMPAS developed its own research program as a response to a need for leadership given "the new complexity posed by the coming of sound."[24] AMPAS was originally created to neutralize conflicts and mediate between opposing parties; as early as 1927 it was mediating labor disputes within the film industry.[25] The research I have done, however, indicates that this role was more pervasive than we have previously considered during the sound transition, and richer than we might have expected.

In the first section of this chapter, I outline the rise of research at AT&T/Bell Laboratories and how noise features in that history. In the second, I show how Bell's research model was applied to the film industry's concerns at AMPAS. And in the third, I explore the legacy of this era of research, in which we can still see vestiges of this early approach at AMPAS today. The model of research AMPAS adopted during these years was more than just a brief interlude in technological culture. It was a genius move that created a necessary perspectival shift as historically significant as the adoption of film sound technologies themselves. Studios began to enable their staffs to think more like engineers. Staff had to do more than just operate sound technologies; they had to understand the logics and the reasoning behind these technologies. And AMPAS wanted more than a good working relationship with the labs; they wanted to in a way become them: to absorb elements of their authority in the risky film sound era. In pursuing this goal, the studios, with AMPAS leading them, made technological laboratory culture a part of their own culture. They made technological culture more familiar, easier to direct toward their goals, and less worrisome to their

THE ACADEMY TECHNICAL BUREAU

ITS PLACE IN THE MOTION PICTURE INDUSTRY

The Academy Technical Bureau represents for motion picture production a development that has become an established feature of modern competitive industry. Similar bureaus are found in the electric light, steel, oil, cotton, and other national industries, each the result of a parallel economic evolution.

The early stages of any new product or service finds a multitude of small companies exploring the market and concerned with outstripping each other to obtain an established position. This early period is always marked by severe competition and waste. It continues to the point where the existing markets have been covered and the competitive relationships established and to some extent stabilized. Further progress depends upon increased efficiency, lowered production costs, and the development of new markets and demands for the product, the ultimate limit depending upon how much of the public's dollar the industry can win in its competition with other industries. During the process of evolution there gradually came to the fore functions to be performed and vital needs to be fulfilled which require organization within the industry for the good of all. The nature and growth of the organization depend upon the particular circumstances in the industry and the vision of its leaders.

Operating in a competitive field, the cooperative organization necessarily has specialized functions which reflect the particular needs of the industry at the time. Several factors in the motion picture industry have determined the form of cooperative organization which can be most effective. Motion pictures may be called an art existing

FIGURE 2.2. Brochure describing the functions and activities of the Technical Bureau of the Academy of Motion Picture Arts and Sciences, July 15, 1930. From the Academy of Motion Picture Arts and Sciences Reference Collection.

stability. Research became a major part of AMPAS's plan to, in the words of Sidney Kent, Fox Film Corporation's president, "keep the business alive with the coming of sound."[26]

THE INSPIRATION: RESEARCH AND NOISE AT BELL LABS

Bell Laboratory/AT&T's influence on the film world just after the sound transition is evident in AMPAS's words and actions from 1929 though 1931. It offered a new model for participation in the sound technology industry. This model was to focus on noise. AT&T was among the very first examples of industrial research and development in the United States.[27] The electro-acoustical industry was at the forefront of the movement to blend applied research into a vertically integrated corporation. It was the second industry globally (after chemical laboratories such as DuPont) to develop research branches to promote empirical knowledge in its field.[28] For Bell, the need to include new research in their business model had been clear.[29] It emerged as a result of the company's drive to establish coast-to-coast telephone service coverage. They adopted "a deliberate policy of supporting the pursuit of scientific knowledge to speed advancement" within the field.[30] Vertical integration meant a chance to control one's own direction.

The study of noise became a prime example of AT&T's emerging model of applied research.[31] The company was able to apply such knowledge to the design of more noiseless products. A vertically integrated system from principles to practices, AT&T, with Bell as its research branch, became a force to be reckoned with. Solutions to the problem of noise became a Bell trade secret, and part of its stock in trade: a way of gaining a corner on the market. With its research system, Bell could beat out competition from smaller makers of telephone components and establish its own dominance in its industry. It also began to hoard patents, securing its future. This "secret" was the additional upper hand Bell gained over any competitors.[32]

Bell was plagued by noise from the beginning. From the late nineteenth century, it called in the nation's earliest research science PhDs to help it with problems of noise in its technologies.[33] These efforts culminated in the formation of an official Research Branch in 1911, under the leadership of University of Chicago–trained physicist Frank B. Jewett.[34] This innovation would have a deep and formative effect on the research scene that AMPAS encountered.

The scientists at Bell used their expertise throughout the 1920s to identify, isolate, and reduce noise. Research physicists made Bell home to the study of the underlying principles behind noise and interference in order to minimize it. They applied their knowledge base and skills to the solution of practical problems and the exploration of sound's "fundamental principles." At the same time, they fed their knowledge into mechanisms that developed products for the corporation.

Jewett's small research laboratory grew, over the course of the 1920s, into the largest organization for the study of noise.[35] Jewett would supervise the work of physicists, chemists, and mathematicians in this developing study over this decade. From the late 1910s to the late 1920s, researchers in the United States investigated the "Brownian-like fluctuations of microscopic charge carriers in electronic tubes and associated circuit components in efforts to understand and quantify the disturbances such fluctuations produced" in the transmission of signals in technologies.[36] The frequencies of such noise, which ranged from several hertz to tens of kilohertz, "slurred the signal," creating factors that interfered with ideal listening conditions.[37] Early research on noise in electronics was also done at industrial laboratories such as Siemens in Germany and G.E.'s laboratory in Schenectady, New York.[38] Their mutual goal was to improve the performance of thermionic tubes and electronic circuits used in the production of their devices. The process of refining, discovering, and identifying noise in the period can be characterized as giving engineers "intellectual tools to make sense of, to quantify, and to define electronic noise."[39] In their pursuit of solutions, they discovered and classified two types of noise, "shot noise" and "thermal noise."[40] Noise therefore played a key role in major elements of research at Bell from the 1910s through the 1950s. That was their sole concern— "the alleviation of disturbances that corrupted signal transmission."[41]

The model of Bell/AT&T's structure, which was set up in the 1910s, attracted AMPAS as much as the similarity in the two industries' troubles with noise. By 1914, AT&T was publishing papers on its fundamental research and developments in engineering.[42] AMPAS would do this later. The *Bell System Technical Journal* spread news regarding innovations throughout the broad-based Bell System.[43] AMPAS would model this with the Technical Digests it published after the turn to sound. Bell was among the early adopters of a model whereby they educated their employees. It and its parent company AT&T rose to become, in the twentieth century, two of the most prolific supporters of graduate education for their employees in the country.[44] AMPAS would imitate this distinctive initiative with its School of Sound Fundamentals. And Bell/AT&T's mission to disseminate knowledge regarding recent innovations to all branches of the system would have been extremely appealing to AMPAS, which also managed a multibranch organization that spanned all activities of an industry.

THE EXPERIMENT: RESEARCH ON NOISE AT AMPAS

Early on, AMPAS recognized the value inherent in AT&T's pet subject of noise. To a "still-adolescent industry," noise had enormous power and meaning.[45] AMPAS seems to have taken this as a chance to uncover a powerful mystery about sound technologies and knowledge and to share a "secret" with its industry that was well worth knowing. AMPAS embarked on fledgling efforts to mimic Bell. AMPAS's representatives were explicit in comparing their new efforts to those of organizations such as AT&T's research branch. The sixteenth report from the Academy's newly formed Technical Bureau compared its activities to Bell's quite clearly, stating that the bureau would conduct a course of technical surveys on sound practices at each of the studios, perform research on technological problems related to sound and noise, host technical lectures and do industrial education, publish a Technical Digest series, present papers at technical conferences and send them out for publication in journals, promote research and collaborate with the electro-acoustical industry to design new experiments, and host meetings at which technical matters might be promoted through interdivisional dialogue. On all these points, they were mimicking Bell's established industrial practices.[46]

It became clear that the SMPE would not fulfill the film industry's expectation to intervene and develop acoustic testing programs, being unprepared or unwilling to do so, according to AMPAS's accounts. Already busy with other projects and disinclined to engage in an industry-wide technological program when their headquarters was on the East Coast, SMPE by default passed the torch to AMPAS.[47] The Academy stepped forward to establish relations with the electro-acoustical labs. It seemed necessary to its technical leaders to, in their words, "do as much as we can"; in the absence of any existing organization for handling a recognized problem," they resolved to "take an interest in it and seek to bring about a solution."[48] AMPAS used its role as an industry-wide umbrella organization as its justification. A speech delivered by the secretary at the Academy states: "It is not logical that a single [studio] company can effectively be expected to do this. It is really not its function. The problem involving co-ordination of so many independent groups can be handled only through an organization such as the Academy."[49]

AMPAS even considered constructing a laboratory of its own. Louis B. Mayer drove for its realization, explicitly recommending it in a joint meeting of the Producers and Technicians Branches because individual studios could not finance or oversee a lab effectively and lacked the overarching ability or intention of benefiting the entire industry.[50] Mayer and others felt that a division for research and development was the missing component of an otherwise vertically integrated film industry. To that end, Samuel Goldwyn offered $5,000 toward its cost, noting, "There is not an industry in the world that needs development that does not spend millions of dollars a year in research." His offer was met with applause. But by 1930, a research laboratory of AMPAS's own was no longer contemplated because of its projected cost. AMPAS would work instead in conjunction with commercial and academic laboratories. However, the Academy's Technical Bureau was officially formed and was budgeted $15,000 per year in order to pursue its research projects—a sizable sum.[51]

At that time AMPAS arguably needed a new justification for its existence as much as the sound industry needed a venue for its products. In 1929, one of its bulletins admitted as much, stating: "Several have remarked recently how extremely fortunate it is for the Academy that this sound recording situation has occurred to give us a new chance to be of special service." Scrambling to correct the impression, the writer added: "It would be more correct, perhaps, to reverse this observation and say that it has been especially fortunate for the industry that there is the Academy to perform this service."[52] Both statements were, in fact, true, but AMPAS hardly did it out of the goodness of its heart. Fred Pelton, chairman of the Academy's Technicians Branch, stated how the introduction of the model of the research laboratory fit into the history of the Academy: "The Academy started off with such a bang and speed, and it was rather difficult to maintain that pace, and a number of people . . . are looking at the Academy to see what is going to happen."[53] Pelton, representing the Academy, claimed it felt "a responsibility as well as an opportunity" for "setting about to systematically spread knowledge of the new tools, and the experience in using them." By acting in this capacity, the Academy could, as Chairman Irving Thalberg put it, "show the benefit of centralized action on these problems rather than individual attempts, spasmodic, undirected, and mostly inefficient."[54] All in the AMPAS leadership agreed that "now is the time to go slow and do all the research that is possible."[55]

A speech by Thalberg at a meeting of the Producers and Technicians branches of AMPAS in May of 1930 explained how sound research and education aligned with the mission of the Academy: "When the Academy was founded vaguely in the minds of the charter members it was hoped that something like this could be realized. There were hopes that the various competing studios could meet on a common ground and help each other on problems that were mutual to them all."[56] Thalberg added that the early work being done on sound was a prime example of what the Academy was capable of in joining the art and science of filmmaking together by joining technologists with the film industry's creative personnel: "I think this is only a forerunner of the kind of work that can be attempted by the Academy in the line of bringing everybody to a point where a scientist can meet on the same ground with the members of the industry."[57] AMPAS president William de Mille similarly told a group of sound engineers and studio staff at around the same time that "the thing of greatest value [is] when we find that you are human beings with every problem in the world before you, and when you find that we are human beings with every problem in the world before us, and we take those two problems and raise them together and call them one." In actively collaborating with sound engineers and with each other, he stated, the film industry was making "the greatest strike that this industry has ever made. . . . I thought it would happen in 50 years and it has happened in 30 days."[58] De Mille ended with "that great word, 'UNITY.' This business now has a chance of real unity," he said, now that Hollywood filmmakers and sound technicians were working together. And when that unity was achieved, research progress would be accelerated: "You can do it so much faster after we have reached an understanding and have a unified purpose."[59]

How they might achieve unity was the question. Research at the Academy had begun, but the model of the organization shifted over time. In October 1929, the impulse for an Academy-sponsored research branch had found its realization in the Producers-Technicians Joint Committee, which was intended to "handle the scientific problems that would benefit from cooperative research, investigation, and experimentation" between the studios.[60] In 1930 the Technical Bureau of the Association of Motion Picture Producers was transferred to AMPAS and began to function under its control. By 1932 AMPAS's research branch had been renamed again as the Research Council. But between them all, the same drive was manifest: the drive to see research associated with the Academy.

Several initiatives mark the beginning of this new role and shift in AMPAS's persona. It became "a place of record": it would supply the studios with "pertinent information on technical problems with which they find themselves confronted."[61] It became a technological clearinghouse to "keep the individual studios abreast of current progress in patents, inventions, and technical developments." And it took charge of reports and publications, funneling technological information from the labs to the desks of the Hollywood executives. Through the work of the Producers-Technicians Joint Committee, the Technical Bureau, the Research Council, and its successors, the film industry picked up and extended the work done by Bell and its partners, working in conjunction with the electro-acoustics companies to suggest new methods and models for the burgeoning film market.

According to their own accounts put forward in their documents, AMPAS intervened during the shift to film sound to produce order out of the disruption that the inclusion of the engineers created.[62] In a 1928 meeting of the Technicians Branch of AMPAS, Fred Beetson stated that when "the talking thing came in," the era naturally became "the age of the technician."[63] Jesse M. Lasky agreed that "the thing we are going through is nothing more or less than a showdown."[64] William de Mille stated that when "the talkies broke," the "whole industry found itself immediately very much mixed up."

At a 1927 meeting of the Academy, Louis B. Mayer remarked that the film industry and the sound industry would need to negotiate the set of concerns that arose and find solutions together: "We all eat the same eggs from the goose that laid the golden egg [i.e., the sound motion picture industry], and it becomes your problem as well as my problem to keep that bird alive so it continues to give us those golden eggs."[65] Mayer criticized his own staff who refused to learn with the coming of sound: "We are little kings, and we are losing today the way of thinking of our perspective and we are losing the happiness and charm of life. Through this Academy that we have got here I think we can iron out our difficulties and our differences. There is an awful lot to be said" on behalf of cooperation between sound engineers and studio staff. To the engineers he stated: "I am heartily in favor of you; I am enthused by you." The problem was, he said, largely one of a lack of understanding. "You are not going to get them by fighting them [the studio staff], but let's coax them into it; let's educate them into the right perspective so that they respect you." The coming of sound, Mayer states, "is our great problem," but "it is our goose and we are all getting the good out of it and we are all getting the damnation from it if it goes wrong."[66] The only solution, he and others asserted, was a sharing of knowledge through a process of research and education that modeled the very electro-acoustical industry that many resented.[67]

That sharing was not easily achieved. An AMPAS memo from Secretary Frank Woods described how "these Bell Lab men were thrown into contact with studio men to work with them, but the difference in attitude and fundamental habits of thought and work between the studio technicians and the Bell Lab men was apparent." The trouble "showed itself in mutual condemnation, the studio men charging the Bell Lab men with being slow, theoretical, and unacquainted with motion pictures—and entirely disrespectful to the ingenuity which has made motion pictures what they are to day [sic]. The Bell Lab men, on the other hand, looked upon the studio men as empirically trained men who knew just enough to be dangerous" and were "therefore incapable of being trusted with the problem."[68]

By 1930, a mythology had grown up around the sound engineer. The conflict between the separate cultures of Hollywood and the electro-acoustics companies is vividly portrayed in the documents circulated within AMPAS.[69] From the account in a memo from the Producers-Technicians Joint Committee, the sound men's presence in the studio system seems to have disrupted its workings notably. For instance, "The majority of the studio personnel did not have a glimpse of a sound stage during the early days of the talkies and being out was discomforting." The memo says that "everyone wanted to go into the sound stage until the studio officials had to place guards at the doors to keep their own people out."[70]

The division of employees into insiders and outsiders created feelings of both awe and resentment. According to the Producers-Technicians Joint Committee memo, "Everyone was humble toward the sound man for he alone understood this strange mechanism which was to play such a vital part in the future." An early draft of this same memo states, in language that would disappear from the finished memo, "Psychologically he was the dictator of the lot and in many cases this feeling of unaccustomed power was detrimental."[71] Supposedly, the engineer relished his adulation: not being used to "so much power and such reverence, [he] enjoyed the orgy of worship and encouraged it by surrounding himself with even more mystery." But "those denied the high privilege of contacting a sound expert reacted as anyone might toward a stranger being which we cannot understand." The feeling was "one of resentment" against the magical bearer of the strange technology, and "this unrest" did not subside "in any individual case until the person became a bit acquainted with [the] mysteries of sound." Education, such memos articulated, would allow for better dialogue between these major players. According to Woods's memo, "The complete subordination to the sound men was not healthy. He was interested in physical performance of his equipment, not in artistic effects. The values of the motion picture that has been developed over years were being sacrificed out of deference to the sound men. The alarm was sounded that the screen was losing its beauty and becoming a mechanical toy. There was a reaction." As the memo describes that reaction, "Sound experts instead of being viewed with awe were maligned as soon as their weakness [of a lack of film knowledge] was discovered. What did they know about motion pictures? What did they know about entertainment?"[72] AMPAS arrived to heal the breach, while also playing the scenario intelligently for its own side. As AMPAS member M.C. Lightman stated later, "It is a well-known fact that we gain more with bricks by laying them than throwing them."[73] By establishing its own research program, AMPAS began to work its way into the high priest's temple and to attempt to share the rituals with their people: to make everyone an "insider" who had become familiar with the secrets of sound. The secret of sound was discussed as if it were a key that would unlock a stable and happy future.

Sound knowledge being made a "secret" seems to be key to understanding the resentments described in such accounts. Studio staff complained that engineers exploited this secrecy. When they could not capture a recording, they provided technical excuses that studio personnel could not evaluate, justified themselves with explanations derived from physics that the studio staff did not often feel qualified to speak to, and alluded to minutiae regarding the specifics of the instruments. To studio staff unversed in such matters, the engineers' behavior read as aggressive. Their specialized knowledge could damage the film industry's productivity and could be used as leverage in disputes on the film set. However, such fears diminished when AMPAS launched a program of research into sound and noise that stole some of the thunder from the engineering companies and taught these subjects to its members. "Director, writer and cameraman began to feel that they were coming back into their own," states a memo from AMPAS's Producers-Technicians Joint Committee.[74] Armed with sound's basic principles, studio personnel could make sound their own purview. The memo finishes: "The present period is one of readjustment. They [the sound men] are becoming sensitive to the demands of the art and are striving to give the director what he wants. On the other hand the director and cameraman have learned to sympathize with the sound engineer's predicament and no longer are intolerantly demanding the impossible," thanks to their recent education. Mutual understanding was achievable, AMPAS's documents suggested, through their projects. But the truth of the situation also went deeper.

AMPAS seems to have comprehended the danger that excessive control by the electro-acoustical companies could threaten the autonomy of motion pictures. The Academy thus sought to gain the engineers' knowledge and repurpose it in order to shift the balance of power and gain control over the application of sound.

One meeting in Los Angeles gave AMPAS a starting point to capture the "secrets" they had sought and begin to reveal them to the film industry. On July 31, 1929, the Producers Branch of the Academy of Motion Picture Arts and Sciences held an extended meeting with a group of sound engineers from Bell Labs, Electrical Research Products, Inc., AT&T, and RCA Photophone. Chaired by B. P. Schulberg, general manager of West Coast production of Paramount-Famous-Lasky Corporation, and attended by multiple officials from the major studios, it was described as a union of the best and brightest minds to discuss subjects of concern to both industries.[75] The purpose, as defined by the agenda, was "considering the Academy as a medium through which certain of the problems which have arisen since the advent of sound might be effectively attacked."[76] It was a meeting designed to transfer at least some of the impetus for film sound research from the labs to AMPAS, specifically research geared toward standardization—always the purview of the technical associations. That meeting represented the point at which AMPAS began its host of new projects.

According to Woods, "When the talking picture revolutionized the industry the studios accomplished wonders in adapting themselves to an emergency"; However, "Now the time has come to lay a strong foundation for future progress. Sound is going to be our business for a long time."[77] AMPAS was positioning itself to take control, having learned many of the lessons it needed from the electro-acoustical labs. Frank Woods stated in a memo from June 1929: "The inquiry into sound recording problems can be best undertaken at this time because the first chaos into which the studios were thrown is giving way to the rapid development of the new technique necessary." The project of an AMPAS-controlled technical program represented what he termed "a step in the self-education which was the response of the industry to the challenge of sound."[78] Education and research were to be based at AMPAS. The lessons would be their own. As Frank Woods stated in a talk given at the Society for Motion Picture Engineers convention in Toronto in 1930:

> The first rush of talking picture production is settling into a longer and steadier stride. We have revolutionized a great creative art and a better business. New methods to use new machines to secure new effects were thrust upon us hardly more than a year ago. It was the work of a good many days and nights as well to get on friendly terms of acquaintanceship with them. Now it is time for an inventory. We need to be sure that we are on a broad foundation. That foundation can be only the widest possible

interest and information in the whole motion picture industry so that wherever each person makes his individual contribution it will be intelligently efficient.[79]

To do this meant to unlock those secrets via a model very much like that of the companies themselves. So AMPAS began a process of research oriented toward identifying the proper methods to standardize sound practice.

The solutions posed at this meeting carried AMPAS into its new role as a bridge in the sound transition. The first step in seizing power through knowledge would be research into the application of new technologies. At least some of the studio reps seemed to believe that this was necessary. First would come a research-style assessment of the state of sound implementation at the studios and their needs. Then would come a period of tests, the results of which would be disseminated to encourage best practices. Last would come a program of education based upon the newly gleaned information. During this period, AMPAS collected data on sound practices at the major and minor studios. It sponsored experiments at physics laboratories in order to diagnose sources of noise and suggest solutions to dampen them. It hosted lectures and organized conferences and symposia on sound technologies used in filmmaking, and it published copies of these lectures for its membership. It took on the role of an educator, creating its School of Sound Fundamentals of Sound Recording and Reproduction for Motion Pictures to teach recording practices to the studios' staff. In an industry where major players were very cagey with their secrets, and at a moment particularly fraught with economic instability, AMPAS found a role to play: that of researcher and educator. However, it had to act very carefully to avoid disrupting power relations between competitors that made up its committees. Acting in this dicey moment, AMPAS created a popular dialogue around noise. It distracted competing companies from the risk of major business decisions inherent in this time of industrial change, and the lack of trust between competitors.[80] In 1929, J. T. Reed of the Technicians Branch of AMPAS said the film industry was in "a condition of chaos due to talking pictures."[81] As Cecil B. DeMille put it at this same meeting: "Yesterday we were snarling at each other. We did have secrets. We were trying to get this and that and the other thing from the other fellow."[82] Noise, then, became the new secret whose truth AMPAS could reveal. AMPAS could also propose a universal solution to that problem in the forms of standardized practices of application for sound recording methods. As Schulberg commented in a transcript from a Producers Branch meeting, "We are, of course, in a competitive industry which means that many subjects are necessarily taboo."[83] The virtue of noise was that it was not. Equally available to and relevant to all, it provided a bridge between the studios. AMPAS then acquired the knowledge of the sound engineers and used it to make tight bonds within the industry and eject outsiders. And while Schulberg stated in that meeting, "You bet you can have our secrets, and we are going to get Lasky's secrets, because there are no secrets," this was not true. All documents drawn upon by this book reinforce the generally held opinion that the sound shift was a historical process full of people who did, indeed, hold a multitude of secrets. But noise was a different kind of secret: one that was meant to be shared, to create unity within a divided business. AMPAS could do this for the industry, helping to create a unified front in an anxious time for the studio system. For this reason, AMPAS created a sort of open secret to distract from the fact of more general secret keeping. It was a secret that was perfect for the moment: a safe secret that united each of the studios with its fellows in a new body of knowledge. Within that context, AMPAS exploited its status as a clearinghouse to educate its members in the mysteries of the sound transition. The aim of this was clear: as William de Mille put it, "This Academy . . . stands for the merger of ideals, stands for friendship, and if I may apologize to the producers for using the word again, that great word, UNITY."[84] He concluded, "We have reached an understanding and have a unified purpose, which is unity, which is this Academy." His speech was met with prolonged applause.

It was at this specific meeting that the idea of the Academy having its own research laboratory was first proposed. But smaller steps were also taken in the meantime. As Reed put it in a speech, sound had been "pretty much a secret," but now, at least, there could be "a lot of worth while [sic] standardizing going on." This would, he writes, "at least get something good out of the chaos."[85] An industry-wide survey of sound production problems was begun in 1929, gathering data from the major and minor studios, with the aim of creating data sets on studio practices large enough to diagnose where programs of tests were necessary. AMPAS again emphasized that the study of noise was a cooperative endeavor to solve a shared problem: the survey was "preparatory to a projected series of investigations and tests to present the basic methods for problems common to all the studios. It is believed many fundamentals can be profitably standardized without affecting the exclusive processes being developed by the various studios."[86] Using technical language, it managed to couch industry concerns as technical concerns, making them safe to discuss.

Out of this process, a schedule of quantitative laboratory tests emerged.[87] Two types of noise came to the fore in the surveys and were attacked in the program. These were "incidental noise," or noises that could be acoustically dampened, and "ground noise," the noise of the recording system. While the former could be prevented on the set, the latter could not. Each presented challenges; each was studied in its turn and had its conclusions disseminated via AMPAS Progress Reports. Progress Report No. 1 laid out the problem of noise and the method of attack for how to study these concerns. The rest of the year was taken up by the publication of data collected on each of the major sources of incidental noise and the descriptions of studies designed by AMPAS and its electro-acoustical partners to address them. The areas of concern were the construction of sets with acoustical dampening materials, the silencing of noisy motion picture cameras, the sounds emitted by lights, and microphone design. On the basis of its research, AMPAS recommended best practices for the industry in dealing with such noise.

Progress Report No. 2 detailed the challenges implicit in the construction of sets. Sixteen studios collaborated in gathering data so as to standardize classification of the studios' practices in reducing unnecessary noise and reverberation. Materials were tested for their properties and classified by such data. Materials tested included cast stone on brick, plaster on burlap, plaster on lathe and flats, plasterboard, and the acoustical material Celotex on plaster.[88] The data gathered was put to use as a preliminary stage in determining which of the acoustical materials would then be tested further in the laboratory of noted acoustician Vern O. Knudsen at UCLA. These tests were sponsored by AMPAS. Progress Report No. 3 discussed camera silencing. Cameras during the silent era were permitted to be quite noisy; it made little difference when no live sound was being captured. In the sound era, however, synchronous dialogue necessitated quiet sets, and the industry's noisy cameras proved a threat to the integrity of the soundtrack. Cameras, then, were enclosed in mobile rolling booths with small windows that allows the camera to look out. They were also enclosed in blimps that were more mobile but still unwieldy.[89] Tests arranged for quantitative noise measurements of noise reduction apparatuses; the effects of heating upon blimped or boothed cameras that would naturally have no means of allowing air warmed by the machine to escape; the accessibility of the camera under such conditions; the ease of operation with booth, blimp, or blankets; considerations of portability and weight; and the effectiveness of these apparatuses as dampeners of noise. Tests were executed at ERPI (Electrical Research Products, Inc., a division of Western Electric), and sixteen silencing methods were tested to determine the distance at which a microphone might pick up the signal without noise. Blimps far outperformed blankets as sound reducers, allowing a placement of the microphone as close as five feet from the camera. Blankets allowed microphone placement as close as fifteen feet and produced a noise level equal to what the progress report terms a "loud whisper," making such plans ineffectual for creating finely tuned soundscapes.[90]

Following these studies of camera noise came an inquiry into the "fizz" or "sizzle" made by arc lamps, with data from yet another survey of the studios leading the way to determine methods to study in AMPAS-sponsored lab tests. It was discovered there was a "hum" caused by the commutator ripple on the power supply. To remove the ripple, which was simply a small amount of alternating current disrupting the direct current power feed, filtering equipment became necessary. AMPAS undertook to determine the degree of ripple in each studio's arcs via testing. This would enable them to recommend the degree of filtering necessary for its removal at each studio, which was especially important, as this equipment was costly. AMPAS engineers made suggestions as to the type of filter that would best do the job, engaging in technical development. Last came discussions of miking with the boom and the cardioid microphone. An AMPAS study in 1931 analyzed how sound was "generated by a vibrating body" in these mikes but how too much vibration created noise.[91] Again, AMPAS fulfilled its mission of gathering information that was noncompetitive in order to standardize methods that would allow the industry to determine its own path in noise reduction.

The next step was to send this knowledge out to the world.[92] The knowledge was disseminated by a dozen progress reports detailing the researchers' work on noise. In each, AMPAS was laying the groundwork for later technical tests on noise to be performed.[93] AMPAS set itself up as a clearinghouse of published information on the sound transition. Its documents indicate repeated communications between Lester Cowan, the secretary, and the electro-acoustics companies, in which the former asked for technical articles and papers to be made available to Academy members.[94] Cowan likewise asked whether Bell Labs had any suggestions for invited lectures that could be given as part of AMPAS's campaign to inculcate greater sound knowledge and understanding.[95]

FIGURE 2.3. The Columbia Padded Bungalow: one of many
solutions film studios devised to attempt to reduce the noise of
the camera. It was one of the eighteen solutions tested at ERPI by
the AMPAS Producers-Technicians Committee in 1930. Courtesy
of the Academy of Motion Picture Arts and Sciences Reference
Collection.

Records indicate that this interest was one-sided; the electro-acoustic
companies seldom answered inquiries from AMPAS. Reading the letters,
one gets the impression that the Academy was attempting to forge a
relationship with obsequious attention and that the research companies
chose to ignore such efforts. Undeterred, however, the Academy pressed
on. AMPAS became a technical publisher again through its Technical
Digest series, which disseminated information to members.[96] These were
the written records of lectures given by sound industry experts and
hosted by AMPAS, engaging not only with the experience of sound but
also with the underlying mechanics of sound waves, reverberation, and

noise.[97] Their publication gave the impression of transparency in matters of sound, welcoming all members from all studios into the "inner circle" to learn the sound secret.

The last component of the Academy's three-part program for 1929–31 was education through the establishment of a School of Sound Fundamentals whose instructors would be engineers brought in from faculty at the University of Southern California and UCLA as well as the staff of the major electrical labs, such as Bell. The school made it possible for studio staff to catch up to the basic understanding of physics they would need to function in the new sound era and to learn the practical methods by which engineers used sound's fundamental principles.[98] It was an education in the kind of applied physics that the labs were doing. In a July 1929 meeting Cowan described how a typical class might work: "The professor would get up and give a general academic talk," and then someone would "explain its practical application to the sound technologies being used in motion pictures."[99] A month later, a supplement to the *AMPAS Bulletin* laid out in more detail a three-part course for studio employees in "fundamentals of sound recording and reproduction." Part One would be a review of the necessary physical preliminaries, which included "the nature of sound; the physical characteristics of music and speech; the human voice," and "analysis of the sense of hearing." Part Two would focus on "electrical recording and reproduction of sound, first in a general way and then as applied in the production of talking motion pictures." This would also include "problems in acoustics and the artistic possibilities of acoustical control." Part Three would deal with the practical application of the laws of physics learned in Part One to the real-world scenarios offered in audio recording for motion pictures.[100] This kind of education, according to Karl Strauss of AMPAS, was an opportunity to bring a "production secret process" into "the new era of brotherhood."[101] An article in an AMPAS Progress Report similarly claimed that the school "will not undertake to make every student a sound engineer, but it will make sound less of a mystery and more of a practical utility to all those whose work touches upon it."[102]

Cowan had stated at the start of an AMPAS meeting on the school that there was a "need for all motion picture creative workers to become intelligently familiar with their new tools."[103] As he put it, "The ideal thing would be to have everybody in every studio equally familiar with the problems of sound." This meant that the entire "creative staff" of the studio should attend: "Directors should go, writers should go, cameramen should go—they should all go."[104] He stated, "Writers and directors especially should be given the opportunity to understand the fundamentals of the work of the technicians so as to be able to at least talk intelligently with technical men and understand generally the tools of the art."[105] Lasky personally encouraged his studio directors to attend, stating: "I am going to learn what I ought to have learned years ago about motion pictures, when I didn't have time and I had other problems . . . I ought to know a great deal more than I do, and I am not too old to learn."[106] William de Mille similarly lent his support, stating: "I am seeking light. My great success—whatever I have attained—has been due to the fact that I have always been like a sponge. I want to absorb; I want to learn; I want to improve, and I can't do that reading books. I can do that [by] listening."[107] Education, enlightenment, and understanding became linked in the discourse of AMPAS at the time.

While this plan of sound education gained enough support to be voted into reality, the transcript of a July 1929 meeting between AMPAS's Producers Branch and a group of sound engineers from Bell Labs, Electrical Research Products, Inc., AT&T, and RCA Photophone indicates that engineers were still dubious about the extent to which studio higher-ups would commit to it.[108] One sound engineer interrupted to ask whether directors truly had any interest in learning about sound, despite the pretty rhetoric, and whether studio heads would force the issue if they did not. The school, he said, "will be looked forward to anxiously by almost every technician on every lot," "but what good will it do" if the studios did not push involvement from their staffs. "On every lot everybody knows—when the director who is his employer for the time being on the picture is not informed [about the limitations of sound technology], it causes the technician great distress." The engineer granted that if educational programs could be "made attractive" to film industry people and could "convince them," real progress toward a fully functioning sound industry might be possible. But top industry players such as directors would be needed if the project were going to succeed. Studio heads did, therefore, encourage employees to enroll, and their efforts proved successful when the School of Sound Fundamentals became enrolled beyond expectation.

The school's aims had been small at first. It was designed to accommodate select employees from sixteen Hollywood studios, with an anticipated enrollment of only about one hundred students.[109] By October 1929, however, the enrollment had swelled to five hundred, forcing AMPAS to add two additional classes. Demand continued to swell. By April of 1930, six sections of the course had been completed, with an enrollment of almost one thousand men.[110] The sound school was so popular that it caused Secretary Cowan to quip: "Our school might even develop a football team."[111]

The idea of a football team of studio men coached by Bell Labs engineers says a lot about their desire to incorporate engineering into filmmaking. Cowan's imaginary football team was only one example of a joke about the engineers designed to make them sound chummier with the studios: very literally, on the same team. A January 1929 letter from J. I. Crabtree at the Research Laboratory of Eastman Kodak Co. to Julia B. Johnson at AMPAS stated, "I am glad that you were able to arrange a joint meeting . . . for discussion of sound matters with Bell Telephone experts. This meeting was even mentioned in the trade papers which is certainly promising." Crabtree added: "I think that after Mr. Hoover gets to Washington the fan magazines may contain notices about the engineers and their divorces and love affairs."[112] His vision of engineers being featured in the magazines that dealt in Hollywood gossip was, of course, a joke. But it was also a joking reference to AMPAS's agenda to make the use of sound technology so integral to filmmaking that its practitioners would even be subject to the Hollywood paparazzi treatment.[113]

A major topic in AMPAS meetings was getting the cooperation of studio directors in AMPAS's sound education program. At a 1929 meeting between AMPAS and sound engineers, MGM producer Harry Rapf recounted how troublesome it was when a director who did not understand sound limitations had to be talked out of his ideas: "The director says 'I am going to have it' [and] we have had to convince him that he can't have it." He continued, "I have had the good fortune to break in one-half dozen directors," adding, "We tried to train them to give them an idea of the limitations." One anonymous engineer asserted that directors' education in sound motion picture technology was particularly vital because the director was the "boss" on set.[114]

Indeed, directors seemed to be one holdout group preventing progress. It was often claimed that directors had to learn how sound technology functioned to be able to understand its limitations. For instance, Rapf asserted that "when we take that director into the soundroom and he hears these things—the mixer says 'We are overloading,'" the director needs to "be told what that word means."[115] AMPAS's Technical Bureau proposed that a glossary be made available for everyday use in the studios, translating common terms from electrical engineering into plain language for the directors, and did end up creating one.[116] An AMPAS memo from 1929 stated that directors "know what the close-up is, what the fade-out is, etc., but in general they do not know what dubbing is, what sound levels are, etc. We feel that if the art side of the business learns enough about the work of the technical aspects to talk intelligently with technical men an understanding will be developed that will be of great benefit to the progress of the art."[117]

Directors' hubris and refusal to consider new sound knowledge was often termed an obstacle for the progress of sound motion pictures, especially since, according to Schulberg, the directors were "wrong most of the time. They are smug, self-complacent about what they know. The wisest thing for the industry is to compel the directors to go."[118] Schulberg complained that directors often operated in ignorance of the facts of sound: "They expect things done—they have been trained that way." Rapf also blamed the studio policies: "I admit that in our own studio for months we kept the doors closed—wouldn't allow any one on the sound stage—this was a mistake. Now we have changed." He stated that now "we allow these directors to go on the stage—before we kept them away—we made it a secret." With the engineers' assimilation into Hollywood, the "secret" became common knowledge. This overcame what Carl Dreher, director of the Sound Department at RKO Studios, described in 1931 as film people's ambivalence toward the sound technician: "a tendency to misunderstand and disparage his mode of thought" while still retaining "equally inappropriate superstitious veneration for his mental processes."[119]

"The significant point," an AMPAS memo reads, "of this whole development was the need for education. The making of a motion picture is a collaboration." AMPAS also concerned itself with educating engineers about film. A report of the survey on sound problems in 1929 stated that "sound has brought into the production industry . . . engineers who have little understanding of the motion picture art."[120] Yet as a paper given on behalf of AMPAS stated, "It is desirable for the sound expert[s] to have an appreciation of screen drama. A mutual understanding facilitates communication and the cooperation that is so vital."[121] Consequently, as one meeting summary stated, a priority should be "developing among the new personnel," specifically engineers, "an appreciation of the art of the motion picture."[122] "The amount of sympathetic understanding," another memo read, was "still [at] a minimum"; "the Bell men" needed to realize that "to be of service, [they] must adapt themselves to m[otion] p[icture] ways that will not change to suit them." To succeed, they would need to be "artist[s] first and engineer[s] second."[123] Consequently, an education in studio work and film aesthetics had to be made available to engineers.[124] To meet this need, the *AMPAS Bulletin* announced "a series of lectures, designed to give the new personnel brought into the industry by sound a broader understanding of the motion picture art," as "the chief feature of the fall education program" for 1930. The course would be "organized and administered in a manner similar to the Sound School."[125]

For the most part, the sound engineers from the electro-acoustic companies stopped coming into Los Angeles as Hollywood began to replace them with its own people, trained in its own way for film applications specifically. J. A. Ball stated in a meeting that "the person who has hold of the mechanical end of the sound should be a person trained along motion picture lines."[126] An internal memo similarly stated that the aim of AMPAS's technological education was "to provide in a systematic manner the fundamental knowledge necessary for an understanding of the electrical recording and reproduction of sound as applied to motion pictures." The goal was "that all crafts collaborating in production have at least a general understanding of the characteristics, possibilities, and limitations of the new tools of the art." Through the courses, the Academy would "offer them the opportunity of securing the added knowledge which they need in their new work."[127]

Expectations of the School ran high. E. H. Allen of AMPAS stated, "If [in] starting these talking pictures we are going to break down practically all of the barriers, we want to know how we can accomplish [this] and put [them] on the screen with sound just the same [with the same methods] as we do with silent."[128] There was hope that the Sound School would begin a new era of faster and trouble-free production with sound engineering better incorporated into Hollywood: a system that would function just as it had before their arrival, only now with sound. The School of Sound, which could not produce such a scenario immediately, met with resistance when it was first described. William Sistrom of the studios interrupted Schulberg at a meeting to voice these concerns: "I mean, there is [the] practicable side and the technical, theoretical side and that is what leads me to ask who is preparing the course and whether the problem of getting immediate results rather than sound fundamental knowledge" may not be a higher priority.[129] Research—the purview of the laboratories—still seemed to be a waste of time to some studio personnel. Sistrom's concern that the "technical, theoretical side" of the matter was gaining too much attention was reasonable. Sound, he argued, should be a straightforward tool rather than an area of intensive study and research. Moviemaking did not require more.

Delving too deeply into the territory of Bell Labs seemed, to some, unnecessary and confusing. It caused discomfort. These "more immediate problems" were those, of course, of day-to-day film production. Critics such as Sistrom worried that an emphasis on research and education that was too abstract could reduce the number of films produced in Hollywood or slow the speed at which they were produced. AMPAS, however, stayed true to its mission of a research program designed for greater unification of the industry. Research was important, Schulberg implied, for its own sake as a process of self-determination for AMPAS and the industry, and not just for an ends-oriented goal of faster filmmaking. "If in the early days of silent motion pictures we had stopped producing to send potential cameramen to school . . . [and] waited four or five years for a class of graduates," those graduates would have been more productive: "I think if these same cameramen would have gone to a school we would have gotten better results quicker." Schulberg had no qualms about taking time for education so as to enable the industry to move more fully and knowledgeably into the future. Such education was absolutely necessary for a new way of making motion pictures that would be better informed by the technical possibilities of the art and more appropriate to an Academy that knew how to research. The School of Sound was an ideal device for AMPAS to acquire the knowledge held by the sound engineers and to begin a process of phasing them out of Hollywood. A new era of cinema sound was beginning in which the film industry produced its own technical knowledge and no longer needed to import it.[130] And this would prove to be an influential model in the years to come. AMPAS was changed by the interactions with the labs: research became a part of its character. Education was a means of acquiring the requisite knowledge so that the film industry could stand on its own in sound without outside incorporation or influence. The goal was ultimately to produce sound pictures that, like the silents, would be under Hollywood control in their aesthetics and the process by which they were produced.

THE RESULTS: THE LEGACY OF APPLIED RESEARCH IN THE FILM INDUSTRY

AMPAS's projects of 1929–35 had a lasting legacy in that they modeled a style of industrial research tending toward standardization of industry-wide technological practice. The Academy first engaged with technological culture on the topic of sound, but that engagement would continue and broaden to other topics. The Research Council at AMPAS lasted through World War II, and by 1938 it had thirty-six technical committees focusing not just on sound but also on projection, lighting, film preservation, and cinematography.[131] The council remained active until 1947, when it returned to the Association of Motion Picture Producers, the home of its predecessor, the Technical Bureau. Renamed the Motion Picture Research Center, it continued there for over thirty years, until 1976. After a spell of inactivity it reemerged in 1989, when it was again given a new moniker and moved to a new home. It became the Technology Council of the Motion Picture-Television Industry and operated as "an independent entity to develop education programs, encourage development of new products, and perform independent investigations and new product development through cooperative industry effort."[132] Its mission has remained the same over these many years, showing how influential that early model was. It has recently returned home to the Academy, being born again as an AMPAS council in 2003. AMPAS's description of the group, now named the Science and Technology Council, emphasizes continuity with its predecessor, reminding us of the necessity of research at moments of industrial crisis due to technological change—most recently the shift to digital: "The current explosion in digital motion picture technology is causing changes more wide sweeping than any the industry has faced since the introduction of sound . . . Movie production, post-production and exhibition are all moving—or have already moved—away from the methods and processes which predominated for the past 100 years. While these shifts hold great promise, they also underscore the need to ensure that technology enhances rather than dominates the art form."[133] Research within the film industry itself has thus taken on a heightened importance, again to protect Hollywood's interests from companies that would enforce their vision on it. The three goals of the council show a startling resemblance to those of its predecessor at the time of the shift to sound: first, "industry-wide projects and collaboration" operated through a "Research Subcommittee" that serves "as a primary forum for discussion and research," to enable studios to better understand technologies emerging from outside companies and create unity in the face of a perceived threat; second, a historical project to "chronicle the development and implementation of motion picture science and technology"; and third, a "Public Programs and Education Subcommittee" that produces "programs to teach industry professionals . . . about the ways in which technology serves the art of motion pictures."

The research methods and education that AMPAS gleaned from the electro-acoustical laboratories allowed the industry to weather a crisis. In creating a noise crisis, AMPAS and the film industry in general also found the models to deal with it. With noise a focus for their efforts, they gained a perspective they needed to thrive. Their legacy is actively with us today, helping us through what AMPAS has termed the industry's next big crisis in its way of doing business. While this chapter has focused on how noise featured on the large scale in the creation of the cinema soundtrack, the next will focus on how it appears in the apparatus of the theater's sound system. Listening for noise there, we find different problems, and the discovery of different solutions for them.

CHAPTER 3

"Machines for Listening"

Cinema Auditoriums as Vehicles for Aural Absorption

The Invisible Cinema, created by filmmaker Peter Kubelka for Anthology Film Archives in 1970, was a daring experiment in architectural acoustics.[1] Its auditorium was what writer Stanley Eichelbaum called "a fascinating and eerie chamber."[2] The experience of entering the auditorium was as alien as if one had opened a door to attempt to view a film on the surface of the moon. Everything was swathed in black velvet—the walls, the ceiling, and the rows of seats extending steeply up into the darkness in amphitheater style. A single beacon shone up ahead: the auditorium's film screen, with the projector's white light illuminating it.[3] As filmmaker Stan Brakhage put it, "People really had a sense of drifting in a black space, a black box, and black ahead of you, nothing visible except the screen. So there you were in this velvet box, watching these jewels of films."[4] Attendees were ensconced like minor moons in the screen's orbit, separated by strange wood-and-cloth frames that were built around their seats. These frames made the spectator's primary companion not his fellow viewer but the screen. When he looked to the side, blinders prevented him from seeing any fellow cinephiles. The alien moonlight of the screen filled his line of sight. If overwhelmed, he could close his eyes and listen to the film; the sound insulation of the frame around his head ensured that nothing but the film's sound met his ears, except possibly his own shallow breathing.[5] The Invisible Cinema was home to a new vision of what it meant to view and listen to films:

one in which the auditorium served as a means of "eliminating all aural and visual impressions extraneous to the film."[6]

The Invisible Cinema is one of several sonic experiments in cinematic architectural acoustics that inspired the writing of this chapter. Structural manifestos, they make a particular idealized mode of cinematic listening visible through their designs. Film critic Ken Kelman stated: "My own feeling is that the Invisible Cinema was primarily a manifesto and once the statement had been made, and it had been put down in the history books, it didn't need to be made again" when Anthology moved house in 1974. Kubelka felt similarly that because his soundscape was built, "the idea is there" and could be picked up by others.[7] So while the cinema existed for only a brief time as an example of Kubelka's "ideal theater" that would "practically not be there" to the viewer, it holds a significant place in the history of cinema's architectural acoustics. Elements of it were adopted by both mainstream and experimental theaters following its demise, and these elements—including its strange means of funneling sound toward an auditor's ears—make clear how cinema design has attempted to use architectural acoustics to enhance spectator attentiveness and provide a pure experience of listening throughout the twentieth century and into the twenty-first.

The genealogy of this kind of acoustic design begins much earlier than most people trace. The style of cinema auditorium that emerged in midcentury America has antecedents as far back as the musical auditoriums of the nineteenth century. This chapter examines the acoustical design of the cinema auditorium that stems from that genealogy and traces how the musical auditorium's soundscape profoundly conditioned the cinema auditor and the understanding of cinematic listening during that time. I examine the creation of the acoustics of cinema auditoriums to craft a soundscape that encouraged attentive listening: a transcendent mode and the style of architectural design that was born to realize it. Both were adapted and applied to cinema from a prior listening culture—that of music culture. One model of cinematic listening is undoubtedly musical, and this genealogy should be traced.

With the widespread popularization of architectural acoustics in the 1920s, design of cinema theaters was shaped by the model of aural absorption. A refined listening experience was enabled by specialized auditoriums that cultivated contemplation like that enjoyed by music lovers attending musical events.[8] By suppressing noise, acousticians crafted soundscapes that pulled the auditor into a transcendent relationship with film sound.

Just how the cinema apparatus encourages visual absorption has been explored at length in apparatus theory.[9] Here I focus on aural absorption, which was the new and stated goal of architectural acoustical design beginning in the 1920s. A clear, unblemished soundscape without noise was an ideal tool for creating a transported spectator in a state of bliss, swimming in sound. Acoustical design aimed to create this effect by reducing distraction via acoustical manipulation. The examples of cinema design I discuss here were self-consciously designed to facilitate "pure" listening and aural absorption. This chapter details the carefully calibrated architectures that emerged to try to create this as a reality, and the serious faults in the project that emerged. Noise manifested as distraction in this scenario. Absolute aural absorption in a purified silent space is, historically, a fallacy, but it is a provocative one in cinema culture because it is pervasive in cinema's aesthetic discourse. Absorption has been presented as a prized mode and has been asserted to be cinema's purview, as it is an art that entrances. With its address, cinema *does* suggest this type of intimacy in both image and sound, but it cannot entirely fulfill it. Rather, something more complex occurs in film listening that involves a negotiation between ideal modes of absorbed listening and distracted modes that acknowledge the imperfect results of the project. Working carefully through the construction of aural experience at such venues, we are able to think critically about something rarely touched upon in scholarship: how the cinema apparatus invites us, in historically specific and traceable ways, to enter the film's sonic world as a transcendent auditor at the expense of the space that surrounds us, and how it attempts to maintain that absorption despite challenges to it, especially by the viewer's own body.

Michael Fried has written about absorption in visual art as the spectator's "state or condition of rapt attention, of being completely occupied or engrossed . . . in what he or she is doing, hearing, thinking, feeling."[10] This results in a myth of the spectator's nonexistence or nonpresence. Aesthetic absorption negates the presence of the observer. It includes states of reverie in someone who, in the words of the eighteenth-century art critic Abbé Marc-Antoine Laugier, "meditates and ponders, and who appears so deeply absorbed in his meditation that it seems one would have a hard time distracting him."[11] It is marked by "an obliviousness to his appearance and surroundings."[12] Fried refers to "instruments of absorption, objects by which the condition of absorption is initiated and sustained."[13] While Diderot's statement on aesthetic experience may be far removed from the film theater in time, the basic

FIGURE 3.1. Magnus Enckell, *The Concert*, 1898. Oil painting.
Finnish National Gallery. http://kokoelmat.fng.fi/app?si=http%3
A%2F%2Fkansallisgalleria.fi%2FE42_Object_
Identifier%2FA_I_740&lang=en.

sentiment animates the structures I will discuss here. He details the virtue of "forgetting myself. Where am I at this moment? What surrounds
me? I do not know; I am not aware of it. What am I lacking? Nothing.
What do I desire? Nothing."[14] When the viewer is immersed in the experience, the "frame" disappears from the painting and the image comes
to life, enveloping him. The spectator becomes one with the world presented on the canvas. The lesson taught by Fried's study of immersion is
that "the fiction that no one is standing before the canvas" must be
established from the very beginning.[15] The cinema auditoriums analyzed in this chapter do that in their own way, encouraging a perspective in which the auditor loses any sense of being watched or even
present in a social situation and instead disappears into the world on
the screen. Feeling completely present to the sounds, the auditor feels no
desire for anything else. Taking Fried's conception of the happily

immersed spectator and placing it in relationship to film sound, I analyze how such absorption comes to be in film culture.

This chapter proceeds in three sections. In the first, I outline a particularly potent historical model of listening. Centering on contemplation, bolstered by scientific studies of attention being done in psychology, and mediated by the acoustical design of opera houses, the "new listening" became a potent marker of a new relationship to music. It was still a dominant model for musical listening with the rise of the picture palace in the 1920s. In the second section, I show how cinema culture adopted a model of the contemplative listener and the acoustical techniques that designers of spaces used to create that listener. In the third section, I outline how these same tactics are being enacted now with new technologies by virtual, rather than physical, architecture that is bolstered by pristine acoustical treatments and increasingly absorptive sound apparatuses such as Dolby Atmos.

"THE NEW LISTENING" AND RICHARD WAGNER'S BAYREUTH

The drive to listen carefully and without distraction—to listen purely— first manifested, in this specific and highly recognizable form, in the nineteenth century. Prior to the 1850s, musical listening had been marked as a social event rather than a purely aesthetic experience.[16] The eighteenth century had understood attending an operatic event as engaging in two performances: the one happening on the stage and the audience's performance of its own social interactions—the chatter and intercourse of what Beat Wyss calls "a gallant seeing and being seen." Theatergoing had pervasive social rituals associated with it, and "at the theater, the public took itself to be at least as important as the performance. The functions of self-performance and the work of art were not yet distinguished from one another."[17] What characterized Charles Garnier's famous Palais Garnier, the single most famous opera house in the world at the time, was its "space for social intercourse," as well as its "place for display, a play where they [i.e., the audience] themselves might perform."[18] A constant buzz accompanied performances. As Anthony Barlow writes, this "reflected concepts of theatre in which impromptu performances and ritualistic social behavior in the audience formed an integral and essential part of the total theatrical activity."[19] The opulent settings of spaces such as the Garnier opera house only reinforced this sense of a "social, festive centre" that was suited to social performance.[20] Lights remained on during performances, allowing the spectators a better view of one another, spectators interacted with each other during the performance, and chatter persisted throughout.

By the end of the century, however, a new form of listening had taken hold. While we discussed listening behavior through the lens of social injunctions against distraction in the first chapter, here we consider it through the aesthetic encounters that a physical environment sparks with the text. Musical culture of the late nineteenth century was newly invested in developing a particular model of contemplative listening. The "new listening," as it was called, marked the thought of the German Romantics, including Richard Wagner, whose work famously emerged as a capstone to the movement. Proponents of the "new listening" could be found across Europe, with prominent advocates such as Baudelaire and Stendhal in France.[21] Composers thought creatively and carefully about the listener and spoke of him warmly in their discourse on the performance of their work. Musical critics discussed his character, what he wanted, and how, really, he ought to behave. Music and the figure of the listener took on increasing cultural prominence in aesthetic debate. The topic even became the subject of art itself. Painters illustrated scenes of auditors sitting in states of psychological absence listening to great works. Listening was, according to these aesthetes, an activity deserving of attention. It was also deserving of one's whole being. It was to be sustained and abstracted from one's immediate surroundings. Words used to describe the experience are familiar to those of us engaged with cinema culture: "immersion," "absorption," and an era marked by the "ascent of inwardness" among spectators. Critics asserted that dedicated listeners experienced "states of pure listening," marked by the concentrated attention that such an activity required.[22]

Crary argues that "spectacle" is not just a visual experience. Beginning in the nineteenth century, technologies of attention are derived from spatial conditions that "separate subjects" within a stimulating environment.[23] Theaters themselves rather obviously comprise these conditions, in terms of not only sight but also sound. They create what Lewis Kaye, speaking about the musical auditorium, calls acoustical "conditions of audience."[24] Acoustical design, he believes, emphasizes a space's social and historically dominant mode of listening and approaching sound. "Acoustically architected space resounds in a very social manner," and acoustical decisions "resonate and reverberate in ways that are as culturally implicit as they are materially audible." They define not only the acoustics of the space itself but also "how it organizes bodies in space," determining "what we are supposed to listen to and how we are supposed to listen."[25] Crary agrees that "spectacle is not an optics of power but an architecture."[26]

This was true in a particular way during the historical moment actively shaped by the new listening. However, we find that attention in these spaces performed in a kind of pattern of oscillation. At times spectators forgot themselves, entering into a state of pure contemplation; often, however, they did not. Contemporary research similarly engaged with attention suggested that the "roots of the word *attention* in fact resonate with a sense of 'tension,' of holding something in wonder or contemplation," with all the "ambivalent limits, and failures of the attentive individual."[27] Wilhelm Wundt found that "such a *periodic rise and fall of attention* can under favorable conditions be directly demonstrated."[28] Angelo Mosso noted that "attention involves modifications of a complex nature," including periodic oscillations: "Experiments have shown that attention is not a continuous but an intermittent process proceeding almost by bounds."[29] Thaddeus Bolton also described attention as possessing a periodic form.[30] The ebbs and flows of attention here undercut the ideal of aural absorption in opera and, later, cinema culture; rather than presenting a perfect sphere for listening, the environment engaged the spectator/auditor in an attempt to win an ongoing battle for attentiveness. It seems it lost, however, as much as it won.[31]

According to William Weber, pure aural contemplation was one of the essential aesthetic "problems" consistently engaged with by artists in the nineteenth century.[32] The new listening was marked by its full concentration "that did not disperse in an instant."[33] Poet Emile Verhaeren described it this way: "It has only been a few years that music is listened to this way . . . with meditation."[34] Listening became an act of turning inward. This model arose in the 1860s, peaked with Richard Wagner's work in the 1880s, and continued up through the twentieth century, when it strongly affected the sort of listening that was encouraged in the cinema house. Cinema architecture helped train spectators in a mode inspired by the late nineteenth century's "art of listening" and the venues that emerged to encourage it.[35] And cinema architecture predisposed spectators to a particular mode of listening that resulted in their silence within the auditorium.

But what role might the body have in this new form of contemplation? While discussions of the body may have still been lively in the early cinema period, as my first chapter suggests, by the 1920s such conversations were scarce. In the new listening, the auditor's was a body registering musical sound not only through the designated organs of the ears but also through the flesh, bones, and, at times, even the erotic organs. Thomas De Quincy referred to appreciating the "deep voluptuous enjoyment" that music brought.[36] Music was said to "engage the heart" more completely than any other art, but also to engage the body.[37] This engagement was frequently, according to accounts, expressed through overt sonic responses. Peter Gay writes that at moments of the greatest musical thrill, spectators would "act out, with passionate gestures and wild exclamations, the bliss and melancholy that music released" in them.[38] The "invitation to ecstasy" that music gave was answered by listeners who engaged not in calm silent enjoyment but in swoons, "fits of trembling," weeping, and even fainting.[39] These states of aural bliss were expressed by the spectator for the hearing of all those around him. Music was even said by various thinkers of the time to be an erotic experience. Stephen Downes notes that in this discourse, stemming from Diderot, "music is highlighted for its biological, visceral power to excite."[40] Stendhal famously had a love of listening to Rossini that was "based on the corporeal excitement it generates."[41] Veit Erlmann states that "the very act of musical listening" at the time was "imbued with eroticism," and he notes a convergence of sex and sound in the discourse surrounding listening.[42] For example, Wilhelm Heinse's "celebration of the ear link[ed], in a mystical, almost Dionysian hypertrope, hearing with sex."[43]

Listening to music was, then, in a certain area of discourse, linked to "intense erotic stimulation." The writer Stendhal referred to Rossini's operas as being worthy of a "ten-day erection."[44] These listeners showed how deeply they were affected through physical, audible demonstration. As Peter Gay writes, there was a "paradox" at work in this mode of listening: "The paradox of the ideology of listening, which imposed on audiences the most rigorous suppression of activity but could [also] be a spur to [physical] action," left a mixed message for those attempting to listen at the opera. One might be an embodied listener who felt sound in the very fiber of his being, and the fibers of his muscles, and cried out accordingly, or one might be an abstracted and silenced listener, experiencing states of reverie, in a state of oscillation.[45] Both of these modes took place in Wagner's ideal opera house at Bayreuth.

Negotiating a tension between socially situated and abstracted listening became a real part of Wagner's mission in the design of his auditorium. His *Festspielhaus* stands as the acoustical/cinematic lineage's original design in the way it engages its auditor. This was then richly interpreted by the designers of film theaters of the twentieth and twenty-first centuries. Ned A. Bowman states that "it is for his architectural innovations that Wagner deserves recognition" and more specifically "for this contribution to development of the *space relationship* which he conceived for the dramatic event."[46] Wagner's innovation was a space that enabled a new kind of auditor. His form of opera entailed what Bowman calls "the need for isolation—both of the spectator from the action, and of the spectator from his fellow audience members." The result was "a drama of introspection" that took place in almost perfect silence and contemplation.[47] As Arnold Aronson puts it, the creation of this environment indicated that Wagner was "the first person to consciously and systematically attempt to alter the consciousness of the audience through architecture."[48] Bringing the auditor closer to the music was one of Wagner's stated and significant goals.[49]

The concert hall itself took on a new role in the context of performance culture's new focus on listening. It provided the structure for a new sort of auditor to be cultivated. Bodies were separated in space and encouraged to listen individually in their own private imaginary capsules. It was within these capsules that stimulation of the senses could occur. Audience interaction was at a minimum. According to Stendhal, rapturous listening was possible only when the listener was "isolated from the proximity of any other human body."[50] And Downes asserts that in order for the listener to have the sort of experience propounded by the musical critics, he or she had to be "in an ideal condition of solitude."[51] Listeners at Bayreuth approached listening with what Gay calls "piety," or a nearly religious fervor. Listening was something to be done, notably, fundamentally alone. Gay writes: "If music was to lift reverent listeners to their finest self, it could do so only if they remained," significantly, "mute" and "virtually unconscious of the world around them as they concentrated on inspiring sounds."[52] Underlying this ideal, writes Anne Leonard, was the philosophy of Arthur Schopenhauer, "rediscovered and much in vogue, which greatly influenced contemporary understandings of listening."[53]

According to Schopenhauer, the social environment had to fall away during an act of contemplation. Part of the architectural ideal would be one of acoustical control. An environment needed to quash noise to the extent it could. For Schopenhauer, noise was the enemy of contemplation:

> If you cut up a large diamond into little bits, it will entirely lose the value it had as a whole; and an army divided up into small bodies of soldiers loses all its strength. So a great intellect sinks to the level of an ordinary one as soon as it is interrupted and disturbed, its attention distracted and drawn off from the matter in hand; for its superiority depends on its power of

concentration—of bringing all its strength to bear upon one theme, in the same way as a concave mirror collects into one point all the rays of light that strike upon it. Noisy interruption is a hindrance to this concentration. That is why distinguished minds have always shown such an extreme dislike to disturbance in any form, as something that breaks in upon and distracts their thoughts. Above all have they been averse to that violent interruption that comes from noise.[54]

A sharp and sudden noise "paralyses the brain, rends the thread of reflection, and murders all thought." But even lesser, continuous noises have a wearing effect: "Occasionally it happens that some slight but constant noise continues to bother and distract me for a time before I become distinctly conscious of it. All I feel is a steady increase in the labour of thinking—just as though I were trying to walk with a weight on my foot."[55] Thus noise is felt as an "actual pain" by anyone with "anything like an idea in his head," it "mak[es] a peaceful life impossible," and it "destroy[s] every moment of quiet thought that anyone may now and then enjoy."[56]

The architecture of performance spaces helped craft Schopenhauer's ideal environment, one that like a concave mirror would focus all rays of attention to a central point. Wagner was a Schopenhauer acolyte, and his design for the opera house that was dedicated to the performance of his works was aimed at intensifying the spectator's ability to listen. Much has been made of the design of Bayreuth in creating what Wagner called a "theatron," a room in which the spectators would look straight ahead at the stage, their vision concentrated via increased visual acuity through the imposition of darkness, the creation of a cone-shaped instead of a fan-shaped auditorium, the reduction of distraction through simple visual decor, and decreased visual distraction by other participants via amphitheater-style seating. The conflation of all these factors has led some humanities scholars to assert a basic similarity between Bayreuth and the modern cinema auditorium, complete with minimalist decor and stadium seating.[57] However, we can also think of the opera house at Bayreuth as a model for cinematic listening. Bayreuth's design is an aural funnel. The amphitheater style of seating produced not only better sight lines but also better audition. The auditorium also featured Wagner's "mystic abyss," the pit in which the musicians sat. Wagner asserted that its sunken placement "mystified" the sounds reaching the auditors by masking their source, thereby increasing their perceived authority. Darkness was an aid both to visual concentration and to hearing. It served as a cue to spectators that the time had come to be

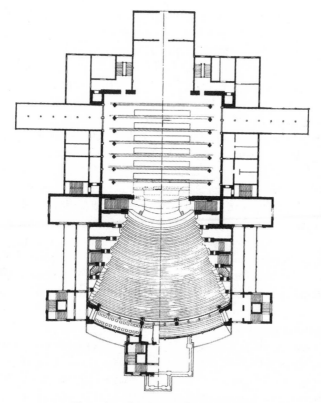

FIGURE 3.2. Floor plan of Richard Wagner's Bayreuth
Festspielhaus. Image published in Edward Burlingame, *Art, Life, and Theories of Richard Wagner* (New York: Henry Holt, 1875).

silent and attentive. This behavior was learned at Bayreuth.[58] The spectator at Bayreuth, Wagner hoped, would be "oblivious to self in the delight inspired by a masterpiece of art."[59] The desired effect of the opera was, for Wagner, a fusion that made one forget oneself. As Beat Wyss puts it, in Wagner's opera house, "so that the appearance of the projected image can reign, the empirical being of the spectator must be extinguished."[60] For Nietzsche, "One leaves oneself at home when one goes to Bayreuth, one renounces the right to one's own tongue . . . to one's own taste, even to one's courage, as one possesses it within one's own four walls against God and the world."[61]

But even Bayreuth, the temple to Wagner's form of listening, was not free of aural distractions. Sounds of sighing and weeping by Wagner's devotees both ensured that others in the audience knew of their meta-phorical transport and belied true sensory transport. Although "the arena of which Wagner had long dreamt ... encouraged, virtually enforced, listeners to listen, and nothing else," these reminders of the social audience snuck through.[62] As Gay puts the matter, "Wagner's *Festspielhaus* in Bayreuth stands as the supreme monument to the lengths to which devout lovers of music could drive the art of listening in the Victorian decades. The Wagnerians elevated ... the experience of music into a cult, a cult strangely able to arouse both Teutonic fervor" in all its noisy manifestations and "soulful inwardness."[63] Wagner distinguished two modes of listening, one characterized as "higher" (deeply attentive) and the other as "lower," or "distracted."[64] The auditor's experience at Bayreuth was a combination of high and low listening, a focus on the thrills of aesthetic transport and but also the sonic engagement available through the social collective of the audience. As Crary notes, "Wagner's aesthetic legacy was inseparable from problems of both perceptual atten-tiveness and social cohesion."[65] Both perceptual attentiveness and social cohesion were active in their turn at Bayreuth.

Fried notes that when the apparatus that serves as scaffolding for an art form reappears, or the spectator notes herself in the act of spectating, aesthetic absorption fails, triggering the feeling of theatricality. The rela-tionship between experiencer and art ceases to be intimate; it becomes artificial as the spectator becomes self-aware. This is the enemy of aural intimacy. But how can a pristine model of intimacy be achieved in the cinema house? In the section that follows, I discuss how the manipula-tion of acoustics performs the work of keeping the framing function of the apparatus outside consciousness. Encouraging a blissful experience of pure sound, the acoustical design manipulates auditors' experience to immerse them in the film text. To understand how architectural acous-tics invite absorption, however, we must discuss what they have to com-bat in order to achieve this: how they make their framing function fall into the background and assert an intimacy between auditor and sound.

In the nineteenth century in America and Europe, the study of the science of the senses informed and provides the context for discussions of models of listening. Jonathan Sterne recounts how, "over the course of the nineteenth century, hearing was constructed as a set of capacities and mechanisms" that were specific to itself.[66] Vision and hearing were newly considered as relatively closed systems in a framework of what Crary describes as "a pervasive 'separation of the senses' and [an] industrial remapping of the body."[67] At the same time, European physiology was making "an exhaustive inventory of the body" that would be turned to use in forming "an individual adequate to the productive requirements of economic modernity."[68] This knowledge would also be applied to what Crary refers to as "emerging technologies of control and subjection."[69] We may place the control over spectators' listening implicit in the design of auditoriums as one of these means.

Robert Jütte writes that the historical period saw the "new, scientifically verifiable basis for the individuation of the outer senses," which formed the basis for a new understanding of how sound and listening were malleable and affected by specific criteria. This study included hearing.[70] Sensory physiology was founded during this time, by Johannes Müller, who "transformed the five senses into a rapidly propagating number of sensorial modalities that could be investigated experimentally."[71] The isolation of hearing from the rest of the senses, and the extrapolation of its functioning, permitted the rise of not one but two areas of a scientific discourse. Müller's discovery of the tympanic cavity's conduction of sound was vital to revolutionizing the understanding of the hearing mechanism.[72] Müller's work did a great amount to allow the scientific separation and study of the senses—including hearing.

This work was followed, historically, by a boom in work on physical acoustics. Hermann von Helmholtz's book *On the Sensations of Tone as a Physiological Basis for a Theory of Music* became the universally agreed-upon standard reference for the study of modern acoustics after its publication in 1863. Helmholtz found that the speed of nervous impulses was variable, being determined by physical conditions. His research also put to rest an outdated theory developed by Georg Simon Ohm that the "human ear could receive only simple harmonic vibrations."[73] Helmholtz determined the presence of overtones in all sounds produced by musical instruments (and the human voice)—a fact that would greatly inflect the possibilities available to acousticians when they came to design auditorium spaces for the separate arts.[74] This was the beginning of an understanding of sound that would give birth to the ability to manipulate tone color and feel via sonic manipulations of space. Lord Rayleigh/John William Strutt in England was at work at around the same time, publishing his enormous work *The Theory of Sound* in 1877. It covered harmonic vibrations, reflection and refraction of plane waves, the vibration of solid bodies, the vibrations of curved shells and planes, and both "facts and theories" of audition. These were the building blocks upon which later, twentieth-century studies of acoustics were built. The twentieth century, however, became the time during which architectural acoustics of the type that most affected the movie theater would be explored. And this all began with a man named Wallace Sabine.

The modern quantitative study of acoustics was born only at the turn of the twentieth century when Sabine, a physicist, determined the nature of the relationship between the acoustical properties of a venue, its size, and the absorption of sound that it offered. By studying rooms that were believed to be ideal listening environments, he determined that concert halls that were best at the propagation of sound had a reverberation time of 2 to 2.25 seconds. Shorter reverberation times seemed too "dry." Lecture hall acoustics, he determined, were ideal at a reverberation time of under one second. He defined what reverberation time had to do with acoustical clarity, formalized it, and quantified it.[75] His formula has been in constant use by generations of acousticians ever since.[76] Sabine designed the Symphony Hall in Boston, still one of the best symphony halls in the world, and the first to be created using quantitative acoustics. Architectural acoustics developed further with the rise of electrical amplification in the 1920s. Both of these developments aided cinema in achieving what music culture sought to achieve: a crisp, clear, and unadulterated earshot of beautiful sounds.

But no one before Sabine had actually taken the trouble to learn and understand the physics of auditoriums. Charles Garnier is an excellent example. As he writes in his book on designing the Palais Garnier, he eventually trusted to chance, "like the acrobat who closes his eyes and clings to the ropes of an ascending balloon." Garnier was as pleased as anyone else that the effect was passable, stating: "The credit is not mine. I merely wear the marks of honor. It is not my fault that acoustics and I can never come to an understanding. I gave myself great pains to master this bizarre science, but after fifteen years of labor, I found myself hardly in advance of where I stood on the first day. . . . I had read diligently in my books, and conferred industriously with philosophers—nowhere did I find a positive rule of action to guide me." He added, "On the contrary, nothing but contradictory statements" were available. "For long months, I studied, questioned everything, but after this travail, finally I made this discovery. A room to have good acoustics must either be long or broad, high or low, of wood or stone, round or square, and so forth."[77] Wagner worked with architectural acoustics without fully comprehending them, and therefore did so highly imperfectly. After Sabine, however, cinema designers knew exactly what they were doing in the design of auditoriums or, at least, some did. The history of aurality is crucial to the history of movie theater design.

CINEMA ADAPTS ACOUSTICAL DESIGN

Acoustical architecture in cinema came into being as a field during the late 1920s and early 1930s and did a great deal to allow designers and architects more perfect control over such spaces. Acoustics gave the architect the necessary tools to create a custom-made, transporting soundscape. This enabled the design of carefully crafted cinemas that controlled noise to produce greater absorption in the sonic text: a cleaner, tighter relationship than had previously been possible. Acousticians became more aware of theater shape as a tool in their fight for acoustical clarity and control.[78] Surfaces within the auditorium, they discovered, must help disperse or "break up" sound waves, nullifying unwanted sound patterns. Angular sections, convex curvatures, and nonsymmetrical offsets were recommended fixes for overly reverberant spaces where sound intelligibility had become a problem.[79] A fan-shaped plan, like that of Wagner's Bayreuth, was considered ideal for reverberation as it allowed reflected sound waves to travel toward the back of the auditorium, rather than getting caught in the middle as parallel walls invited. Control over unhelpful sonic reflections was accomplished through the use of segmented wall and ceiling splays, "full or partial surface tilts, or. . . angular or broken contours." Sound was thus more effectively and beneficially spread out, with sections "'turned away' from the source of sound in such a manner that a part of the reflected energy [was] evenly distributed over the seating area." "Through the proper arrangement of surfaces and the planning of surface contours," acoustician C.C. Potwin wrote in 1940, "the beneficial sound reflections can be retained and their destination controlled."[80] Similarly, the more harmful reflections that produced echoes and areas of "excessive or deficient loudness" could be manipulated. When auditorium shape and design did not entirely do the trick, acoustical dampening materials were introduced into a space.[81] Acoustician N. Fleming wrote in 1943 that the goal of good acoustical technique in both the theater and the studio was to facilitate the spectator's absorption in the fictional scene: "So long as the sound is good it is accepted without conscious attention," he wrote, but "if through unnatural quality, dialogue or poor intelligibility, inadequate loudness or excessive loudness, it continually and irritatingly proclaims its artificial origin, the best picture in other respects may be completely spoiled." The aesthetic effect was ruined.

According to Fleming, the requirements for good acoustics that enable self-forgetfulness were an absence of echoes; "adequate and uniform loudness"; "a suitable degree of reverberation"; and "absence of extraneous noise."[82] When noises intruded, attempts "should be made to suppress the noise at its source. Failing this, the next method of attack is to isolate the source." Engineers quieted ventilation systems as best they could. They silenced projection booths. They tended to heating systems. They insulated auditoriums so they would not have sound leaks that allowed noise in from the outside. They might also resort to absorptive acoustical treatments. This was the "last method of attack," however, as it was deemed preferable to prevent noise rather than to treat its presence.[83] Surprisingly, however, a complete elimination of noise was *not* generally desired. A certain amount of reverberation, undesirable in its excess, was necessary to preserving a sense of what acousticians described as "vitality and naturalness" in the soundscape.[84] A severe lack of reverberation resulted in a "dead" theater, which was "useless" to the purpose of creating fictive realism.[85] If reverberation was too tightly controlled, the cinema would be unable to produce full, rich, and believable diegetic sound that would spark the auditor's belief in the spectacle. The aim was to have, not zero reverberation, but an amount that would read as natural to the fictive scene. This encouraged absorption in the tale being told. Echoes and volume, Fleming states, were "mainly bound up with the size and shape of the auditorium."[86]

While modes of listening carry across venues, and cinema auditorium acoustics in many ways mirror the same problems and respond positively to the same acoustical tactics as other auditoriums (for music, or for speech performed live) this is not true in every respect. The projection of sound via loudspeaker is the defining factor that enables us to extend these principles to a uniquely cinematic set of goals and problems. Cinema theaters, Fleming stated, had loudspeakers that were permanently positioned. This allowed for a consistent and careful avoidance of the problems uneven loudness would cause and allowed engineers to avoid the presence of distracting echoes through careful placement in a manner unequaled in traditional auditoriums designed for live performance. The cinema form, however, had its own drawbacks for acoustical design. Amplification proved to be both a blessing and a curse for the acoustics of the cinema auditorium. The worry was added reverberation, considered a curse early in cinema's history. Sound recordings themselves brought the reverberation of the spaces in which they were recorded into the auditorium, thereby doubling the amount of reverberation heard. S. K. Wolf, a theater acoustics engineer, stated that because the recording would have reverberations that were

not in the original speech, "the period of the reverberation of the reproduced speech must be brought down."[87] Loudspeaker placement and
arrangement enabled the engineer to avoid the nasty scenario in which
"the syllable which is dying down to the threshold of audibility" was
still being heard as the next syllable began, which of course damaged
dialogue's intelligibility.[88] "To help with this situation," he wrote,
"energy must be absorbed so that each dying syllable will be so feeble
as not to interfere with its successor."

Sound projected in a cinema auditorium, engineers found, decays at
a rate somewhat slower than the slower of the two sources of reverberant sound, so "for an auditorium there is a preferred degree of reverberation which increases with the size of the auditorium," and that
degree is less for cinema auditoriums than for traditional ones housing
speech or music.[89] For this reason, they argued, the reverberation of a
cinema theater should be minimized so it would not enhance the effect
and distract the spectator. As Fleming noted, the recorded sound should
also lack reverberation as much as possible, making the sound recording slightly unnatural. To calculate the ideal amount of reverberation in
the theater, it was necessary to determine the amount of insulation
present as well. While the greatest absorptive factor by far was the audience, the variation from one screening's audience numbers to another
could not be left to determine a space's final acoustics. Fleming stated
that the volume per seat needed be quite low to ensure that reverberation would not occur even when there were empty seats. So the seating
area was treated in such a manner that it accomplished the same task as
a human body, whether or not the seats were filled with auditors. Seats
were, for this reason, plush and soft, upholstered in velvet and like
materials, drapery abounded in the auditorium, and carpets were heavy.
Absorptive materials such as these were particularly useful for preventing reverberation in mainstream movie palaces that had formerly been
vaudeville houses. Here the original architectural and acoustical decisions could not be undone. So the interiors were modified through the
judicious use of absorptive materials like red velvet swing curtains. Sat-
isfying the drive for opulence of exhibitors such as Samuel "Roxy"
Rothafel, they also provided necessary acoustical treatment that helped
create spaces for immersive listening.

In 1928, *Photoplay* published an article that perfectly illustrated the
link between the movie palace's acoustical sound-dampening treatments
and the way they invited silence from the spectating body. Titled "How
the Screen Hypnotizes You!" the article outlined the criteria for a cinema

that would reduce noise by encouraging a sense of removal from a social scene and alienation from one's own sounds. Author Louis E. Bisch established the situation in which silence was achieved: "Two striking situations," he stated, "affect you the moment you have dropped your ticket into the box and the swinging doors have closed behind you."[90] The first, "and the more impressive, is the absence of human voices." Second, as in Wagner, was "the darkness." Bisch states: "No matter how excited or buoyant or jovial or noisy you have been in the street, this peculiar hush, this quiet immediately gets you." Music played, "but it accentuates the absence of the human voice all the more." It produced an atmosphere in which "you become sober at once." "The soothing melodies sort of engulf you and shut you in," Bisch wrote. "The strangeness of the place may even appear ominous."[91] Other aspects of the auditorium's environment—the acoustical treatments he suggested—affected you just as powerfully. Each of them reminded you of the demand for silence already suggested to you. "Thick, velvety carpet [that] deadens sound also helps to increase this same feeling." And "As you walk, you walk noiselessly. You may even be struck by the fact that you do not hear yourself walking." The quiet environment created a feeling of quiet within you. "Your own state of calm and quiet corresponds with the atmosphere in which you find yourself, which, in turn, tends to make you want to be more quiet still. At any rate, it checks any tendency on your part to give way to any emotion or behavior that is loud or boisterous." Instead of resisting the silence of the cinema environment, "You become a part of it." Bisch concludes, "You are a different person!" or, as we could rephrase it, a silent auditor, created by the enterprises of acoustical design.[92]

But how can this sound arrangement be seen to inflect one's relationship to one's fellow viewers? The end of the chapter will focus on how these aural formats can be applied to deal with the problem of one's relationship to other people. Through acoustical treatment and speaker placement, an immersive acoustical design comes into being to remove us from the social scene of the cinema house to an even greater extent.

One of the clearest examples of an avant-garde designer's creation of an auditorium to ensure aural total absorption was the Invisible Cinema described at the beginning of this chapter. It was created in 1970, when Anthology Archives in New York commissioned filmmaker Peter Kubelka to envision an ideal screening space. This space has been discussed in film scholarship by figures such as Peter Decherney, Annette Michelson, Juliet Koss, Rob White, and Barbara Rose, but always in terms of its use of techniques of visual absorption and never in terms of

FIGURE 3.3. Andy Warhol at Peter Kubelka's "Invisible Cinema" at Anthology Film Archives, New York. Photo credit Michael Chikiris. Courtesy of Anthology Film Archives, New York.

its use of sound. The space of the Invisible Cinema was small, unimpressive, and unadorned. The designer crafted a pure visual and aural experience, made possible by the enterprises of interior design. He sought to create a space for high art within its walls, so the atmosphere was very controlled. As noted earlier, its ceiling and walls were coated with light- and sound-swallowing black velvet. Fixtures and doors were also black, allowing no light to enter the theater to detract from the spectator's feeling of visual immersion.[93] Strangely, and significantly, around each seat was a black fabric partition that surrounded the head, shoulders, and chest of the spectator seated there. Blocking out visual information from the periphery, these partitions focused the spectator's attention toward the screen. They also blocked his view of the other spectators, creating solitude in the viewing experience. Kubelka had designed his cinema to embody a particular theoretical position on the nature of film art. A film showing there was meant for an individual spectator to experience in stimulated sensory solitude.

Based upon the idea that "an ideal cinema should not at all be felt, should not lead its own life," the Invisible Cinema was designed to allow the cinema to disappear from one's peripheral vision and to

FIGURE 3.4. Spectators at Peter Kubelka's "Invisible Cinema" at Anthology Film Archives, New York. Photograph by Michael Chikiris. Courtesy of Anthology Film Archives, New York.

ensure that the auditorium, with its participants, remained at most an audiovisual background reality for spectators.[94] "In a cinema," Kubelka wrote, "one shouldn't be aware of the architectural space, so that the film can completely dictate the [audience's] sensation[s]."[95] As Decherney describes the space, the "members of the audience, then, like the theater itself, recede" from the cinemagoer's consciousness. Rose has described Kubelka's cinema as one in which film would truly become an art like other arts, "in as much an individualistic one-to-one communication from artist to viewer as the high arts of painting and sculpture."[96] Kubelka called his cinema "a machine for viewing."[97] But it was equally a machine for listening.[98] Besides the noise-absorbing velvet, another detail unlocks Kubelka's sonic intentions.

The velvet partitions, according to Kubelka were not just visual blinders. He was inspired by particular listening devices that had been developed by militaries across the globe for antiaircraft intelligence during the First World War. Called "acoustic locators" or "sound mirrors" and nicknamed "Big Ears" by the press, they were designed to allow their operators the greatest possible aural acuity to pick out a desirable

FIGURE 3.5. Acoustical device crafted by the Dutch Army in the 1930s. Image courtesy of Museum Waalsdorp of TNO Research, the Netherlands.

sound in a noisy environment. They were in common use in western Europe, Russia, the United Kingdom, the United States, and Japan by World War I and continued to be used through the 1940s, with versions such as the Japanese "war tuba" joining a host of strikingly strange devices.[99] These horns serve as a testament to the commitment to the perfection of listening to only a desired signal. And it was these that the Cinema was designed to recreate. Kubelka explicitly stated that the partitions in the Cinema were "simulations" of these "big ears which concentrated the sound coming in directly from the screen and subdued sounds coming from other directions in the room, thereby creating a maximum of silence within which the sound from the film would be undiluted."[100] They created an individual experience of pure listening.

The listener sat in the middle of an aural funnel. And on the faces of the operators in the military photos we see an absent-mindedness that we recognize in the description of auditors given by W. Stephen Bush of *Moving Picture World* and quoted in chapter 1.[101] They were in the middle of a vortex of sound directed straight at them. This led them to a state of concentrated listening that abstracted them from their

FIGURE 3.6. Acoustical device used by the Engineer Regiment of the Dutch Army in the East Indies. A later version of the device shown in figure 3.5. Image courtesy of Museum Waalsdorp of TNO Research, the Netherlands.

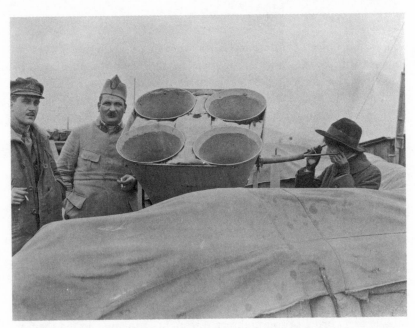

FIGURE 3.7. American photographer Helen Johns Kirtland experiments with a World War I acoustical location device as two European soldiers look on. Photo is dated as being taken between 1918 and 1919. Country is not specified.

environment. The hoods worked to enhance the intended signal of the soundtrack and decrease spectators' hearing of all extraneous sounds, including the surrounding audience.

It was in fact the other viewers that the hoods were designed to block out. Kubelka stated: "In the average cinema . . . where I hear them crunching their popcorn . . . and where I have to hear their talk, which takes me out of the cinematic reality which I have come to participate in, I start to dislike the others." Acoustical design, he explains, can work to craft a different relation among the spectators, but to do so it "has to provide a structure in which one is in a community that is not disturbing to others." Kubelka was actually quite interested in the concept of aural community and discussed it several times during this interview, stating that the design was oriented toward creating "a community in which people liked each other."[102] This, he believed, they could do only if they were inaudible to one another. So this leads us to ask: What form of sonic community did Kubelka intend to realize? Filmmaker Ken Kelman states that the auditorium's design "discouraged people from talking to the person next to them," and in those terms of counteracting disturbances "the theater largely succeeded."[103] However, Kelman states that while the Invisible Cinema may have discouraged talking, it did *not* discourage the noises of persons gathered in the same space. The Cinema did not reduce the sounds of physical shuffling and shifting, or "heavy breathing and coughing." "In fact," he states, "I felt and still believe" that the theater made such things worse.[104] Kubelka himself noted that one could both hear a muffled version of other people's noises and movements and also touch one's neighbors. Stan Brakhage commented on the theater that one could easily touch the knee of the auditor one seat over. He stated, "There was always a joke that the seats got very erotic in the Invisible Cinema"; one could "play with someone's feet and hold their hand," or even "have sex on the floor or ceiling of those little boxes."[105] This suggests Annette Michelson's interpretation that the Invisible Cinema suggested a pornographic environment from the first.[106] The sounds of others made one part of a type of community: a physicalized and fully sonic one, even when it lacked speech. Kubelka certainly did not intend this type of awkwardly corporeal community; rather, he sought an abstracted collective of inwardly focused individuals—a community of sensitive auditors all listening at the same time, focused together on the sounds provided for them. Listeners sitting in their velvet hoods were like soldiers listening with total dedication to their devices for the sounds of enemy aircraft.

VIRTUAL ACOUSTICAL ABSORPTION: DOLBY ATMOS
AND SURROUND SOUND

In all of the preceding, I have outlined how the acoustical space of the auditorium serves as an apparatus for mediated listening: one that encourages the auditor to absorb himself in the sounds of the text and ignore all other sounds. Now, however, we find ourselves in a moment when much of this work is done virtually, within the soundscape of sound mixing. The soundscape crafted through speaker arrangement has almost eclipsed the acoustical role of the auditorium as a means of controlling reverberation and creating spectator absorption. Thinking through how the drive for aural absorption manifests itself now, we need to turn not to physical but to virtual aural architecture in the construction of the film text and its forms of spatial address. Jean-Louis Baudry has written in a related way of the "Transcendental Subject," which emerges, he writes, from an encounter with the *dispositive*, or the apparatus. The spectator's eye joins the perspective of the camera and the projector to enable a consciously created sense of mastery over space, and his perspective slips into the place of the "transcendental subject whose place is taken by the camera." The spectator identifies his own perspective with "what stages the spectacle," "obliging him to see what it sees."[107]

Jean-Pierre Oudart and Kaja Silverman posit the spectator to be perspectivally aligned with the "Absent One." This "Other" enjoys "transcendental vision" unlinked to any specific viewpoint and is able to flit between primary and secondary identification—an identification with the apparatus and with characters within the narrative.[108] The spectator becomes a pure perspective, situated "at a window, an *aperta finestra* that gives a view on the world—framed, centered, harmonious," the point "of a sure and centrally embracing view."[109] The result of the visual system that uses Quattrocento perspective is "that of a scenographic space, space set out as spectacle for the eye of the spectator."[110] The sound space designed by modern-day sound architects deals less with reverberant materials (although such preconditions must be met) and more with the auditor's absorption in an invented sound space. The aural subject is made absent to himself and affiliates his perception with the sound apparatus: as Christian Metz puts it, "The spectator identifies with himself as a pure act of perception (as wakefulness, alertness): as the condition of possibility of the perceived." The text "inscribes an empty emplacement for the spectator-subject, an all-powerful position which is that of God himself," identifying himself as look. As Jay Beck puts it, using Michel

Chion's terminology, "The Dolby [surround] sound space becom[es] an 'acoustic aquarium' where sound 'magnetizes' the fragmented diegetic space into a concrete whole."[111] What's more, a position can be claimed within this space for the auditor, whose surrogate is the apparatus.[112] The promotional posters for new surround sound system Dolby Atmos evoke this "Absent One." In each image, an empty seat invites you to adopt its position. An airplane flies right overhead, and jungle vines grab at the chair. You, it is implied, are the inhabitant of the empty seat: the one who is absent and yet present, listening with his perspective situated within the film text. As Metz notes, "He can do no other than identify with the camera, too, which has looked before him at what he is looking at."[113] In sound, we find the same thing occurring. The apparatus, again, makes this process possible. Creating an ideal placement for this auditor is increasingly possible through the situating function it enacts. With the installation of cinema sound meeting THX Certification standards, acoustical designers have turned again toward creating immersive environments.

Sound certification system THX arose to more fully realize the dream of complete absorption in a film text. THX's Theater Alignment Program was designed to create the ideal environment for aural immersion. James Cameron calls it a savior for the filmmaker creating a complex soundscape, stating that TAP can "minimize the damage" caused by imperfect sound: "All that stands between us and [this] entropy is TAP."[114] A cinema that has received "Professional Cinema Certification" has guaranteed that "through its standards for acoustic performance, background noise, sound isolation and image quality . . . every seat in the house is a good one," fully ready to immerse the spectator in the soundscape.[115] THX certification offers several components that create this design. First is a "feasibility study," which determines how THX's design can be taken into account with the cinema's architectural plans. Next is the THX "baffle wall"—a "massive wall of speakers enclosed in an acoustic baffle speaker system enclosure" that ensures that the auditor's perception within the soundscape will remain smooth as it moves from speaker to speaker, preventing awareness of the sound's construction.[116] "This makes panning shots and off-screen sounds more believable and natural, helping to pull audiences into the storyline," states THX. Also, there is "auditorium isolation" service—a review of "exterior noise sources, such as adjacent auditoria, street traffic and concessions, to ensure nothing distracts audiences from the feature presentation."[117] According to the website, "THX Certified Cinemas are quiet.

They feature massive wall structures to isolate the cinema from the out-side world—creating a pristine audio sanctuary. With these walls, audi-ences can focus on the movie experience in front of them, as opposed to distracting sounds from neighboring cinema auditoria, outside traffic and lobby activity." Also included is "reverberation control." THX cer-tification requires "the placement of absorptive materials on the side-walls, down to the audience's ear level. This reduces the amount of side-wall reflections."[118] Last is the measurement of background noise in the theater to ensure that it "does not mask the subtle effects in a movie's soundtrack." All of this also goes toward executing the THX "high-fidelity sound reproduction standard." The goal of such environments is to have the viewer "placed 'inside' the filmic space" by eliminating her connection to the aural space surrounding her.[119]

Dolby Atmos, the newest product from audio juggernaut Dolby Lab-oratories, is bolstered by this deadened acoustical treatment and does what previous models have tried and failed to do: it negates the frame around the film's sound entirely, nearly eliminating auditors' awareness of speakers and apparatus and immersing them entirely in genuine sound space. Atmos, in the history of sound systems up until now, is the clearest example of this impulse. The Atmos system bathes the auditor in sound that emanates from what amounts to an immersive sound sphere.[120] Designed to be an improvement upon Dolby's now-wide-spread Dolby Surround formats, Atmos gives a new meaning to "sur-round."[121] Rhetoric from ad campaigns refers to "sound that truly envelops you and allows you to hear the whole picture."[122] As Dolby engineer Nick Watson, creator of some of the most impressive Atmos installations, puts it, there are two crucial differences between Atmos and all the systems that came before it. These are the ability to place sounds overhead, thus creating a sound sphere that mimics real-life sonic experience, and the ability to place sounds with great accuracy at any point within this sphere, placing the auditor in a precise relation-ship to the sounds heard. In an Atmos-equipped cinema, speakers line each sidewall from the screen to the room's rear. Lines of them run along the ceiling. The rear wall is lined with speakers, and many speak-ers cover "screen sounds" as well.[123]

One's position in cinematic listening has always been determined by what cinema studies calls "sound perspective"—the sense that one is positioned in a larger space or a smaller one, based upon the amount of reverberation, or the sense, relying on aural cues in volume or pitch, that one is near to or far from, to the right or left, in front of or behind,

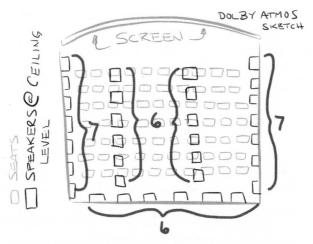

FIGURE 3.8 Sketch of a Dolby Atmos sound system in a review of Pixar's 2012 film *Brave*. In T.J. Wolsos, "*Brave* Movie Review: Dolby Atmos," *Pixar Post*, June 29, 2012. Courtesy of PixarPost.

the sound heard. Such cues have always placed the auditor within the film's sound space and offered him aural information to understand his involvement in that world. However, the new apparatus provides advancement in this technique. Atmos is a pinpointing system, producing an environment that can place sound in an exact predetermined relation to the auditor. Sounds emanate from a "point source," and in a discrete channel, rather than in an array as they did with Dolby 7.1. In contrast to 7.1 Surround, first-generation Atmos can support up to sixty-four speaker outputs for a single cinema space, with up to 128 tracks.[124] When a sonic event occurs, the auditor is able to "pinpoint this sound," accurately using cues active in real life; whether the sound is a whisper in one's ear or a punch landed on a villain's chest, Atmos performs the role of placing the auditor precisely within an imagined space.[125] A gunshot heard in the theater "will now be heard precisely in that one speaker in the middle rather than traditionally on the entire wall," placing the sonic events in a more intimate spatial relationship to the auditor. Cinema magnate Rudyard Coltman describes Atmos in this way: "When the wind blows, the leaves rustle all around you." He states: "You'd occasionally think someone in the middle of the auditorium stood up and started talking."[126] Such are what one technical manager of a multiplex describes as the "little bits and pieces of audio that make you feel like you are there."[127]

This desire is very consciously oriented toward the effacement of the physical body and the creation of a phantasmal one by the sound system. In Disney Pixar's *Brave* (2012), the first film to utilize the technology, little protagonist Princess Merida's sound perspective governs what we hear in the auditorium and how we hear it. Birds sing higher overhead, since she is shorter than an adult and our sound perspective is situated lower to the ground.[128] Atmos is designed to create an aural extension of the screen world and its sounds into physical space. In the words of Dolby engineer Ian Tapp, you "come off the screen with sounds."[129] Much of Atmos's virtue lies in its ability to make a smooth transition between what are called "screen sounds" and auditorium sounds. One transitions from sounds associated with viewed actions to the sounds of an immersive aural space.[130] The aim is to produce a subject position that creates unity between the two worlds. The auditor becomes a central player in a world that is laid out perfectly all around him. In fact, this sound perspective substitutes for suture's formulation of the Transcendental Subject, "as the point of a sure and centrally embracing view," in Heath's words. This is the "steady position," the "unique embracing center" that, as Heath puts it, sees (or *hears*) within a space, a space set out for the ear of the auditor.[131] The system puts the auditor in the role of the organizing consciousness that creates the world. The position, its creators state, is that of the sound mixer. Senior design engineer Steve Martz of THX states that the auditor's placement is "all actually related to the mix room. We want to make sure that the audience is sitting in the same location that the mixer is sitting in when he mixes that movie in his mix room."[132] Of course, this is a fabricated placement: the auditor sits at the font of all sound. This is an impossible position, an ideal. If the camera in cinema suture provides us with the God's-eye view, then we may think of Atmos as an attempt to simulate God's ear.

Listening to a soundtrack in Atmos gives a sense of what Kaja Silverman calls "an imaginary plenitude."[133] The distinct pieces of the soundscape are effectively stitched together to give the impression of a whole, unbounded and unmarked by difference. We "lose ourselves in it" and "allow it to envelop and absorb us." We become a "ubiquitous observer," getting at each moment "the best possible viewpoint" on the action.[134] We are God, centered in the world of sound. Stephen Heath refers to the suturing process as "the give and take of presence and absence, the play of negativity and negation, flow and bind" that we find to mark our relationship to cinema sound, and I believe specifically, to Atmos.[135]

But what if we rejected such possibilities of complete control? What if we reasserted the reality of the auditorium and its social scene? Throughout this chapter, creating private listening environments has been a means of increasing the distance between actual spectators—making spectators listen silently in a virtual environment that makes them feel less connected to one another. What if it were possible to use a sound installation to reinforce our sense of what these theaters usually suppress—the embodied, physical and communal nature of moviegoing that reinforces theatricality and prevents the cultivation of intimacy with the film? Canadian installation artists Janet Cardiff and George Bures Miller answered this question with their 2006 installation piece entitled *The Paradise Institute*.[136] It produces, not an "Absent One," but a highly embodied auditor. Ironically using technological techniques of aural immersion that operate through the same methodologies as Dolby Atmos to place the auditor in space, this piece produces just the opposite effect. Rather than removing us from the community of spectators at the cinema house, it returns us to that environment, reminding us of it and its complexities.

Cardiff and Miller crafted a project that directly opposes the expectations of aural intimacy in the auditorium environment. *The Paradise Institute* negates the previous models of silent and absent viewers and reasserts the sound of the social audience. The exterior of the installation is unimpressive: a large, plain plywood box. The interior of the space, however, performs the magic of illusion. It meticulously simulates a 1930s movie palace, giving the installation's participant the impression that she sits in the balcony of an enormous and richly outfitted theater. Tiny seats lie seemingly far below the viewer in rows as she sits in her own plush red velvet chair. However, she is certainly not alone. Around her are a dozen other participants of *The Paradise Institute* who are similarly situated. All don headphones attached to the backs of the seats and sit down. The film these participants view is, as Cardiff and Miller put it, "part noir, part thriller, part sci-fi, and part experimental," and it is the artists' own work.[137] But the film is far from being the primary attraction. This is not a cinema house but a cinema *simulator*—a simulation that is created largely through sound. The aim of our experience here is to understand, not a particular film, but moviegoing itself. The viewer's expectations are confounded by Cardiff and Miller's use of binaural sound. Binaural recording is an attempt to replicate the experience of true hearing. Two microphones are placed inside a dummy head during the recording process to ensure that there are naturalistic differences in the interaural registering of a sound's position, loudness, direction, and timing.[138] This produces a lifelike replication of the sound of actual space. Cardiff and Miller use this to the hilt in their installation. Piped into the headphones is not only the "film's" soundtrack but also the binaural soundtrack of a phantasmal "audience," placed with such precision that one truly feels one is surrounded by that audience. Cardiff and Miller create aural characters whose existence does not extend beyond the installation's soundtrack. Their presence, however, deeply affects our experience of watching the film. A female spectator described in the installation's notes as your "friend" leans over to you and whispers directly in your ear: "Did you check the stove before we left?" You hear her breath whistling through her teeth as she speaks to you. A person behind you gets up and leaves in the middle of a scene. We hear her body brush against the back of the seats as she leaves. A man coughs periodically to one side of you. You are caught in a vortex of audience sounds. The Paradise Institute's script includes "sounds of cell phone ringing beside you in the audience" and the "rustling sound of someone going through their coat pockets." A spectator nearby states: "Here's your drink. Did you want some of my popcorn?" The hushed question is immediately followed by the uncomfortably close, wet-mouthed smacking noise of the spectator consuming her snacks.[139]

In a conversation with the filmmaker Atom Egoyan in *Bomb* magazine, Cardiff admits to achieving "an immers[ive] experience for the audience." But she also adds: "I want the pieces to be disconcerting in several ways, so that the audience can't just forget about their bodies for the duration of their involvement."[140] The Haus der Kunst program states that Cardiff and Miller deploy "the expectations of cinema . . . in order to simultaneously undermine them."[141] What's more, Cardiff reports that it is the body, and not the screen, that serves as the primary object of her audio work in pieces like *The Paradise Institute*. She responds to Egoyan's question: "You've hit on it with the body being the medium. Our Western investigations in virtuality over the centuries have been about getting closer and closer to the experience of the photographic image, bigger screens, more immersive sound, until as an audience we want to go further and be inside them with our bodies."[142] Her work, arguably, does just the opposite. While Cardiff is right, I think, in asserting that the body is the medium in the case of her work with *The Paradise Institute*, I must really disagree with her that the point is the ever-greater fusion of the human body with the image or the art piece.

That has been the point of many of the pieces described prior to this, but it is not the necessary lesson of Cardiff and Miller's piece. This installation is not only about absorption; it is also, and simultaneously, about everything that absorption attempts to negate. *The Paradise Institute* is, strikingly enough, about the exact opposite of "going inside the medium." In the interview, Egoyan states: "There's nothing more annoying than being in a first-run theater and listening to the ambient sound of people eating popcorn, or whispering to themselves." He adds: "It's amazing how you allow discrepant noise to infiltrate your track. Do you actually find yourself listening to other audience members when you're watching a movie—allowing that to become part of your sonic experience in a John Cage sort of way [referencing Cage's famous "silent" piece 4:33, which encourages an awareness of the sounds of the audience]—or do you find extraneous noise as irritating as I do?"[143] Cardiff answers, significantly, that she and Miller "wanted to create an intimacy, so we have the person sitting next to you bothering you, but when she leaves . . . you become almost worried about her, so there's different levels."[144] Through the inclusion of a soundscape that is devoted exclusively to the sounds of spectators, the individual participant in the project is drawn into a community. Rather than experiencing a transcendent space of the fiction, she listens to those all around her.

Cardiff says that she "wanted *The Paradise Institute* to be about the whole experience of the cinema," including "the background noise in the balcony" and "audience comments." It was, she states, about "undermining" what people have been trained to expect of the sounds of the film experience.[145] As Haus der Kunst puts it, "the outside world" of the cinema "remains present and prevents the viewer from concentrating exclusively on the fictitious plot on the screen." The point, she says in a response to one of Egoyan's questions, was to "[frustrate] people's attachment to the established consensus" of what the film experience was. "As a culture," she says, "we are used to agreeing to be silent when listening to a film, agreeing as a whole audience that it's not appropriate" to make oneself heard.[146] All of this, Cardiff states, implies "that we take our play very seriously." Our established norms of behavior at public entertainment functions are quite fixed. In their Artists Statement for the National Gallery of Canada, Cardiff also states: "I think for any art piece, it wouldn't be complete without a spectator, but for our pieces the spectator takes a more active role." She adds, "They sort of make the piece."[147] Indeed, Cardiff and Miller's project includes precisely the element that has been downplayed and excised from the "aural architectures" discussed throughout this chapter. No art, what-ever the venue, is complete without an active and social listener who strains to listen purely.

The last chapter will focus on how, in a historical moment when the movie theater is no longer our dominant mode of engaging with motion pictures, we can see the practice of listening to noise adapting to new forms that place the responsibility for negotiating the line for ourselves.

CHAPTER 4

Cinema Theaters as Antiquated as "Edison and His Wax Cylinders"

Mobile Technologies and the Negotiation of Public Noise

In the winter of 2017, spurred by a new behavior I had noted in myself, I created a survey for my students about the act of listening to video on a mobile device. I had found myself engaging in the behavior of viewing video often while walking in the city. My earbuds had become an aural prosthesis that accompanied me on my various engagements throughout the day, finding a comfortable spot in my pocket and in my ears. While I was in motion I was engaging with media that in the past I would have stayed home to watch, and this led me to a conclusion: if I was doing this, I could not be the only one. My listening was actively changing, and this made me curious: Did others listen like this? If they did, when and where? And what did it seem to offer them? My students' answers sometimes surprised me. When asked if there were ever times when she just listened to audiovisual content, a student replied, "Yes, there are often occasions in consuming content when I can only listen to it." In response to the question, "Do you watch your screen the entire time you are consuming audiovisual media on your smartphone?" another student answered that he often did not look down while "watching": "No, I'm usually distracted by what's happening around me and look up often. I'd much rather people-watch than watch my screen while in public." Did they feel connected to the public space in which they stood while viewing media? "I don't feel connected to my immediate environment when viewing media in public," stated one. "The places I would choose to view media in public are likely environments I am trying to escape as opposed to feel connected to." Another student stated that he most liked to wear one earbud in and one out, so that he could hear both the city and the soundtrack of what he was engaged with on his smart-phone.[1]

At the end of the second decade of the twenty-first century, our ways of listening to media are changing. We may be entering a new media moment when it comes to how we consume our film and television media, especially aurally. This brand-new mode of mobile viewing and listening on mobile should not be ignored. It connects us back to a much longer history of mobile listening to music. As we become more mobile in our viewing habits, sound comes to the forefront and our consumption of video becomes based more on the history of listening than that of viewing. Mobile viewing encourages a new and different engagement with sound.

The previous chapters of this book have all argued that, via either the impositions on the audience placed by a cinematic venue or the way the film industry has constructed a clean and noise-free soundtrack for its listeners, cinema culture has historically constructed a limited sound-scape that allowed only certain kinds of sounds and promoted only certain sorts of listening. This soundscape has encouraged us to listen to the sounds of media in a narrowed way. It has been constructed to pro-mote certain kinds of absorbed listening and not others. Brick-and-mortar venues were absolutely vital to this process of conditioning. The sounds of everyday life surging around the listener fell away. Those of the film gained prominence through the careful acoustical engineering of the cinema environment by cultural authorities, reformers, and acoustical designers. The apparatus of the movie theater—the audito-rium's architectural acoustics, the decor, and the etiquettes created for the moviegoing experience—encouraged us to engage in a particular sort of sonic negotiation. Our listening was mediated by the practices of legitimate theaters, opera houses, symphonic halls, art house cinemas, and multiplexes. They each placed us in a relationship to the film text that encouraged us to consider all other sound not intended by them as noise. We are now well into a moment when all of this is changing because of the decline of the public venue as the primary way in which we engage with media, and the rise of privatized, individualized, and mobilized experiences. Now it is possible to carry our film venues with us. With the rise of smartphone technology, we enter into a new mode of aural engagement with desired sounds and what we feel to be extra-neous noise. This is the scenario of mobile viewing of film and television on smartphones—and the manner in which it draws on a history of mobile listening, activating these practices for a new practice that is developing now.

Focusing not on the past but on the present, this chapter investigates the phenomenon of listening to cinema on our smartphones. This produces a new set of answers to the questions regarding listening, the public, and the private that each chapter has previously explored. These questions include: How are we being encouraged to listen to films in different exhibition contexts? What noise exists within the listening scenario? And how do we create aural contemplation in the face of this type of noise? Listening to cinema and television is a practice that troubles some of the distinctions we might hold about the separateness of audiovisual and aural media. And this, too, has a great deal to do with noise.

The prospect of mobile media users who view the majority of their media content on their smartphone has troubled discussions within the film exhibition community for some time. These viewers are perceived as harbingers of the beginning of the end of conventional moviegoing. Andrew O'Hehir, writing in 2007 for *Salon,* warned that the "specter that's haunting Indiewood and Hollywood alike" is "the shambling figure of some semi-shaved, post-collegiate 22-year-old watching movies on his cellphone."[2] In 2014, cinema attendance in North America was the lowest it had been in two decades.[3] While some box office dollars are still rolling in in the late 2010s, thanks to the attempts of the film industry to attract viewers with visual innovations in 3D as well as aural innovations such as Dolby Atmos, the practice of moviegoing still seems to be in decline.[4] Home viewing was the most commonly identified culprit in this decline in the early 2000s. The revolution that began with VHS in the 1980s and 1990s continued with DVD in the 1990s and 2000s. The popularity of home viewing was powerfully enhanced again by the rise of digital streaming. With the appearance of Netflix, followed by Amazon Prime, Hulu, Fandor, and other streaming media platforms, we have increasingly decided to remain at home to experience our media. Indeed, the home viewing experience is holding strong in 2018; in 2017, 92 percent of all video viewing was done on a television or television-connected device.[5] However, changes are also afoot. Some films and media content appear only on these platforms, especially with the rise of original content for both Netflix and Amazon Prime—*Trans/parent, Orange Is the New Black, The Unbreakable Kimmy Schmidt, House of Cards, Stranger Things, The Get Down, Master of None, Mozart in the Jungle,* and *The Man in the High Castle* being recent examples.[6] And the apparatus of the

FIGURE 4.1. Andy Singer, "The History of Motion Pictures." Cartoon. Courtesy of the artist.

home theater is complete enough, with widescreen televisions and 5.1 or better Dolby surround sound systems, to effectively rival the conventional moviegoing experience. As a result, an average twenty-year-old, market studies indicate, is much more likely to have watched Hulu, Amazon Prime, or Netflix in a given week than he is to have attended a screening at a movie theater.[7] That is behavior for a special occasion, and those events are chosen sparingly rather than habitually. Streaming media is supplanting moviegoing, and audiences ranging from the most casual viewers to the most devoted cinephiles depend upon streaming for a significant portion of their viewing pleasure. In the last five years, streaming media providers have also developed their own smartphone apps for viewing their own original and other licensed content. Now this mode of experiencing media, previously yoked to the home theater system, is mobile. In the 2010s, we are not seeing an out-and-out overthrow of the movie theater by any means, but we are seeing new and emerging technologies, and with them new and emerging practices. These practices offer us new means of understanding the way we listen to films. The apparatus of the smartphone, and the modes of listening in which it is inscribed, form a new type of configuration that must be studied so that we may better understand how, in the era of a film that is held in your hand, modes of listening change.

The use of video apps for smartphones, combined with a normalization of media viewing on the go, is changing the ways in which we use our media. O'Hehir states that when this shambling, smartphone-carrying twenty-two-year-old bogeyman is called up, he appears as a frightening possibility for the exhibition industry that they do not know how to negotiate. "What people are really saying is that a big, weird change is coming. They don't quite understand it and they can't do anything to stop it, but they're worried that the whole business of selling $10 tickets to go sit in a dark room with some strangers and a movie projector is suddenly going to seem like Thomas Edison's windup gramophone and its wax cylinders."[8] In 2018, the traditional form of public viewing is becoming antiquated. As consumers of media products we can see that some form of this "big, weird change" is happening all around us. People on public transportation, on the street, and in lines at the bank and the grocery store are actively watching films, television programs, and short-form video content on their smartphones. And so are we. We all have earbuds in our ears as we move through public space, and many of us are quite pleased about it. A former student of mine writes on Facebook: "I watch almost all of my TV/movies on my smartphone. I'm always on the move, so I like knowing I can watch something wherever and whenever I want. Long lines at the bank don't bother me if I can get through an entire episode of *Kimmy Schmidt*. And my level of enjoyment doesn't change drastically when I'm watching on a smaller screen versus a television."[9] Another friend writes that she has "recently gotten in the habit of bringing headphones to a bar alone and enjoy[ing] a drink/meal with *Star Trek*."[10] This practice produces a barrier between herself and the immediate environment—one that may be especially welcome for a young woman alone at a bar. She adds, "I can't bring myself to watch movies on it, though. Not sure why murder procedurals or *Star Trek* are less sacred." Another friend, a creative executive in television, states that he watches programs on his smartphone while he is in bed. This is something that I do, as well; I have viewed films and entire seasons of television, parceled out into those bedtime moments. They are peaceful times, "me" times that rejuvenate me for sleep. But I equally often watch while I am on the go. In either case, watching has a mediating function; my phone becomes a tether, one that connects me to my media sphere and, slightly, disconnects me from my physical one as a comfort mechanism.

We find ways to negotiate public space even while we listen to a television program. We continue to listen even as we take our eyes off the screen for a moment to pay for our purchases, open a door to a building, check the traffic light, or cross the street. As we increasingly watch our own small personal screens while on the move, we inherently listen more than we used to. Listening comes to the fore in this experience. We rely upon it more because the medium allows us to lean upon it more. Our eyes are off our screens for practical reasons at various moments; our ears are always connected to the sounds. This is the sound I *choose* to hear. I fall asleep listening to old episodes of beloved TV shows with my eyes closed. I clean the house with my earbuds in my ears, listening to television programming. I follow old episodes of *America's Next Top Model* mostly by listening, stopping only at the episode's vital moments to pull my phone out of my pocket and see the final photo shoots and evaluate the contestants' performance. But what does this new form of listening have to do with our mode of engagement with the cinema that we experienced in brick-and-mortar venues? What can it tell us about the history of listening to music as it affects film viewing today? This project has often focused on how noise manifests in the movie theater environment. In each instance, the matter of how the public met the private came to the fore. Listening served as a negotiated practice of the public and the private. When we listen to our mobile devices, we are still negotiating these concerns. The sounds of the public become noise, and the sounds of our device are the desired sound: the signal. The smartphone becomes a tool for contemplation. In giving us a new platform that encourages us to focus amid a welter of sounds, it also gives us a means to negotiate it.

This chapter proceeds in three parts. The first focuses on how we have shifted to a more personalized negotiation with cinema sound via smartphones. The second aligns this shift with a concurrent shift in our cinephilia: the serious engagement (which will, in this case, be sonic) with motion picture media by its devotees. In this shift, listening comes to the fore as vision takes a backseat in mobile viewing. The third section proposes the introduction of the smartphone as a surprisingly versatile tool for the user in negotiating sound, and more specifically, noise, while experiencing media within this new listening context. In this section, I also analyze how our current mode of viewing has much in common with the history of mobile listening created with the Walkman and continued with the iPod. Using the smartphone as a tool and not just as a novelty, we consciously engage with our environments to mediate them through sound. This continues on through the publication of this book in new and exciting ways with the coming of a new age of podcasts and a new golden age of what was once thought of as radio. When we encounter cinema and television not in a brick-and-mortar theater, or even in our own homes, but in our hands, while we are on the move, we are negotiating the sounds of the public and the private, as we have in each chapter of this book. However, we are doing so in a way that offers new answers to ongoing questions regarding contemplation, negotiation, and the prioritizing of some sounds over others.

Mobile viewing lacks the conventional constraints that the moviegoing experience had. In the mobile scenario, listeners cannot rely on as uniform a boundary between themselves and the outside world as the theater's architecture provided. Acoustics are unpredictable when one is watching video on the street. And the space may be changing even as we watch (consider a person watching media on a smartphone while walking down the street during a morning commute and then boarding a bus). We are no longer within a sphere of control arbitrated by authorities—the designers and producers who could monitor and shape our aural experiences of cinema to produce contemplation. Rather, we experience a device that has certain modes of engagement inscribed within it. And these are modes of listening. The device conjures up, not the history of cinema, but the history of mobile listening. The smartphone app is not simply an extension of the movies into public space; it is also the infusion of mobile listening into the sphere of cinema. With the removal of these walls and the lowering of these barriers, we now begin to negotiate for ourselves the tension between ambient noise and the desired signal. While we formerly entered into a cinema environment that operated upon us via architecture, these contemporary viewing experiences (which are also, of course, fundamentally listening experiences) lack such clear-cut architectural and acoustical tactics. Rather, tactics are built into the use of the device itself by cinephiles, and they come to life in the way in which we use it. They do not directly participate in the conventions of audience conditioning common to the movie house. Instead, we find ourselves in a new scenario: one in which the boundary between sound and noise is mediated by a new technology and its users' listening practice. This depends upon our actions of determining sound versus noise for ourselves at a given moment, and our negotiations between the two. We begin to screen out undesired content with the help of a mobile device, which allows us a new means of controlling our aural environments and making sense of our own experience with our ears.

As David Beer puts it, speaking in the context of musical listening, the question becomes not just how we are listening but also "Who is tuning out of what? Where are they doing it? Why? With what consequences?"[11] These acts of listening take place in a broad range of environments, ranging from the home to, more significantly, public space. Drawing upon a dialogue on listening in urban space, I will speak in this chapter about listening to films in urban space. Whereas the moviegoing era was marked by its separation of listening practices from the business of living, the mode of listening that this chapter focuses on takes place deeply embedded within its noise.

FROM MOVIE THEATER TO MOBILE VIEWING

The shift from listening in the movie theater to mobile listening is a transition from a listening of surrender to one of negotiation. We negotiate the experience of the public and the private together. Perhaps it is best, then, to show how the traditional cinephilic mode differs from the experience of mobile viewing. For the most part, the environment of the cinema house invokes a sense of specialness.[12] And this functions to encourage a sense of removal from the immediate in the ways we interpret this experience. In his 1929 essay for *Photoplay* quoted earlier, Louis Bisch describes how the imposition of darkness, the separation of the auditorium from the outside world via techniques of decor (the heavy doors, the thick carpets that deaden sound, and the sound-absorbing velvet seats), and the ritual of the movie's beginning in silence all work to create what he calls an effect of hypnosis. Bisch alludes to the fact that "your own state of calm and quiet corresponds with the atmosphere" created by such tactics.[13] Cinema going is, among other things, an act of separation—and once we are separated from the outside world, it is an act of disciplining and concentrating our attention. We are disciplined by the venue. The rituals that allow us to engage fully with the film, to the detriment of all surrounding aural stimuli, are a large part of that conditioning.

Movie theaters' habit of drawing a bit of velvet rope around the cinema experience and creating a separate sphere was formative for the experience of cinema for decades. Listeners engaged with cinema in a mode of aural contemplation thanks to theaters that concocted environments that were suited to this practice. Now, however, this now seems to be shifting. Users *handle* new media technologies in a way unavailable to traditional movie theater audiences. They may place their media device in their pockets and bend it to their preferences, determining when and how its content will appear in their daily lives. And they negotiate space, rather than entering a space preordained for the practice. They lack the boundaries that were established to help them cultivate their contemplation. This is both a challenge and a moment of a new beginning. Either way, a new mode of viewing and listening is forming. People's viewing and listening practices are mutually imbricated with the sights and sounds of daily experience in flux around them. So how do we as listeners now draw the lines we need to draw to be able to distinguish desirable sound from noise, and hence pay attention to what we hear? How do these sounds of everyday life mediate our aural experience of film?

Smartphones help change our listening modes in profound ways. We use mobile devices as a means of achieving a personal relationship with film while holding the rest of the sonic environment at bay, as we did in conventional cinema venues. We achieve contemplation with our smartphones, using the lessons of a history of mobile listening to guide us. With the iPhone as the most popular, smartphones arose as a major platform for entertainment and a tool for our viewing habits quite recently. Brian Stelter of the *New York Times* writes that the rate of home-based television viewing has notably decreased in the last five years, particularly among Americans under thirty-five. Americans aged twelve to thirty-four are spending less time in front of TV sets.[14] Young people are still watching the programs that the rest of the public does, "but they are streaming them on computers and phones to a greater degree than their parents or grandparents do." A 2012 study by the Nielsen Company was the first to give conclusive evidence of this shift.[15] As a result, Stelter states, "There is a growing sense of urgency within the industry to make online and mobile viewing as measurable as traditional couch-bound viewing."[16]

As early as 2013, websites such as *Business Insider* were publishing articles such as "The 11 Best Streaming Apps to Turn Your Tablet and Smartphone into a TV." This particular article states that "most of us can't live without a subscription to Netflix or Amazon Prime."[17] It adds: "With busy schedules and other issues that arise, the ability to stream content to a multitude of devices from anywhere has become a perfect tool." Arguing that such apps permit one to "catch up on shows like *Mad Men* and *Dexter*" while on the run, *Business Insider* suggests a series of apps that "have helped make this process simple," including VUDU, Watch ABC, Comcast XFinity, TV Go, Crackle, the Roku app, and HBO Go, as well as more specialized apps such as SnagFilms (intended for the cinephile community specifically, with a wider variety of films, including those "that never stood a chance in theaters"). Since that article was written, two giants have entered the game: Netflix and Amazon Prime. These, of course, legitimized the practice and showed its profitability. Mobile viewing of video was a new market.[18] Since the publication of the *Business Insider* article, some of these services have disappeared, and many more have been subsumed by larger companies, as the mobile viewing market consolidates.[19]

Consumers today spend 59 percent more time watching video on their phones than they did in 2009—and they are watching the same media shown on their home theater systems. There was a marked increase even from 2012, when the percentage watching these media on their mobile phones was just 11 percent. In 2014, that figure was 23 percent of Netflix users. Of the content Netflix users watched on their mobile devices, 34 percent was taken up by movies in 2013. Television seems to be gaining ground as a major player in what people watch on these devices, with 44 percent of users saying in 2013 that they watched television and movies equally on streaming, whereas this number was just 35 percent in 2012. In keeping with what Nielsen calls "the new two-screen minimum," connected mobile devices such as smartphones have become integral parts of our TV viewing, constituting what Nielsen calls "constant companions to consumers on the go."[20]

In 2012, media research corporation MWW conducted a plan of research of immediate import regarding this movement toward mobile viewing. Their report, "Smartphone vs. Tablet-Based Video Viewing," breaks down how and where, precisely, we watch our media when we are on the move. It also shows how fast things change. We may apply this data to the context of our discussion of listening. In February 2012, MWW surveyed more than 1,100 US consumers eighteen years and older regarding who used a tablet and/or a smartphone to watch video. To qualify for the study, users needed to have specifically watched a piece of "long-form" media, meaning either a TV program or film, on their device within thirty days of the data collection. These forms of media were held in distinction from shorter pieces of video, such as those found on YouTube or Vine.[21] The stated objective was to "determine the words and images most strongly associated with watching mobile video" in each instance. Armed with such knowledge, MMW sought to determine "how people think of their smartphones and tablets as it relates to when, where, why and how they use their devices in what context."[22]

MWW's findings offer us exactly what is missing from most data-driven accounts of mobile media use, which this is how users feel about their mobile viewing experiences. How high is their level of satisfaction, and, at least as importantly, what are their feelings about the device and the interactions they have with it? MWW found that mobile viewing on smartphones was associated with words such as "kill[ing time]," as well as "pass[ing] time," "travel," and watching while at "work." These were opposed to the much more leisure-associated words that they applied to tablets, which included "relax," "wait," and "travel," but also "home" and even "bed." The difference between these two sets of terms indicates one important difference: that is the difference between travel, or mobility, and leisure—being in motion and being at home. The report corroborates this finding, stating: "Tablets are associated with periods of relaxation and personal time, while smartphones are associated with times when respondents are waiting, killing time or taking a break."[23] The report then goes on to break down where, precisely, we are doing these kinds of viewing. The breakdown is instructive in aiding our understanding of what we believe ourselves to be doing when we do this. How actively engaged in the business of life around us are we as we view and listen? The evidence is wonderfully clear. On an airplane, 33 percent of the polled users said they would use a smartphone to view television or films, whereas 45 percent said they would use a tablet. In bed, 20 percent of the polled users used a smartphone, whereas 38 percent used a tablet. In a hammock, 24 percent used a smartphone, whereas 34 percent used a tablet. In a waiting room, 21 percent used a smartphone, whereas 26 percent used a tablet. In a train station, 25 percent of users used a smartphone (as opposed to 20 percent who used a tablet). On a park bench, 15 percent of users polled used a smartphone to view long-form media. In line at a store or other business, 22 percent used a smartphone to view this media, and only 10 percent used a tablet. In a coffeehouse (in a set of numbers surprisingly low, to me, considering my own use habits), 13 percent used a smartphone as opposed to 9 percent using a tablet. At a bus stop, 14 percent would whip out a smartphone to watch a favorite piece of media. In a restroom, a mall, a school bus, or a lecture hall, the smartphone kills the tablet's numbers. However, it is relevant to note that in 2018 the age of tablet users seems to be increasing. As one of my students put it in her responses to my survey, "I'm not a dad, so I don't use a tablet."[24] The tablet, the device of a dad, is being phased out. The smartphone, then, seems to be a valued tool for time spent on the move and is a fairly constant companion to those young people who are watching while moving about in their daily lives.

The 2012 study also investigated the number of times these frequent mobile media viewers watched different types of media. Fifteen percent of users polled had watched a full movie on their smartphone at least once; 18 percent had viewed a movie three to five times in total; 9 percent had viewed a movie six to ten times; and 9 percent had viewed a

movie more than ten times. Numbers were higher for television programming, with 32 percent having watched a program "once or twice";
18 percent, three to five times; 11 percent, between six and ten times;
and 11 percent, more than ten times. In contrast to either of these, the
numbers of viewers who had watched short-form video on YouTube
were much higher.[25] Numbers of users who viewed media on a smartphone or tablet tended to constitute roughly half the number of those
who viewed shorter forms of media. So while the smartphone or tablet
is not evidently taking over a mode that conventional cinema going
covered, it is clearly accentuating it and extending it.

These findings suggest several very important ideas to those of us who
are invested more in questions of user interpretation than in data-derived
sales or the more effective pairing of users with brands best suited to
their lifestyles. For one thing, they suggest that viewers do clearly use
mobile media while they are on the move. Further, they imply users'
overwhelming satisfaction; while the numbers suggest areas with potential for growth and change in the current model, they also indicate a
growing number of users who are quite content with what they have—at
least, enough to motivate them to come back. Viewers have committed
to the form, at least in part. And a statistically significant portion of the
media-viewing audience is doing so.

The data on mobile streaming changes incredibly quickly, and numbers that once seemed impressive are now dwarfed by larger ones. Since
2014, the smartphone as a video device has exploded in popularity,
especially among millennial users. Video is fast becoming the smartphone's reason for being. Millennials watched less connected television
than ever in 2016 and watched 18 percent more on their mobile
devices.[26] Over the last two years, millennials have cut their TV watching by 25 percent and upped their viewing on mobile devices by almost
50 percent.[27] The smartphone is gaining dominance as the way to reach
the demographic of eighteen- to twenty-four-year-olds, which is especially relevant to distributors, as this is the demographic that watches
the most programming. Richard Iurilli states, "People spend more time
watching video" now even "than they do on social media, and Cisco
projects that 90 percent of all Internet traffic will be video by 2019."[28]
According to a recent report, mobile video plays since 2011 have a com-
pound annual growth rate of more than 116 percent. Indeed, they have
increased an astonishing 2,084 percent over the past five years.[29] Use of
smartphones to watch video has "skyrocketed," according to Nielsen.[30]
In just the first quarter of 2016, the daily amount of time users spent on

smartphones to consume media went from sixty-two minutes to ninety-nine minutes per day.[31] On average, 57 percent of users watched video on a mobile phone each day in 2015.[32] Statisticians predict further growth. Nielsen Comparable Metrics for 2014–16 predicted that 2017 would be another year of boom numbers, and they were correct: in 2017, monthly US video consumption jumped 81.5 percent, from 151 minutes in 2016 to 274 minutes in 2017.[33]

Some users are very enthusiastic, and the specter of the shambling twenty-two-year-old who views films exclusively on his iPod and never attends the cinema or watches at home seems to be an active threat to conventions at this point in the game.[34] However, not all of us are watching entire films this way. Movies are still twice as likely to be viewed on a connected television device as on a mobile device.[35] Still, nearly one-third of smartphone users who were millennials did watch videos that were longer than ten minutes.[36] Sixty-two percent of eighteen- to twenty-four-year-olds report watching television shows on their mobile phones several times a day or even more.[37] And 58 percent of all mobile data traffic was video in 2017, with an expansion in the number of viewers who watched long-form content. Viewers watched long-form videos between twenty and forty minutes to completion 57 percent of the time. They viewed what is now termed ultra-long form content of more than forty minutes to completion more than 45 percent of the time.[38] This does constitute a genuine change in our way of working when it comes to media. The share of viewers accessing television, and even film, may well continue to increase. As Knect365.com put it in 2017, "As we look back to last year, it's safe to say that video delivery in 2016 looked absolutely nothing like it did a few short years ago."[39] This marks the potential for a new way of viewing—a new expression of movie love. We may now engage in a more personalized cinephilia that is more like our long-standing engagement in mobile listening.

Feeling that the newest possible data regarding young people might shed light on these practices, as stated above, at the end of 2017 I engaged in a survey with some of my own students as the subjects. They responded to a survey designed to describe their use of mobile media: whether they used it at all, and if so, how and when. Respondents ranged in age from eighteen to twenty-two years. The data set from my students produced some interesting trends. Among them was the fact that while my students rarely viewed films on their smartphones, they fairly often viewed television programming. (Most of all, my students viewed short-form video content on their smartphones, with most respondents indicating that they viewed this material daily.) From there, however, the questions yielded interesting results. The question, "Do you spend some time *just listening* to the content [on your smartphone]?" produced a surprising number of "yes" responses. According to the data set, many college-aged people just listen to audiovisual content. One student stated that she did so "a great amount. Often times I would start a video, but then go do homework while listening to what the video is saying." This person added, "I would say that it is an even balance between watching and listening and simply just listening to the content." It is "bad," another student stated, "that I do not see what is being shown," but "just listening lets me use my own imagination to envision for myself what is happening just from the sounds themselves." Yet another student stated that she often literally listened to an entirely separate soundtrack when she was viewing a film, stating that she generally wished to curate her own experience via mobile technology while watching. She stated: "Sometimes the music enhances the scene, or creates a more personal experience with it, particularly when a song that means something to me meets a scene that also means something to me." Only occasionally, she stated, was there a scene "that I feel I need to listen to, so I'll pause my music [on her phone] and turn up the volume on my computer" to listen to the film's original soundtrack. She defended this practice, stating, "One might argue that I'm missing something by experiencing film without [the original] sound or with different sound, but I prefer to think of it as having a different experience. If I want to, I can add more feeling to scenes by choosing music that makes me emotional." She added that she did not see this as all that different from what others did in lesser ways. "Many people choose to alter their viewing experience when rewatching at home and/or on their personal devices." This was just one example. She finished "It is not the same experience as going to a movie theater—but that does not mean that it is less valuable."[40]

Another student said that she enjoyed walking around while listening to her audiovisual content. This same student mentioned that she used podcasts in a very similar way. "I have recently gotten into podcasts," she stated. "I don't know why I wasn't into them before." In fact, the two experiences—listening to videos that were intended to be viewed and then listening to podcasts, which never had any visual component— were felt by a number of respondents to be contiguous. Both enabled listening while moving. One student said, "I used to watch videos but only listen to them; now, I mostly listen to podcasts." Another student said, "Just listening to videos . . . allows the listener to view their surrounding environment when being aurally connected to the media on their phone." Still another referred to it as "a little escape into something else." This same student mentioned that she used "videos to pass the time, often relying more on the audio stimulation than the video." Mobility was key to much of this feeling. When listening in this way, students stated that they "focus on the words and the exchange," of the clip, adding, "I will often just listen to the rhythm of the speech." This, one student commented, "is what drove me into podcasts." She added, "You catch other things. . . . I still catch new things when I'm *only* listening." This, of course, indicates that there is something new and potentially very interesting happening with mobile video and its relationship to audio. It is evidently beginning to intersect with listening practices that are active in multiple forms of aural media. The behaviors that focus on listening tie this behavior rather clearly to radio, as well to more contemporary audio forms such as the podcast: hence the multiple mentions of the podcast as a contiguous activity to television and short video viewing. Many students noted that they rarely looked at their screens when they were viewing television or short-form content, stating in their surveys that they might begin by watching but then were often drawn away by homework, walking around, or thinking other thoughts. This is the beginning of evidence that I feel confident will grow over the coming years, indicating that changes in mobile technology will allow a greater and pervasive overlap between audiovisual media and aural media.[41] This is just another example of how cinema culture now connects with a wider range of audio technologies and practices. It suggests a new intervention in terms of how we discuss the use of mobile viewing apparatuses. This relates directly to a recent rise in audio-only media.[42] Podcasts have mainstreamed the listening media of our day, allowing access to audio in the car, the office, and on the street via earbuds. Video listening has followed suit. When it comes to watching film and television, we are now in a new sound era that is mediated by its concurrence with the podcast era, or the new "golden age of radio." The data also allows us to observe that this use of mobile technology for experiencing media on the go lends itself to a new type of aural imagination. The act of using one's "own imagination to envision for myself what is happening" was precisely what listeners did during the golden age of radio. They do it now with podcasts. Listening also seems to be increasing users' appreciation for dialogue and language, thereby increasing the radio aesthetics of what we usually think of as (and what is) an audiovisual medium. In this way, the new use of smartphones is creating an opportunity for a variation on mobile viewing practice. With a variation on smartphones' use, and inflected by the practice's context in a new era of smartphone *listening*, smartphone *viewing* becomes even more like mobile listening—to the point of mimicking a podcast experience.[43] And podcasts are booming; a 2016 study by Edison research indicated that an estimated fifty-seven million Americans listen to podcasts each month. Twenty-seven percent of users between ages twelve and twenty-four years had listened in the last month, and 24 percent of users between twenty-five and fifty-four years had. Thirteen percent of respondents listened on a weekly basis, an estimated thirty-five million Americans. Of podcast listeners who listened on a weekly basis, 12 percent listened for ten or more hours per week; 17 percent for between five and ten hours per week; 19 percent for between three and five hours per week; and 40 percent for one to three hours per week. The majority of podcast users listened to four or five podcasts per week. And in 2016, 71 percent of this listening was done on a smartphone or other mobile device.[44] The experience, according to *The Cut* writer Sirena Bergman, had become "part of my daily routine." She stated: "I listen while I'm traveling, commuting, working, cooking, cleaning, and sometimes even when I'm showering." It got to the point that, for Bergman, "I couldn't remember how to exist in the world on my own, without a stranger chattering in my ears at all times."[45]

All of this may seem to be rather tangential to the cinephile experience. But it does relate the act of mobile listening to being a lover of audiovisual media. To get back to that cinephilic experience, we can now discuss how these same practices come to be applied directly to acts intended to explore an affective relationship with cinema, rather than short-form media. How do we use cinematic listening, in this new era, to expand our emotional relationship with films?

Francesco Casetti and Sara Sampietro have begun to explore this territory of mobile viewing of cinema on mobile technologies with their conception of "relocation" of an experience from one technology to another. They ask "whether, and to what extent, film spectators' experience may translate to devices such as the iPhone."[46] They note that the rise of cinema in the late 1800s "created a clearcut opposition" between spectacles based on fixed images (such as the museum or the panorama), with users that were free to move, and spectacles based on moving images (such as cinema) that required the immobility of their participants.[47] Today's technology, they believe, makes the opposition less apparent. These technologies enable us to move while we watch moving pictures, "constructing 'existential bubbles' that allow the subject to create an individual space even within collective environments." The iPod attracts the user's attention and maintains the user's focus, even when it is used in public. In this way, it excels at "constructing an 'existential bubble'" so that "the spectator can find refuge while remaining exposed to the surrounding environment."[48] As Sarah Atkinson and other theorists argue, we can say that in "what could be considered to be a post-transmedia, post-platform-specific," and increasingly "platform-agnostic age," we are met with new problems of the public to solve when it comes to the ways we view and listen to our media.[49]

CHANGES IN CINEPHILIA

The importance of the stand-alone motion picture venue is made surprisingly clear as we shift into a mode of media experience that does not require it. Such venues set the rules of engagement that governed encounters with films; they were the disciplinary institutions that set the etiquettes that became bedrock for future etiquettes in the cinephile subculture. They taught their patrons how to listen and how to negotiate noises. From this we can now see new sound etiquettes for listening to a new mobile scenario emerging. While previous modes of encounter with cinema encouraged surrender, these new digital modes of engagement promote negotiation between the public and private quite overtly. We have been negotiating this in many ways since the beginnings of cinema history; movie theaters have always been sites of distracting noise. We now only have a new tool to enable our modes of listening; the motivation to control undesired sound is much the same. As we shall see in this section, we borrow those lessons learned from brick-and-mortar contexts and place them in the service of a mode of negotiation. This section discusses how cinephile movements, with their interactions with venues themselves, crafted a system of etiquette that governed the engagement with films. These etiquettes, which would seem historically restricted to their historical moments, have actually reemerged to govern our interactions with mobile media.

In each of the major moments at which cinephilia coalesced in particularly famous venues in the twentieth century, the experience of moviegoing at a curated or commercial institution featured centrally. In the 1920s and 1930s, French cinephiles Jean Epstein and Louis Delluc began a cinephile movement, encouraging film attendance for the purposes of expressing as well as broadening one's love of cinema.[50] By the mid-1930s, Iris Barry had instituted a film library at the Museum of Modern Art in New York and was curating screenings of films. In France, Henri

Langlois was doing the same with the creation of the Cinémathèque Française.[51] This was to be the birthplace of the *Nouvelle vague*. In each scenario, every major movement implied the spectator's surrender to the experience, but also to the institution. MoMA, or the Cinémathèque Française, was the financial and aesthetic sponsor of the film experience, and adherence to the institution's etiquettes was a prerequisite for being permitted access to these works. Part of the experience of cinephilia was a devotion to the practices of the institution, and learning the rules of viewing within a specific exhibition space was almost akin to learning the rituals of a religious service; in order to be a member, one *had to* know these things and behave appropriately. The affiliation with the institution was strong; attending the Cinémathèque Française was sufficiently political that when Henri Langlois was sacked by the French government, cinephiles who closely identified with its project, including Jean-Luc Godard and Francois Truffaut, gathered there and proceeded to protest.[52] Filmgoers at MoMA prided themselves on learning the proper etiquette for cinephilic behavior, as established and regulated for the venue by Barry, who often attended screenings and who could therefore enforce quiet listening upon spectators.[53] Devotees of any major venue took pride in knowing the ropes, as their identity as cinephiles was formative of a greater sense of personal identity. Film viewing meant, quite literally, an outing to the film theater, which was a controlled and a controlling environment. As Girish Shambu puts it: "The terms of this screening . . . the place, time, and spatial set-up of the viewing experience—were determined not by the viewer but by someone else (e.g. the exhibitor or curator)."[54] The "viewing contract," as Shambu puts it, therefore entailed "a certain surrender" by the cinephile to the cinema experience, or, as he puts it, "a submission to the terms of the viewing experience."[55]

As Shambu notes, the venue's conditions "produced a high level of likelihood for *sustained engagement* with a film" (emphasis in original).[56] Because the apparatus of the architecture and decor suggested contemplation, "A viewer was likely to pay full attention in the darkened theatre and stay for the duration, her attention rewarded by the scale of the big-screen image and sound—and the immersion in detail these conditions made possible."[57] The feeling of transport was precisely what today's mobile cinephilia lacks, and it was lamented, unsurprisingly, by Susan Sontag in her famous essay "The Decay of Cinema," appearing in the *New York Times* in 1996. Sontag mourns the loss of the moviegoing ritual as much as the films themselves, and in her essay the decline of moviegoing becomes metonymic for cinephilia's general decline. Sontag suggests a rhetoric of surrender in her work; she believes that "what you appropriated for yourself was the experience of surrender to, of being transported by, what was on the screen." She asserts: "To be kidnapped, you have to be in a movie theater, seated in the dark among anonymous strangers."[58] Even Sontag (despite writing in 1996, before the marketing of a handheld digital streaming device was even imagined) laments that "images now appear in any size and on a variety of surfaces," and she concludes that as a result movies have become just "one of a variety of habit-forming entertainments" that fill our empty time, rather than a ritual that fills us up like a vessel.[59]

This discourse shows a shift from the language of "surrender," used by conventional cinephilia, to the language of "negotiation." This is a mode I consider more appropriate to the twenty-first-century cinephile, armed with her smartphone, even while she may be enjoying (at least, clips of) the same films. We do not lose ourselves in these experiences; rather, we maintain an awareness of our surroundings that inflects our feelings about the media to which we listen. The user focuses on that and the world around her in a sort of relay, reminiscent of the ebbs and flows of attentiveness described by William James and other researchers on attention in the nineteenth century, cited in chapter 1 of this work. Attention is divided, and noise consistently reminds us of all that exceeds the boundaries we are currently choosing to place upon the experience. Whereas institutions previously regulated this, now we are on our own. With our personal mobile devices, we draw these boundaries for contemplation for ourselves.

Cinephiles have a long history of resorting to any venue to see their films. While auditoriums were eventually designed specifically for the Cinémathèque Française, Langlois also projected films in all available spaces to an audience greedy for more films than there were screens in the building. Claude Chabrol recalls films being screened in the two theaters of the Cinémathèque's home at the palatial Museum of Mankind on 7 Avenue de Messine, while *Diary of a Lost Girl* played to movie-mad youngsters on the walls of the stairwell as cinephiles sat staring up at the images.[60] Sound would have been, at best, poor in such an environment, bouncing off highly imperfect acoustical walls and mixing with the sounds of everyday movement throughout the Cinémathèque. Cine-clubs in the 1920s and 1930s in Paris, Berlin, and London were often hosted in cafes or coffee shops, where the intellectuals who filled them spent their time engaged in kaffeeklatsch, and films were projected onto a sheet or a plain wall.[61] Sound, again, would have been a confused welter of noise. Controlling a public space such as a coffee shop would be an aural nightmare: an impossibility. A highly mixed aural environment would have resulted: one that encompassed the sounds of socializing and cinema both. Movie enthusiasts have long understood the necessity of home viewings for fare that is not generally marketable enough to gain a wide audience or that is experimental or countercultural. And museums, churches, and libraries have long had film screenings in basements and worship spaces ill designed for the practice.[62] A love of motion pictures has generally found a way to thrive even in environments inhospitable to it. Not all environments for viewing are ideal, especially when the desire for motion pictures outstrips the availability of exhibition sites. If we are to position mobile cinema viewing within this context, then the history seems more contiguous than not. Mobile viewing becomes the exercise of experiencing films as one can and where one can. The viewer no longer makes a pilgrimage to a perfect venue; rather, films come to the viewer where the viewer can encounter them. This has always been so; even the temple of the New Wave experienced it. The cinephile on the train, intent on gleaning moving images and sounds with a cell phone, may be the new version of the cinephile crouching on the steps of the Cinémathèque. Access, rather than perfection, becomes the order of the day when one simply wants to *watch movies*—especially when this desire strikes often, and there is personal technology (in past decades the 16mm projector, but today the smartphone with a streaming app) to realize the aim. The cinephile on the steps of the Cinémathèque had to negotiate a welter of sounds with the film experience. So does the mobile viewer. To fully understand the implications of this, however, we must add the missing piece of the puzzle: What does it have to do with listening?

MOBILE LISTENING AND THE NEW CINEPHILIA

How does listening become a part of our new way of loving media? What follows analyzes how the history of public listening practices, exemplified by the Walkman and the iPhone, also serves as a necessary theoretical antecedent for understanding mobile listening to films on smartphones. Listening practices, as they are enabled by the smartphone's rise, showcase that the smartphone enables a new form of listening to visual media. It makes a new form of engagement possible that has the power to shape our sonic experience of the movies. The smartphone,

I argue, represents the beginning of a culture of convergence with regard to listening practices. A multimedia device that encourages listening across platforms, it enables easy access to multiple forms of sound media. The history of movie listening offers us some answers as to where this all might lead. Public, mobile listening through music has been possible since the 1950s when the transistor radio was invented, with its trademark "tinny" sound that users attempted to counteract by placing it directly by their ears.[63] The transistor radio established the "public" trend early; it was meant to be heard by surrounding listeners. The transistor radio was followed in that vein by the boom box, invented in the late 1960s but appearing around 1975 in the American market.[64] One could broadcast one's music to the surrounding neighborhood for the cost of nine D batteries. In the history of public listening, debates over the introduction of unnecessary noise into public spaces have suffused conversations for some years. Boom boxes became an aural marker of noisy urban culture in the 1970s and 1980s, and debates over boom boxes also became debates over noise's relationship to class and race.[65] Noise was marked as "other" to a white middle class operating according to an etiquette of public decorum that maintained a value on personal silence. Debates emerging with the rise of the boom box then continued into later decades, even up until the mid-2000s with the ongoing debate over the phenomenon of "sodcasting," in which users now continue to loudly listen to their own music in public spaces, including, most famously, those of public transportation, only now using mobile phones.[66] Publicly broadcasting their music for all surrounding listeners to hear, with no headphones and without consideration of those auditors' own desires, constitutes a clear and evident example of the problem of noise in modern public aural culture and its cultural negotiation.

As Wayne Marshall has written, "Such assessments do often politicize particular sounds and sonic practices in the ways 'noise' sometimes entails." "Critiques of mobile music," as Marshall writes, "frequently express anxieties about the social order, ... bringing class and race and age either implicitly or explicitly into the debate."[67] The ultimate representative of such an activity is the "London kids listening to grime on their phones on the bus."[68] Their "trebly, tinny reproductions" reflect a belief that their cell phones may operate as "mobile sound systems," broadcasting their musical choices. Implicit in the decision to so broadcast is "a fuck-you, anti-social element" that makes such broadcasting seem offensive to some listeners.[69] But other interpretations of public listening doubt whether such behaviors are in fact anti-social. The sharing of music could be considered a social act, which would make it, not noise, but communally enjoyed sound. Perhaps, these critics write, we have simply lost track of a sense of aural community. As Dan Hancox puts it, "Others hear in treble culture a reclamation of public space and an impulse toward communal musicking."[70] For Hancox, "Sodcasting represents a vital, politicized re-socialization of public culture" in a way that this book has argued happens in cinema culture as well: a desire to "make the music public again, to have it listened to . . . in groups."[71] It reintroduces the communal element of the listening experience. In this, it acknowledges sound as something to be enjoyed together.

Normally, however, it is not. In the United States in the twenty-first century, we tend to prefer to enjoy our sound privately. We engage with it alone. The model of public listening that the smartphone follows is the track of mobile listening described by Shuhei Hosokawa in his 1984 study of the Walkman.[72] The Walkman, says Hosokawa, created a private realm within public, urban space. One was sonically stimulated while remaining in a state of relative isolation. This description has been taken up by Michael Bull in his work on the personal stereo and the iPod. Hosokawa's study of the Walkman contains several points relevant to the case of mobile viewing on smartphones. First, it is a phenomenon that finds its purest expression in the urban environment; this is true in the case of mobile videos as well. Hosokawa refers to the use of the Walkman as an "urban strategy" of the "autonomy of the walking self" and to the Walkman itself as an "urban sonic/musical device."[73] The Walkman's use was marked by the user's ability to negotiate urban space in a manner that allowed him to mediate his surroundings sonically. Hosokawa describes the mobile listener as a "minimum, mobile, and intelligent unit" moving throughout the city. He quotes Jean-Francois Lyotard: "The *self* is small, but it is not isolated; it is held in a texture of relations which are more complex and mobile than ever before."[74] The Walkman's listener listens to music alone, yet he is still a member of the public.

Being able to listen to music while doing something else makes both of those activities more pleasurable, but it also allows the user to negotiate options and cycle back and forth between them, rather than remaining open to all stimuli. When we are walking down the street, we have the potential for our attention to be redirected by other people, and in that way we are aurally available. The user of the Walkman who does the same activities while listening to music gives off the exact opposite impression; rather than available, he appears occupied, busy already, producing the effect that an engagement by others becomes an interruption. This particularly decreases the risk that others will attempt to engage the user; attempts at interaction are reduced, as the listener may not hear the interlocutor. Headphone listeners glide through public space with a semipermeable membrane surrounding them. Through the practice of what Phil Patton and Bull call "auditized looking," users of a personal audio device may even escape eye contact with others when desired and thereby make themselves seem unavailable for social interactions.[75] The rules of social engagement are severely modified by this addition to social interaction. Users may assume that a person is "busy" simply because of his or her practice of private listening. This is, in certain evident ways, analogous to the practice of mediated togetherness that we have been talking about throughout this book. We never looked at other viewers when we were at the cinema, but we knew that they were present. Here the cinema provides the aural model that we need to best understand our more current mobile practice.

SONIC NEGOTIATIONS OF PUBLIC AND PRIVATE

Aural signals may be better suited to negotiation of public space than visual signals. We can listen and attend to another task more easily than we can watch. Take our eyes off the screen—especially with a film (rather than, say, a soap opera, which accounts for this phenomenon in its style)—and we might lose a narrative thread. But the soundtrack may give us that thread in another form, so we may even rely on it as we move about our space freely. We are still engaged with the film or television program as we move, but in a manner that allows some flexibility. While the Walkman has been criticized for enabling users' detachment from the social environment, it also allows greater control and the possibility of negotiating that world in a way better suited to one's own media-based desires. This section argues that the phenomenon of mobile listening depends upon what Kenneth Gergen terms the "absent presence" that arises in the context of mobile listening, and allows us to "tune out" of our surrounding environment.[76] It demonstrates how this phenomenon of absent presence allows us to draw a sharp line between desired sound and noise.

Headphones are now a ubiquitous part of the mobile experience. Phenomenologist Rainer Schönhammer has argued that wearing headphones in public disrupts the expectation of shared sensory experience that we assume arises when we are in public. He writes that they violate "an unwritten law of interpersonal reciprocity: the certainty of common sensual presence in shared situations." He argues that the Walkman user creates "walls of separateness" by wearing headphones: an act akin to wearing dark sunglasses, as one creates a veil of privacy.[77] The result is a "figure-ground" relation that is in constant flux. Walkman users "confess" that they have an aural secret that keeps them apart from their surroundings, and they pull a curtain of privacy around themselves, evidently private in the public space. From within this semipermeable membrane, users are free to interact with the world—but only as they choose.[78] The "figure" and the "ground" of their consciousness may alternate, with the sounds of the music or the sound of the environment coming to the fore at a given moment in time. They may alternately dominate users' experience; these users experience a "simultaneous absence and presence" while in public.[79]

Beer has noted this same phenomenon. He in fact views it as a positive though complicated scenario of negotiation. He states that the act of listening to music in public enables "users to tune out of the immediate landscape—by prioritizing the musical information overlay over the physicality of the urban environment."[80] He adds, however, that this process is always imperfect, being "often interrupted by the complex imbrications of the pervasive sounds of the city." Beer emphasizes the constant negotiation of this process; he suggests "an alternative vision of mobile music device use," in which "the user remains an integrated yet distracted part of the aural ecology and informational structures of the city." The primary discourse on the MP3 player describes it as "a device for shutting out sound thus generating an isolated and detached listener." But Beer rejects this in favor of "a vision of the mobile music device (and its use) as an integral part of the audio web in which we are constantly enveloped." Listeners remain, he writes, "an integrated yet distracted part of the aural ecology."[81]

Hosokawa writes that mobile listening can be considered "an *additional* listening act." "Listening is incidentally overlapped by and mixed up with different acts: as a listening act it is not exclusive but inclusive, not concentrated but distracted, not convergent but divergent, not centripetal but centrifugal." Music is "incorporated with alien elements which are usually taken as non-musical."[82] Drew Hemment has similarly argued that the mobile listening experience is "never hermetically sealed but incidentally overlapped by and mixed up with different acts: walking, eating, drinking, playing. Because the Walkman is designed for use in the street, on the bus, etc., any use of the Walkman is going to be bound up with different places and other acts. They are as much a part of the Walkman experiences as the intermission is a part of the experience of theatre, or, in a stronger sense, the bricks and mortar of a concert venue are a part of the acoustics of a gig."[83] The mobile listening act constructs the lived experience of the user. In this way, the user "occupies two spaces at once."[84]

Michael Bull has dealt extensively with the changes wrought in our culture of listening by the introduction of the iPod. He repeatedly uses the term *bubble* to describe the experience of mobile listening. iPod users are, he states, very sensitive to "urban noise" and therefore create havens of desirable sound for themselves. They "have successfully reclaimed not merely the private domains of the city but also public space. They have transformed the public spaces of the city into private enclaves of saturated sound."[85]

Bull writes that technologies like the iPod "produce for their users an intoxicating mixture of music, proximity and privacy whilst on the move."[86] Citing Adorno, he states that the aim is ultimately one of simultaneously distancing ourselves from the social scene and still retaining a sense of contact with the humanity around us. Adorno, he writes, "recognized that sound technologies, in particular, transform our understanding of connection and proximity" to others.[87] Jonathan Sterne has similarly noted that a "construct of acoustic space as private space" occurs with MP3 listening.[88] Bull's arguments in general align with those proposed by James E. Katz and Mark Aakhus, whose collection of essays on mobile media also posit competing desires for sonic privacy and publicness. Gergen, who coined the term *absent presence* for this mode of engagement, explains that mobile technologies such as the smartphone permit their users to create a private sphere within the realm of the public, thereby crafting the "emergence of a world of meaning cut away from the pragmatics of everyday life."[89] Bull argues that "iPod users tend to be non-interactive" in that the pleasure of their experiences is marked by their distancing function. He writes that users take control of their experience by "privatizing it." As Bull notes, "Users tend to negate public spaces through their prioritization of their own technologically mediated private realm."[90]

Beer's approach softens some of the more troubling conclusions made by Bull, arguing that listeners, far from being perfectly removed from a sphere of noise, are negotiating with it, and that such negotiations ought to be the focus of our study "Sound generated in their ears by the mobile music device is not the only sound they hear: they are still exposed to soundscapes of the urban territories through which they pass, and in fact, if the earphones are loud enough, may also be contributing to other people's experiences through sound leakage."[91] He writes: "The background hum is always there, despite our temporary moments of otherworldliness where we submerge ourselves in the soundtracks that we give to certain places, journeys and activities. To put this back into Bull's terminology, our 'bubble' is often burst by heavy or noisy traffic, alarms, shouting, doors slamming, car horns, dogs barking, construction work, louder music, Muzak, sirens, the list goes on." For this reason, he writes, "We can think instead of people attempting to tune out the complexities of the city—for any of the reasons Bull (2000) lists in his work—by overlaying sounds that they wish to hear on top of the existing soundscapes of the territories through which they move. In other words, rather than being lifted out of aural ecologies, mobile listeners are constantly and inescapably integrated or networked in these territories."[92] The practice of mobile listening also permits the creation of a sphere of comfort and contact with an absent set of reference points. Gergen similarly argues that "as the technologies of absent presence divert and redirect attention, so they expand the range of relationships (either real or imagined) in which the person is engaged."[93]

As Carolyn Marvin notes, and Max Dawson affirms, media technologies themselves are in fact never "discrete objects," seeing as they lack "natural edges."[94] Rather, it is the *practices* that accompany the array of devices that are of interest; these allow continuity between one form of viewing (or listening) and another, enabling us to engage in similar forms of practice across contexts. In this case, the mobile cinema that travels with us forms a bubble around us and is composed merely of our devices and ourselves. As Dawson writes, media are "constructed complexes of habits, beliefs, and procedures embedded in elaborate cultural codes of communication."[95] Barbara Klinger argues that cinema, as an "old" medium in the 1990s, at this point transformed into a component of the "media saturated household."[96] Her work showcases how DVDs, cable, and the Internet have affected the encounters we make with media in the home. In the 1990s, audiences began to think of home video as an option for the exercise of their moviegoing impulse. Cable movie channels, DVD collections, and Internet downloads all offer the cinephile cinema, available at any time. The situation that Klinger described in 2006 is realized to an even greater extent today. In this era of mobile viewing, we find that even home viewing has become complicated by the entrance of more viewing technologies actively used by consumers *as* they use their conventional televisions. While viewers at home engage with their films or television programming, they also often have a smartphone or a tablet on their lap in or in their hand, enabling them to engage with their community online, either by posting content to cinema-based websites or by posting to social media sites such as Facebook and Twitter. Twitter, in particular, has come to have a real force in the media world when it comes to the viewing of television, since viewers become devotees of certain shows and then tweet about them at length during the show's broadcast, as well as over the course of the season. This, we might argue, is the new online chatter that is the "new noise," replacing chitchat between viewers or, equally, lobby talk.[97] It is one territory of a new version of cinephilia.

Listening, then, is becoming an individual activity made public as a spectacle through acts of conspicuous and highly branded consumption for the modern mobile technology user. Not only are we negotiating public sounds of traffic, car horns, and pedestrians, but we are publicly negotiating sounds. We make a spectacle of our own listening. The headphones with which we approach this activity both privatize our experience and enable it to become a public activity, one that is easily consumable by onlookers. It becomes a form of self-presentation and thereby dances between the public and the obviously private aural experience. The headphone era allows us to make other sounds, which we usually engage in regular life outside our headphones, into noise.

When we do this, we are creating our own privatized and perfected venue for viewing and listening to our own media. We do so, obviously, however, within the sphere of public space. Flirtations, laughter, and chitchat have always marked film theaters as private/public spaces where tension arose between contemplation and distraction. Hence the need for rules to enable us to better contemplate, and the range of institutional practices to increase focus within venues themselves. The city bus, I believe, is another version of this strange sort of hybrid space. Carving out aural privacy within the space of the public is the work of a combination of tactics; one of these is simply ignoring the presence of others. Mobile devices help us enormously in this respect. Another tactic is absenting ourselves until we find a moment when we desire to be present. By engaging in auditized looking, we disengage from our environment—that is, until we wish to re-enter at a moment of our own choice. This is an apparent negotiation between two modes of attentiveness, enabled by the management of our attentiveness as performed through the mobile device. In the previous models we have discussed, the venue did this negotiation for us, encouraging the necessary split

FIGURE 4.2. Tracy Mosley, *Casual Style*, 2017. Photograph. From Flickr, with image permission granted by the artist. https://www.flickr.com/photos/burntdirt/32006692244 /in/photolist-23xw8Nw-25exvoL-QLjEvs-REyLRq.

between the public and the private via its tactics. Now we ourselves impose the mandate of neutralizing social noise, turning what is undeniably public space into private space via the "privatization" of our own bubbles. We import the values and restrictions of the cinema house into our mobile behavior, where they previously would have been the antithesis of what was expected and/or required. Making a space for contemplative listening in a busy world, we manage to revive practices of a platform we are in the process of turning away from (this being the movie house). Turning social space into private space, we recreate the movie theater's sense of separateness to listen to our private sounds in a controlled environment, on our own personal devices.

In our desire to engage with our own private world, we make the rest of the world a type of noise that is then blocked out. All sounds surrounding us become beside the point as regards the cinematic sphere we have decided to engage in, or at least a secondary concern, necessary only for successful navigation. We listen for the sounds of honking cars, or traffic signals, or other necessities, but we block out anything else. Via our silent assertion of our private space within the public, we take the rules of the movie theater—that silence is appropriate, decorous,

FIGURE 4.3. Tracy Mosley, *The Metro Wait*, 2017. Photograph. From Flickr, with image permission granted by the artist. https://www.flickr.com/photos/burntdirt /33557112176/in/photolist-T8jYkA.

and necessary—and apply them to the public. The headphone era may not mean that we don't make noise as we listen, but it does mean that we begin to see all that is outside our headphones as noise. The world, attractive as it is, in many ways, becomes an aural background for our chosen type of listening. But this can also be complicated, for as we have discovered over and over in this book, no attempt to block out noise is ever entirely successful. Rather, we negotiate noise here too.

NEGOTIATING NOISE: LISTENING ON OUR SMARTPHONES

Our experiences of noise are akin to the figure-ground scenario outlined by Schönhammer; sometimes noise is the background sound to our listening, while at other times it rises to the fore as we need to re-engage with where we are. In the dialogue on listening culture there is a notable focus on the act of listening on buses. This, I believe, is because the bus itself is a perfect encapsulation of the public and the private, much as movie theaters have been throughout this work. They function because we craft imaginary walls via media and choose not to engage, even as we sit together in a communal space. We listen in our own private, public space. No longer limited to just the sounds that come from our iPods, we now watch images too. We watch movies on our phones on the subway. We also do so while waiting to be called in for our appointments at the doctor's or dentist's offices, or waiting in line at the post office or the local takeout place.

As Beer writes, "It is worth emphasizing that it is not only music that has a transformative impact upon the city, but also that the city has an impact upon the experience of the music as new narratives and experiential connections to place become attached to the music through mobile listening."[98] As we listen to movies in public, the social scene inflects these movies. We are watching films as background—as filler for our daily activities. Under such circumstances, we are engaged, not in pure contemplation, but in negotiation. And some texts lend themselves better than others to this task. For example, full-length films still do not offer themselves quite as readily as television. TV episodes are well timed to run the entire length of a morning or afternoon commute, and short videos are perhaps best suited to the act of watching while waiting in a line for a hot dog from a street vendor. Clips we watch may be directly inspired by events happening around us. An event occurring around us may trigger a memory, which provokes the Google search for a favorite film clip. Our cinephilia may, in this way, be inspired by our immediate surroundings as well as serving as an escape from them. We are inattentive and attentive, distracted and compelled to listen to what we listen to. We are modern-day cinema listeners and are highly mobile. As William J. Mitchell puts it, when we use these devices, we construct "a virtual mise-en-scène on the substructure of the immediate physical one."[99] We do this quite readily. In the next section, I will examine how the cinephilic ideal of audiovisual quality comes up against a contending ideal of media accessibility, and how we negotiate our media when we decide that sacrificing quality is indeed worth having the convenience of the smartphone.

Cinephile culture has long been obsessed with the question of visual and aural quality of the user's experience. This question was fervently discussed during the rise of the home theaters and drove, as Klinger writes, the culture's acquisition of a "hardware aesthetic." In fact, as mobile viewing becomes more mainstream and much more popular, the cinephiles are doing it in greater numbers. While Klinger, in the words of a review by Dawson, "contrasts the web short's 'uncommitted' viewer to the figure of the 'contemporary cinephile,' the home-theater enthusiast or film collector who zealously scrutinizes the transfer quality, aspect ratio, and sound mixing of special editions DVDs, and Laser Discs," such a distinction is challenged by current practices as we settle into this new mode of listening.[100] I and other cinephiles like me are listening in this way. As Klinger notes, debates over visual quality—of both the visual texts themselves and the equipment necessary to play them—became prominent in cinephile culture. The experience of viewing at home had to rival the cinema experience, so larger and more high-definition television sets became necessary equipment. DVDs were supplanted by Blu-Ray in order to get more visual and audio information per experience. In this home media environment, with its fetishization of audiovisual quality, sound took on a new and necessary role. Surround sound became a cornerstone of any home theater system worth discussing. The 1980s saw the implementation of the Dolby sound system in many theaters around North America, and a love of superior film sound resulted in a multitude of home theaters equipped with Dolby 5.1 surround, as well as its successors. Such a system was easily marketed and became a popular feature of many home theaters. By the early 2000s, many homes across America had 5.1 systems, and mainstream electronics stores such as Best Buy offered extensive options for widescreen home theater systems as well as large speakers for the sound. Good sound at home was achievable; indeed, it became a serious point of pride.

In the first decade of the 2000s, however, the handheld digital device became a marked second option. Undoing much of the work that had been done to create a simulation of the quality of the moviegoing experience, the handheld device *lacked* everything the film theater and the home theater had: size, visual clarity, a wealth of visual information, and broad-frequency surround sound. The handheld device had only one thing going for it, and this was convenience. Quality came up against convenience in a new battle over what consumers wanted most. Would they prefer the home theater experience, or the smartphone experience? Barbara Klinger wrote that viewers streaming media at home tended to "reject the 'value-laden' binary that construes domestic [or, in this case, public] exhibition as an inferior alternative to the immersive experiences offered by the multiplex."[101] This same kind of choice is now evidently being repeated with the switch from the home theater to that of the mobile device. Now more than ever, we are sacrificing "quality" by prioritizing convenience.

Filmmaker David Lynch has long spoken out against the practice of listening to films on smartphones, arguing that the old-fashioned theater experience was integral to film sound. He has stated that he finds viewing films on smartphones offensive because of its lack of respect for the original film text; films, he explains, should be given a dedicated amount of time as well as the listener's full attention. Lynch considers screening films on a smartphone anathema because of the same respect for sound design that leads him to his rather complex collaborations in his own films. He bemoans the notable reduction in sound range and quality of the smartphone, declaring, "Now, if you're playing the movie on a telephone, you will never in a trillion years experience the film. You'll think you have experience it, but you'll be cheated. It's such a sadness, that you think you've seen a film on your *fucking* telephone. Get real." The vehemence of his rhetoric has been such that in 2007 a video clip of Lynch addressing the matter in the DVD special features of *Inland Empire* was cleverly transformed into a parody of an Apple iPhone ad and went viral on YouTube.[102] In a later 2013 interview he restates the "transport" thesis propagated by thinkers earlier in this book, arguing that "if you have a chance to enter another world, then you need a big picture in a dark room with great sound." Viewing a film in a theater with the sound done correctly is "a spiritual, magic experience. If you have the same movie on a little computer screen [of an iPhone] with bad sound—and this is the way people are seeing films now—it's such a shame. It's a shameful, shameful thing. It's so pathetic."[103]

Pathetic it may be, according to Lynch, but if it is, then many of us are pathetic. When the review was published, it appeared all over the Internet and the reaction was generally not agreement but amusement at Lynch's Luddite perspective. Users poked fun at what, arguably, seemed to be a form of cine-mysticism; when online outlet *Gawker* posted the video clip, user Cam/ron wrote in response, "I've always wanted to watch *Eraserhead* on an iPhone during family picnics in the sun."[104] He added, "The kids would just love the mutant baby," mocking the idea that users would not know how to choose their modes of engagement more carefully than that. And some went even further. User mathnet wrote a small manifesto for the viewer's rights: "When a thing is complete, it's complete. It's mine now. I'll watch it with my eyes closed if I want and don't go thinking you're the boss of me."[105] We can choose a degraded experience, such users asserted, and find meaning from it. An unwillingness to surrender to a perfect experience marks the new, mobile user's cinephilia. The tone of users' comments was light, but their assertion of the user's very active role was clear. This might be, as Roland Barthes and Michel de Certeau propose in very different contexts, a cinema not of writers but of readers, not of the overwhelmingly powerful cinema experience but of the myriad ways in which we may comfortably, and cleverly, fit films into our daily lives for a deep and profound experience or a light one, as we choose.[106] There is a sense of play to the ways the film is received, and a range of actions, both physical and metaphorical, are made possible by these active readers. While users may or may not literally "watch with [their] eyes closed," some certainly do, and many are certainly performing a range of practices in their mobile listening that exceed Lynch's vision of appropriate listening.[107]

These users allude less often to the sound quality of a video or film as a major concern than to the visual, though it very obviously suffers from a series of problems of degradation similar to those posed by the visual. Audio file size is reduced, and speakers (in an analogue to the viewer's problems with the iPhone screen) are insufficient for creating the full "cinema experience." Even listening on headphones cannot approximate the experience of theater sound in its full dynamic range, with its full directionality executed via the use of multiple speakers. However, Lynch's concerns and those of other users with high expectations for cinema sound are actively being addressed by companies such as Dolby Laboratories, which is attempting to inch its way into the mobile technologies market for mobile device–based viewing and listening. Marketing its software and hardware as the "Anywhere Entertainment Center," Dolby claims to make your smartphone your "portable movie theatre" through the implementation of cinema-worthy sound.[108] The company that brought us excellent movie theater sound now brings us a vast improvement in personal cinema sound. These projects include Dolby Atmos for your smartphone, which can be used with either Netflix or Amazon Prime.[109] Among its benefits are the creation of improved surround sound and clarity in dialogue. The "surround visualizer" creates a surround sound experience either through headphones (for mobile listening) or, in a pinch, through the cell phone's own built-in speakers in a design prefigured by Dolby's theater setups. The "dialogue enhancer" allows for increased clarity in hearing spoken language in one's favorite densely crafted audiovisual texts.[110] And the "intelligent equalizer" adjusts the audio dynamically to achieve the tone you want, even as the "volume leveler" maintains a constant volume across all content and applications so one does not get blasted with high audio levels on YouTube while Amazon Prime remains at a normal level. With such devices, Dolby works to make mobile listening a cinephile's (and audiophile's) experience, asserting that "a smartphone featuring Dolby Audio offers a richer audio experience for your movies."[111]

These technologies remain nascent, however, and Dolby sound is not yet an established part of all brands in the mobile listening experience. Sound is not at this point a widespread selling point for smartphones. Rather, when we make the choice to view and listen while we are in motion, we tend to be sacrificing a tradition of quality that we associate with conventional cinephile culture. So in what scenarios do we find this trade to be a worthwhile one?[112] Anecdotal evidence and the numbers from recent studies suggest that we are happy to sacrifice the higher quality of the at-home experience for the convenience of a pocket cinema that brings us our movies as we move. We are less concerned with audiovisual quality than we are with maintaining the experience we desire: the experience of personal listenership on an intimate scale while in public space, executed with whatever methods are available.

What effects might this have on traditional cinephile viewing and listening culture? Project Cinephilia, an online venture that includes critics and scholars, held an "online roundtable" on digital cinephilia in the era of changing viewing habits that are affected by not only streaming services and changed platforms but also mobility. In response to an early statement by one of the roundtable members, film and media scholar Genevieve Yue states that the continuity of new and old practices of engaging with media is much greater than discontinuity. She writes: "The end of the cinematic century has only opened new questions as to what cinema was, or continues to be in augmented forms."[113] Inquiry should be controlled by concerns not about format but about motivation and continuity of use. "In an era of multiple viewing platforms, how might we reconsider the history of cinema as that of a screen practice?"[114] Of course, I ask this same question. How might media be considered a sound practice, a speaker practice, or an earbud practice? Addressing the questions this chapter alludes to in the form of different viewing environments and practices, Yue writes from an age group that is my own, in between the Baby Boomer cinephilia of the 1960s and 1970s and the new, emerging mobile cinephilia of the younger millennials and Generation Z. The memories and thoughts she describes are much like the ones I have related here: "I came of age, like many in the newly ascendant generation of cinephiles and critics, in the home-video era, and like many others, I had already taken for granted that movies were malleable art forms that functioned differently in different spaces (theater/home/classroom)." As Yue writes, perhaps the matter of discussion should be not *how* are we watching but what continuities of practice and desire carry across those contexts. As we leave venues behind, the aim of getting what we want with the maximum of intimacy continues. She writes: "Against the gloomy predictions of its end, the misty-eyed nostalgia for a heyday those of my generation have only read about, and those pesky pronouncements of cinema's (deathless) death, it endures. And I think," she says, "this is because cinema, at heart, is an activity."

I find myself looking up favorite scenes of beloved films on my iPhone as I move through my day, treating this time like a check-in with friends. It is a personal experience, for me, in fragmented and fragmentary cinephilia: a sort of grab bag of clips that are emblematic of my memories and fleeting thoughts. This is, in itself, a practice in cinephilia. And it is one that is created largely through my listening while I am traveling somewhere else. I wear earbuds and delve into *Before Sunset* to check in with Jesse and Celine. I listen to the Robert Mitchum–Lillian Gish duet of "Leaning on the Everlasting Arms" from *The Night of the Hunter,* and Mitchum retelling the story of the battle of "right hand, left hand."[115] And this, surprisingly, does not seem separate from my own history of cinephilia but forms a real and constantly manifesting part of it. My phone and my earbuds form my own minitheater: the ideal of many movie lovers' dreams, it is my own private auditorium in which I listen. Closely connected with my dreams, desires, and feelings, it allows me to screen any film I like on my dream screen. I negotiate this with the world around me, and I carve out a space for the practice. Christian Keathley has argued that cinephiles have a tendency to collect filmic moments. He argues: "Such details remain one's own, no doubt in large part because the initial encounter was a private one." Keathley quotes Roger Cardinal as saying that this obsession assigns to individual filmic moments a "wholly unreasonable priority and value."[116] It can manifest in a focused—almost compulsive—return to scenes from memory. With ubiquitous access to films, on our own terms, and absolute convenience in this form of access, this minicinema is available to me as a sphere of movie memories at any time. At any time that I may call it up, I can use this audiovisual device for my own personal pleasure. Cinema is an archive of images; it may also prove to be an aural treasure trove for cinephiles who want to listen to the sounds of beloved films.

One of the respondents to my survey wrote in support of this idea: "Sometimes I don't want to or don't feel the need to sit down and re-watch a whole movie, especially if it's a movie I know well. Sometimes I just want to taste it. I want to see or hear a specific scene or sequence, maybe during a study break or with friends in the dining hall." She added: "Though revisiting a favorite scene is a very different experience than watching a favorite film start to finish, it is fulfilling in its own way. Picking out these favorite scenes is like assembling my own little collection. It feels more intimate, in certain way, than compiling a list of my favorite movies." She finished: "It's like underlining favorite passages in a book—it makes the copy your own."[117]

As a cinephile, I am still, evidently and obviously, engaging with films. However, now my cinema theater moves. I carry it with me. And when it speaks to me, I don't always need to look. Films speak intimately in my ears. They converse. I listen. I am in a hurry. Our mobile devices help us tune out what we do not want to hear, and, as Bull argues for musical listening, they craft a sense of personal continuity through the creation of our own soundscape. We have our own soundtrack, and it consists of beloved voices, music, and memories that overlay our current experience. Now, this is not new. We can argue, looking at the whole of this book, that the encounter with cinema has *always* occurred in a space of vacillating attention and distraction, of choosing to listen to the sounds of the film screened or to one's own, more private, desires. The tools that enable our construction of contemplation vary historically, but the negotiation is not new. It finds a distinctive and unique meaning in our current era, and it is one that focuses on listening.

In the last days of this book project, because such things were on my mind, I sent some questions to former students who are friends of mine on Facebook. While the degree of rigor in this call for information did not rise to the level of ethnography, I found their responses helpful for understanding elements of my own cinephile community—one that I, in fact, through my teaching, had helped create. I asked them: "Do you watch clips of films on your smartphones? If so, do you consider this to be an extension of your cinephilia, or is it, perhaps, something else?" The responses I received were varied; many students asserted that they preferred to use their smartphone only as a last resort for film viewing of any kind. They preferred the home theater of their own apartment, or their own laptop screens, with their greater resolution and (with headphones) better sound. Smartphones were still considered a poor substitute for such experiences. But, it became clear, the former students tended to assume that I was asking them as a teacher—and, in that mode, they were considering their most serious viewing experiences—the ones they would be most comfortable speaking about in a classroom. The practices that they then brought out as relevant to the discussion, in response to my gentle prodding, became more specific. Some responses homed in on precisely how the phone, unlike other methods of viewing, relates to this question of personalized experience. They related it directly to memory and to personal feeling. The cinema in your pocket dovetails well with more intimate reflection. A student of mine wrote that he consistently considered his smartphone to be an extension of his own memory of films: "I sometimes watch little clips (five minutes or less) of specific scenes or moments." He added, however, something important: "But it's always something I'm already familiar with. I do this with TV shows and games, too—re-watching how a specific moment/feel/interaction was executed." In this, he writes, he feels there is a "blurred line between Cinephilia and . . . I want to see it again."[118] Another student, I believe, hit the nail on the head. His statement is a fine ending to this chapter that focuses on the exercise of movie love in the age of the digital. He wrote: "I think watching the clip of the scene on [your] phone is just a small form of worship in a grand scheme of worship of a movie. One rehashes the scene poorly in one's head if you love it enough; the phone, if anything, is an improvement on that."[119] Mobile screens become screens of memory, reminding us of moments that hold personal import for their watchers. And watching them, we perhaps exercise a love of movies that shows a different set of rituals from, but a continuity of feeling with, modes of cinephilia from twentieth-century history. We may watch in moments rather than in sustained attention. We bring our etiquettes with us, and sometimes we recreate that sense of surrender even in a mobile form. We cultivate it: now, through sound. And in so doing, with *Night of the Hunter* in our pocket, our earphones at the ready to listen to the duet of "Leaning," we begin to move into a new negotiation of an old desire: the desire, which we have perhaps always had, of bringing movies closer, closer, closer . . . even in a public place, until they whisper in our ears as we fall asleep, to quote the song, "safe and secure from all alarms," "leaning on the everlasting arms" of familiar films to resonate within us at moments when we most want them. And like parents speaking downstairs while we as children fell asleep, listening, sometimes it is just the film's familiar voices and sounds that carry us over into sleep—the voices that stay with us as we close our eyes. We are still negotiating noise, holding the device in our hand as all sorts of sound occur around us, but in the notes of that song, we hear the forms of noise that linger on in our current self-determined listening practices.

Conclusion

Noises We Will Be Hearing Soon

The examination of the soundscape of cinema culture via noise that this book has done has showed certain ways in which we might expand our boundaries to include a far-reaching definition of sound and noise—one coming from a broader sound studies—in what we consider to be cinema sound. The soundscape of cinema culture is broad, and it is historically and socially grounded. Understanding this, we come to recognize the methods by which the sound culture of the cinema is created, sustained, and maintained during certain moments. We also discover how it is connected to the structure of a broader culture with its own beliefs about sound and the act of listening itself. Widening the net in terms of what constitutes "cinema sound," beyond the sounds of films themselves or even film technologies, to include the sounds made by the audience in the auditorium, styles of listening that came from elsewhere, and the acoustical engineering that went into creating "silent" cinema auditoriums, we find that many sounds we had previously discounted combine to make up a meaningful soundscape that animates many of the social, technological, and aesthetic concerns of cinema culture. Sounds present in the envelope that surrounds the film event add to our understanding of the life of the medium. By focusing on noise specifically, I have argued that when it is analyzed through aural culture and history it can reveal important details about the conflicts upon which motion picture culture is structured. These include the power dynamics that are present in its cultural envelope, the politics internal to the industry, the ideological construction of cinema's venues, and the modes of engagement we bring to the listening act. It reveals the struggles that animate the definition of the boundaries of film culture, as well as cinema culture's assumptions about what is and is not socially acceptable, technologically productive, or personally pleasing. These conflicts make it clear where we set limits on expressiveness through sound in cinema culture. In this way, they connect the struggles over noise in cinema's sound culture with their activity in the broader context of American aural culture.

As my case studies have indicated, the study of noise presents an opportunity to analyze the underlying factors that produce the film cultural context. Chapter 1 explored how the male middle class wielded its power to term the sounds of women and the working class "noise." As Goodwin, Attali, and Bijsterveld assert, this means the "audiosocial play of power" was at work in film culture. The drive for quiet played into a gendered, classed, and sexed sphere out of which a new aural etiquette emerged. In chapter 2, noise appeared as a technological key to the film industry's continued success. AMPAS enacted a process of transformation to enable itself to turn noise into an industry asset rather than a liability. Taking the obstacle as an opportunity for changing course, the Academy saw it as a chance to shift the film industry in a productive new direction. In chapter 3, noise served as a motivating factor behind the establishment of an immersive apparatus for cinema environments. It motivated the design of theaters, both mainstream and avant-garde, to deal with the concern. And it interacted with modes of spectatorship and listening to craft a new assertion of the necessity of contemplative silence when watching a film. Noise, then, served as a cue for the creation of a perfected architecture that enabled a new mode of listening. In chapter 4, I followed the premises laid out by previous chapters into the present historical moment and explored how such etiquettes as those established in the moviegoing era come to affect our listening practices in a range of new technologies for mobile viewing. I thus explored noise in media outside the range of cinema proper and moved into the digital and mobile era.

I have chosen four examples, but these are far from being the only examples one *could* choose in a study of noise's role in cinema culture. This book is a first step in a project that I will continue, on how different modes of listening have inflected one another and how certain modes of listening stretch *across* media practice, uniting musical listening with new techniques of cinema listening, for example. My upcoming work will jump off from chapter 4 of this project, and will be on the form of what I call "listening convergence," which functions across media platforms. While I have focused on four significant moments in which noise reflected cinema culture, a great many more moments readily suggest themselves for exploration and analysis, especially as we look to the present and the future rather than to the past. The matter of noise and media gains a new life in sound culture as we face a changing paradigm in our media consumption. That is, I have here focused almost exclusively on cinema. As a cinema scholar, and as a historian, I find the cinema era important. But it may be one object of interest rather than a way of focusing on this question of noise indefinitely. The future mediascape appears more hybrid than a mere study of "cinema" would suggest. And the notion of a soundscape that unites different media becomes especially enticing.

If we take Rick Altman at his word and take cinema's sound to be an "event," then that event is changing in profound and potentially unrecognizable ways based upon our listening practices. Media use is more fluid, and young users often think of films, television, and other audiovisual media produced for alternative platforms as contiguous, rather than distinct, spheres. While my focus has been on how film theaters have crafted a range of listening experiences around the films themselves, I recognize that the context is now changing to incorporate an array of options that lie outside the movie theater's doors. There is now a drive to combine our media in terms of how we engage with them together. We begin to navigate, rather than to succumb to a single dominating film text or environment. I alluded to this trend in chapter 4. However, other media that are not accounted for here would also be relevant to our discussion. There is the rise of video game culture, which boasts a whole new interpretation of the soundscape that is meant to be interactive rather than immersive. This changes the nature of listening to allow the listener greater say over what is the "signal" and what is noise. The interactions are simply not the same. Video games such as *Proteus*, developed by Ed Key and David Kanaga, allow their users to actively play with the soundscape of the game by collecting small sounds that originally read as nonmusical noises and orchestrating them in a virtual environment, creating music: order out of chaos.[1] By manipulating her path through space (which is the entire point of the game, to create a trajectory and orchestrate these sounds), the user constructs the soundtrack of the game for herself. Exploring a new soundscape, we are placed in a more active relation to what we hear. And we are pushed to do so especially when the form of media encourages interactivity. Video games here provide us with a powerful and, admittedly, understudied example in the context of media's sound studies. Since they are a medium with growing social presence and force, and with great potential for applicability to sound studies due to their creation of different types of relationships between the image and sound, they and their culture offer us a new and exciting territory in which to study the workings of noise and the interaction between a medium of art and the greater sonic culture surrounding it.

Music listening's conjunction with cinema listening, which animates elements of chapters 3 and 4 of this book, will also be a major concern of mine moving forward. How is media listening becoming more hybrid—particularly as more and more people are using mobile media devices for listening purposes? Studies of noise may continue to make a particular intervention in this field, to show us how we are interacting in new ways with new media and with our surrounding environment. Cinema venues have obviously been very important to this project. As more and more people view films on their smartphones, the relevance of the cinema theater environment to our listening culture obviously lessens, even as new sound experiments are tried to retain the cinema-going audience. This, too, opens up new territory for sound studies. So do new sound technologies to be used across platforms.

Much of what I have spent time analyzing here are the techniques developed to encourage a feeling that, even while seated in a room filled with other people, one is fundamentally alone. While multiple scholars have suggested that the new mobile technologies also encourage this feeling, they obviously function in different ways. Media, and not cinema, are what we will be listening to, and this will undeniably be a profound shift—so much so that the questions motivating such media studies will need to be different, and reformulated, as well.[2] It may be necessary to think of sound as something that unites otherwise diverse media practices. What would the nature of that constellation look like?

In our new media context, screenings occur while we are moving, walking, talking, eating, and among family or friends. They take place on the street. While much of the work done in this book traces the rise of a series of viewing etiquettes, platforms, and spatial/acoustical designs designed to make viewing an experience further removed from the everyday, with their imposition of silence and their detachment of audiences from the context of the social environment through devices such as established rules of conduct, the last chapter leaves us at a new moment when these rules of etiquette are changing. Whereas the period of this book's events was a time of constructing the rules and increasing a sense of ceremony by borrowing elements of etiquettes from entertainments and activities associated with the higher arts, we are currently in a moment of reconfiguring them into new, more casual, and more interactive etiquettes. This includes habits of where we sit, how prolonged our viewing times are, and how we literally watch and listen (on headphones, for example, or on a bad smartphone speaker). And more devices become involved in the screening's scene, with smartphones, tablets, and games not only being the main attraction but often being played during screenings. This adds measurably to the noise of the "screening." As our screen time increases and our nonscreen time decreases, the sense of ceremony surrounding viewing, the public rituals, and the set of manners designed specifically to cater to certain public film screening situations becomes less necessary and perhaps less relevant to our everyday media experience. Certain thinkers have written about this extensively in terms of mobile technologies, speaking about the "cellularization" of aural culture.[3] While I recognize their point, what I mean is something different: How will we continue to think about the act of encountering sounds as they imply a desired signal and undesired noise? What will constitute the new signals? What sounds in this context will form the new "noise"? Will we consider them a problem at all? Or will we, already immersed in a sphere of noise, simply find them to be the new normal? How will we mediate them in our new listening practices? These questions remain to be answered as we move forward into a rapidly changing media culture, although they are beginning to be answered by cinema and audio culture. Throughout this project, it is not just noise that has consistently interested me, but what noise tells us about the manner in which we interact with each other through the culture of motion pictures. As these practices change so much that they are no longer recognizably moviegoing at all, the brick-and-mortar venues and official etiquettes I have found so fascinating here lose their sway and we look to new events and spaces.

When I was teaching my senior seminar on the history, practice, and potential future of cinephilia, conversations about media love often expanded to include mobile musical listening, as these forms of media seem separated more by history than by necessity. And although I find the history of the rise of etiquettes in cinema culture fascinating, telling us how we reached the point where our media culture is today, I find the present equally intriguing if not, increasingly, more so. My students were intent on thinking of modern cinephilia in terms of other media—especially "audiophilia." Our techniques of listening to audiovisual media cannot be as cinema-specific in the future as they have been in the past.

My next area of research will focus on the notion of listening convergence, in which the practices of listening in one medium begin to touch upon, and fuse with, the practices of listening in another. Musical listening and cinematic listening have been fused, in some ways, from the very beginning of film culture. This is true in new ways in the twenty-first century, with the formation of new sound platforms that enable us to cross from one listening medium to another. Dolby Atmos, mentioned in chapter 4, provides one clear example. Originally designed for cinema, Atmos is fast becoming a platform for crafting three-dimensional soundscapes in electronic and dance music. In both cases, sound forms a cohesive and coherent diegetic world that places the listener, spatially, in a complete sound bubble. The techniques of mixing and of listening are the same across media and using the same platform. Podcasts are booming, and those who listen to podcasts most are also statistically most likely to also listen to their audiovisual media while on the move. And new models of sound media are emerging in what we can call a new golden age of audio, including voice and recording apps for social media and podcasts that involve the audience via immersive techniques to create a sense of "absent presence"—as if one were truly present in the text. If noise continues to serve the historical role it did with cinema, of causing us to think more carefully about our relationship to the social dynamics of our surroundings in acts of spectatorship (to others, and to our environments), then I believe that it may yet have a role in the analysis of new patterns of spectators' listening in this new media culture—and that it may be truly illuminating.

Analyzing the nature of this media environment sonically and culturally could hold real promise. Noise serves a new purpose here, and one worth comprehending. When we think about how we engage with aural environments and this new welter of noise, and what that has to say about our attitudes about one another as we engage media, noise remains an active and critical tool for figuring out what we are hearing, how we are positioning ourselves with regard to sound, and what we make of our place in the dynamics of media culture. Making sense of how we listen is a valuable exercise as we engage with new forms of media, on new platforms, and in new constellations of relations between viewers in public and private space. What we are listening for, and what we are hoping to block out, remain real questions. As new practices emerge, so will new ways of categorizing what is desirable and what is noise, and so will ways of avoiding the latter and seeking out the former. As with cinema culture, those distinctions will have as much to do with us as listeners as the sounds we hear, and will reveal as much about our powerful audiosocial distinctions as the aesthetics that guide such judgments. As we move into a new era of listening that is marked by fluidity over discontinuity, and connectedness over separateness, listening practices may yet be a common way of understanding just how we negotiate the media sphere and how we negotiate the public and the private in a newly unified twenty-first-century media world. As we move into that era, one of increased convergence between sound media, there is a great deal more to hear.

The Static in the System Mobile Listening Survey

The following was sent to participants in the survey cited in chapter 4.

STOP. Before you answer these questions, please fill out the release form, indicating that your responses may be used in Meredith Ward's book, *The Static in the System: Noise and the Soundscape of American Cinema Culture*, to be published by the University of California Press. Your anonymous responses may be used in the book's fourth chapter, on the mobile viewing experience.

This questionnaire is estimated to take approximately 30 minutes.

It is requested that you answer all questions fully. Please be precise and specific in your answers. Also, please offer all information that is implied by the question.

Demographic information is for the purposes of establishing the nature of the data set, in terms of its heterogeneity/homogeneity and specific characteristics. Your individual demographic information will not be cited in the text, nor will it be used in any way without express permission.

If you have questions, please contact Meredith Ward at meredith.ward.athopkins@gmail.com prior to answering the questions below. When the questionnaire is complete, please email it to meredith.ward.athopkins@gmail.com with the subject line, "Questionnaire." You will receive a confirmation email that it has been received.

If you have any additional comments on the topics discussed, there is space for that at the end of the form. Please do feel free to use it as well. Thank you.

Demographic information:

Your age:

Numerical Questions:

*x indicates "times," as in 1x = 1 time, 2x = 2x. "/week" = per week, "/month, /mos." = per month, per months.

How often do you do the following:

Attend the movies (at a commercial movie theater)?

__ Multiple times/week

__ 1x/week

__ 1x/2weeks

__ 1x/month

__ 1x/2–3mos.

__ 1x/3–4mos.

__ 1x/6mos.

__ 1x/8mos.

__ 1x/year

Watch movies or TV on your television set at home (via streaming or any other platform)?

__ Every day/most days

__ 3–4 times/week

__ 1–2 times/week

__ 1 time/week

__ 5–6x/2 weeks

__ 3–4x/2weeks

__ 2–3x/2weeks

__ 1x/2 weeks

__ Never

Watch movies on your laptop?

__ Every day/most days

__ 3–4 times/week

__ 1–2 times/wk

__ 1 time/week

__ 5–6x/2 weeks

__ 3–4x/2weeks

__ 2–3x/2weeks

__ 1x/2 weeks

__ Never

Watch movies on a tablet?

__ Every day/most days

__ 3–4 times/week

__ 1–2 times/week

__ 1 time/week

__ 5–6x/2 weeks

__ 3–4x/2weeks

__ 2–3x/2weeks

__ 1x/2 weeks

__ Never

Watch movies on your phone?

__ Every day/most days

__ 3–4 times/week

__ 1–2 times/week

__ 1 time/week

__ 5–6x/2 weeks

__ 3–4x/2weeks

__ 2–3x/2weeks

__ 1x/2 weeks

__ Never

Watch television programs on your phone?

__ Every day/most days

__ 3–4 times/week

__ 1–2 times/week

__ 1 time/week

__ 5–6x/2 weeks

__ 3–4x/2weeks

__ 2–3x/2weeks

__ 1x/2 weeks

__ Never

Watch short-form video content (e.g., College Humor, Facebook videos, etc.) on your phone?

__ Every day/most days

__ 3–4 times/week

__ 1–2 times/week

__ 1 time/week

__ 5–6x/2 weeks

__ 3–4x/2weeks

__ 2–3x/2weeks

__ 1x/2 weeks

__ Never

What content do you prefer to view in this manner?

__ Comedy

__ Drama

__ News

What are your feelings about viewing the following on a smartphone? Please answer for each of the following:
  a. Short-form video
  b. Television
  c. Films

Why would you watch movies or television on a smartphone?

Why wouldn't you?

Where is the strangest place you've watched media on your smartphone?

Where are you generally when you view media on your smartphone?

Why do you generally do it, when you do?

What forms of media do you believe are suited to the smartphone experience? Unsuited to it?

What about for the tablet experience?

The laptop experience?

The television/home theater experience?

The movie theater experience?

Do you enjoy the experience of viewing media on a smartphone? Why or why not?

How is it different from viewing media in other ways (the laptop, television, movie theater)?

Do you see this as a valid way of enjoying the media experience? Why or why not? What do you lose with it? What do you gain?

What, if anything, is uniquely positive and good about the experience?

If you watch movies this way, do you watch them all the way through, or in pieces?

Same with television?

Do you consider your smartphone to be a multimedia device? How do you like to use it?

If we only watched movies on smartphones, would you be upset? Why?

Do you watch content while you are mobile and out in the world? Where? How? Why?

Do you miss the movie theater, ever? Why? Why not?

What content do you feel is ideally suited to the experience of mobile viewing?

Would you feel self-conscious about watching video/television/films on your phone in public spaces? Why or why not?

Do you personally feel connected to the space (the immediate environment) in which you are viewing, when you watch media out in public?

Why or why not?

Do you look at the screen all the time under these circumstances? Explain/describe.

Do you spend some time *just listening* to the content?

Mostly just listening?

How does this change your experience?

Thank you! Your responses may be included in the data set, and your words may be quoted in the book. Thank you for your help!

Notes

INTRODUCTION

1. I engage extensively with James Lastra's work throughout this book. His *Sound Technology and the American Cinema: Perception, Representation, Modernity* (New York: Columbia University Press, 2000) has provided me with insight, perspective, and a keen appreciation for the fraught discourse on the representation of sound in culture. The work of Rick Altman also remains a major inspiration. Last, the far-reaching cultural analysis done in film sound work, including but not limited to that of Don Crafton, with his excellent and rigorous *The Talkies: American Cinema's Transition to Sound, 1926–1931* (Berkeley: University of California Press, 1997), has had a real impact on my conception of the soundscape of American cinema culture. Also of interest has been Douglas Gomery's *The Coming of Sound: A History* (New York: Psychology Press, 2005). Showcasing the rigorous and exciting ways we can explore a broader sense of the cinema soundscape began, for me, with my reading and rereading of these texts.

2. Although Crary's work is visual in character, his model is vital to what I do here. If Sterne's focus is on our culture's understanding of the nature of hearing, then Crary's is on how we consider the question of sight and, extending from sight, attention and perception. His study of the cultural and historical situatedness of the culturally current notion of attention has been an inspiration for my project, particularly in chapter 3, where I discuss how modes of listening in the nineteenth and twentieth centuries can be seen to extend his theories about disciplined attentiveness via sight into the realm of listening. I have also found helpful Crary's approach to the study of the senses as historically and culturally situated.

3. Douglas Kahn, *Noise, Water, Meat: A History of Voice, Aurality, and Sound in the Arts* (Cambridge, MA: MIT Press, 2001), 22.

4. Oxford English Dictionary, s.v. "Noise (n.)," www.oed.com. See also Nick Smith, "The Splinter in Your Ear: Noise as the Semblance of Critique," *Culture, Theory and Critique* 46, no. 1 (2005): 43–59. "Noise, from the Latin *nausea,* suggests an unpleasant disturbance lacking musical quality" (43).

5. Paul Hegarty, *Noise/Music: A History* (New York: Bloomsbury Academic, 2007), 5.

6. Caleb Kelly, *Cracked Media: The Sound of Malfunction* (Cambridge, MA: MIT Press, 2009), 62. For more on how electronic music and other forms of sonic art interact with our conception of noise, see also Caleb Kelly, *Sound* (Cambridge, MA: MIT Press, 2011).

7. Jacques Attali, *Noise: The Political Economy of Music* (Minneapolis: University of Minnesota Press, 1985), 27.

8. Michel Serres, "Noise," *Substance* 12, no. 3 (1983): 55.

9. Many of the most influential extant works on noise approach it via the fine arts. Kahn's *Noise, Water, Meat* is likely the most influential of these. See also Kelly's *Cracked Media* and *Sound*; Hegarty, *Noise/Music*; and a host of works, inspired by the writings and practice of John Cage, that focus on aesthetic texts, analyzing how noise becomes an aesthetic choice for practitioners of *musique concrète* and our contemporary forms of experimental music—for example, Joanna Demers, *Listening through the Noise: The Aesthetics of Experimental Electronic Music* (New York: Oxford University Press, 2010).

10. Hegarty, *Noise/Music*, 3.

11. Kelly, *Cracked Media*, 72.

12. Hegarty, *Noise/Music*, 3.

13. Kahn, *Noise, Water, Meat*, 3.

14. Attali, *Noise*, 26–27.

15. See R. Murray Schafer, *The Tuning of the World* (New York: Random House, 1977). For a book that gives a more comprehensive impression of the range of Schafer's work, see *The Soundscape: Our Sonic Environment and the Tuning of the World* (Rochester, VT: Destiny Books, 1993).

16. Marina Guzzy, "The Sound of Life: What Is a Soundscape?," *Smithsonian Center for Folklife and Cultural Heritage Magazine,* May 4, 2017, https://folklife.si.edu/talkstory/the-sound-of-life-what-is-a-soundscape.

17. Schafer, *Tuning of the World*, 4.

CHAPTER 1. SONGS OF THE SONIC BODY

1. For the original account referred to here, see Louis Reeves Harrison, "Jackass Music," with a sketch of the girl pianist by H. F. Hoffman, *Moving Picture World* 8, no. 3 (January 21, 1911): 125. He is the origin of the description of the girl pianist, "Lily Limpwrist," who is flirting with her boyfriend. Smaller elements of the rest of the account describing the peanut shells and the noise come from other accounts from *Moving Picture World* during these years.

2. See, for one excellent example, Scott Curtis's "The Taste of a Nation: Training the Senses and Sensibility of Cinema Audiences in Imperial Germany," *Film History* 6, no. 4 (1994): 445–69.

3. Jan Olsson, *Los Angeles before Hollywood: Journalism and American Film Culture, 1905 to 1915* (New York: Columbia University Press, 2009). 236. For more on the relationship between light and a sense of physical safety in early motion picture theaters, see Martin L. Johnson, "The Well-Lighted Theater or the Semi-darkened Room? Transparency, Opacity and Participation in the Institution of Cinema," *Early Popular Visual Culture* 12, no. 2 (2014): 199–212.

4. Quoted in Olsson, *Los Angeles before Hollywood*, 237.

5. Quoted in ibid., 236.

6. Olsson, *Los Angeles before Hollywood*, 236.

7. Rick Altman, *Silent Film Sound* (New York: Columbia University Press, 2004), 279–80.

8. Ibid.

9. Ibid., 390.

10. Ibid., 281.

11. Ibid., 283.

12. Steve Goodman, *Sonic Warfare: Sound, Affect, and the Ecology of Fear* (Cambridge, MA: MIT Press, 2010).

13. For more on the rise of the etiquette manual in middle-class American life, see Arthur M. Schlesinger, *Learning How to Behave: A Historical Study of American Etiquette Books* (New York: Macmillan, 1947).

14. Gwendolyn Audrey Foster, *Troping the Body: Gender, Etiquette, and Performance* (Carbondale: Southern Illinois University Press, 2000), 30.

15. See Karin Bijsterveld, "The Diabolical Symphony of the Mechanical Age: Technology and Symbolism of Sound in European and North American Noise Abatement Campaigns, 1900–40," *Social Studies of Science* 31, no. 1 (February 2001): 37–70, and *Mechanical Sound: Technology, Culture, and the Public Problems of Noise in the Twentieth Century* (Cambridge, MA: MIT Press, 2008). For more on the noise abatement campaigns, see Emily Thompson, *The Soundscape of Modernity: Architectural Acoustics and the Culture of Listening in America, 1900–1933* (Cambridge, MA: MIT Press, 2004), 115–30.

16. See Tom Gunning, "The Cinema of Attractions: Early Film, Its Spectator and the Avant-Garde," in *Early Cinema: Space, Frame, Narrative,* ed. Thomas Elsaesser and Adam Barker (London: British Film Institute, 1990), 60. See also Jean Chateauvert and Andre Gaudreault, "The Noises of Spectators, or the Spectator as Additive to the Spectacle," in *The Sounds of Early Cinema,* ed. Richard Abel and Rick Altman (Bloomington: Indiana University Press, 2001), 183–92, and Miriam Hansen, *Babel and Babylon: Spectatorship in American Silent Film* (Cambridge, MA: Harvard University Press, 1991), 84.

17. Gunning, "Cinema of Attractions," 58, 59.

18. Hansen, *Babel and Babylon*, 33. Hansen describes early film's address to the spectator as predicated upon distraction, in comparison to later films' mode of "absorbing him or her into a coherent narrative by way of a unified spectatorial vantage point" (54).

19. Ibid., 60.

20. Ibid., 2, 23, 105.

21. Mary Ann Doane, "'When the Direction of the Force Acting on the Body Is Changed': The Moving Image," *Wide Angle* 7, no. 1 (1985): 44. The "classical

mode of narration" that marked this shift in the way in which films involved their spectators can be seen as early as 1907 but was cemented by 1909. "Transitional" films began to clearly articulate "the spectator's perceptual placement *within narrative space*" by means of "different camera set-ups and editing devices such as shot-reverse-shot, the 180-degree rule, eyeline match, and point of view." Hansen, *Babel and Babylon*, 23, 81.

22. Hansen, *Babel and Babylon*, 90.

23. Ibid., 44.

24. Ibid., 81.

25. Ibid., 81. See also Nick Browne, "The Spectator-in-the-Text: The Rhetoric of *Stagecoach*," in *Narrative, Apparatus, Ideology: A Film Theory Reader*, ed. Philip Rosen (New York: Columbia University Press, 1986), 102–19. See also David Bordwell, *Narration in the Fiction Film* (Madison: University of Wisconsin Press, 1985), chaps. 1 and 7.

26. See Jean-Louis Comolli, "Technique and Ideology: Camera, Perspective, Depth of Field (Parts 3 and 4)," Jean-Louis Baudry, "Ideological Effects of the Basic Cinema Apparatus," and Stephen Heath, "Narrative Space," all in Rosen, *Narrative, Apparatus, Ideology*, 421–443, 286–98, and 379–420 respectively.

27. Hansen, *Babel and Babylon*, 23.

28. Ibid., 44.

29. Altman, *Silent Film Sound*, 281.

30. Ibid., 283.

31. Rollin Lynde Hart, *The People at Play* (Boston: Houghton Mifflin, 1909), 126–27. See also Joseph Medill Patterson, "The Nickelodeons: The Poor Man's Elementary Course in the Drama," *Saturday Evening Post*, November, 23, 1907, reprinted in *Spellbound in Darkness*, ed. George Pratt (Greenwich, CT: New York Graphic Society, 1973), 46–52, and Walter M. Fitch, "The Motion Picture Story Considered as a New Literary Form," *Moving Picture World* 6, no. 7 (February 19, 1910), quoted in Hansen, *Babel and Babylon*, 306n54.

32. Hansen, *Babel and Babylon*, 23.

33. Altman, *Silent Film Sound*, 284–85. This transformed "each spectator from recognized (audible) interlocutor in an overtly discursive situation" to an "(invisible) voyeur and (silent) *écouteur* [eavesdropper] of a distanced history." Removing the direct address to the audience, films also "removed overt interpellation's invitation to respond."

34. Chateauvert and Gaudreault, "Noises of Spectators," 183. They write: "Early cinema commonly involved a resolutely public space between screen and spectator. It is not, then, an individualized spectator but an audience, a collective entity, that is implicated in the viewing situation specific to this period" (183).

35. Ibid., 184.

36. Ibid., 184–85.

37. Ibid., 185.

38. Stuart Blumin, *The Emergence of the Middle Class: Social Experience in the American City, 1760–1900* (New York: Cambridge University Press, 1989), 5.

39. Melanie Archer and Judith R. Blau, "Class Formation in Nineteenth-Century America: The Case of the Middle Class," *Annual Review of Sociology*

19 (1993): 22. It coincided with the "convergence of socioeconomic status, living patterns, the culture of work, and social perceptions and self-identity" of nonmanual workers. The creation of the middle class involved the decline of master artisans and skilled, self-employed manual laborers, and the demise of the "old middle class" or the small-scale merchant class.

40. Ibid.

41. John Kasson, *Rudeness and Civility: Manners in 19th Century Urban America* (New York: Hill and Wang, 1990), 5, 7. For specific examples, see also Karen Halttunen, *Confidence Men and Painted Women: A Study of Middle-Class Culture in America, 1830–1870* (New Haven, CT: Yale University Press, 1982).

42. Kasson, *Rudeness and Civility*, 6, 112–32. Kasson and others link middle-class self-discipline with the concept of embarrassment. According to Kasson, "Embarrassment became a normal, even an essential part of American urban life. Embarrassment thrives upon the unfulfilled expectations of the kind that frequently occurred in novel social situations and with individuals of shifting or indeterminate status" (114). Kasson writes that it served as "a subtle and routine form of discipline" (114). Certainly it was used by the press to govern behavior during a period of upheaval of social standards—for example, when the press complained about noise. For more on embarrassment, see Erving Goffman, "Embarrassment and Social Organization," in *Interaction Ritual: Essays in Face-to-Face Behavior* (Garden City, NY: Doubleday/Anchor Books, 1967), 109. See also Edward Gross and Gregory P. Stone, "Embarrassment and the Analysis of Role Requirements," *American Journal of Sociology* 70 (July 1964): 14; Andre Modigliani, "Embarrassment and Embarrassibility," *Sociometry* 31 (1968), 313; and Richard Sennett, *Authority* (New York: Knopf, 1980), 46–47, 94–95.

43. Kasson, *Rudeness and Civility*, 5.

44. Archer and Blau, "Class Formation," 31.

45. See Arthur M. Schlesinger, *Learning How to Behave*; Norbert Elias, *The History of Manners*, vol. 1 of *The Civilizing Process* (New York: Pantheon, 1982); Marjorie Morgan, *Manners, Morals and Class in England* (New York: St. Martin's Press, 1994); Stephen Carter, *Civility, Manners, Morals, and the Etiquette of Democracy* (New York: Basic Books, 1998); and Michael Curtin, *Propriety and Position: A Study of Victorian Manners* (New York: Garland, 1987).

46. Zhiwei Xiao, "Movie House Etiquette Reform in Early-Twentieth-Century China," *Modern China* 32, no. 4 (October 2006): 531.

47. Kasson, *Rudeness and Civility*, 4, 7.

48. See Bijsterveld, "Diabolical Symphony." See also Raymond Smilor, "Cacophony at 34th and 6th: The Noise Problem in America, 1900–1930," *American Studies* 18, no. 1 (1971): 23–28, and "Toward an Environmental Perspective: The Anti-noise Campaign, 1893–1932," in *Pollution and Reform in American Cities, 1870–1930*, ed. Martin V. Melosi (Austin: University of Texas Press, 1980), 135–51. See also Thompson, *Soundscape of Modernity* 120–30.

49. Bijsterveld, "Diabolical Symphony," 38, 50, 51. American antinoise societies, Bijsterveld notes, proved more successful than their European counterparts.

50. As Bijsterveld and others, including Emily Thompson, have noted, antinoise campaigns tended to be originally inspired by the industrialized noise of a changing economy, which far exceeded that of individuals. Yet in a fascinating turn, individuals remained the focus of concern, and "Public education continued to be seen as the ultimate way of creating silence: it kept dominating the rhetorics of noise abatement," to the detriment of practical measures of city planning, technological advances, and industrial regulation (39).

51. Arthur Schopenhauer, *Studies in Pessimism*, trans. T. Bailey Saunders (New York: Cosimo Classics, 2007), 77. Schopenhauer believed that repulsion from noise was actually a sign of deep mental cultivation. People who showed no sensitivity to noise were insensible to "argument, or thought, or poetry, or art, in a word, to any kind of intellectual influence. The reason of it is that the tissue of their brains is of a very rough and coarse quality" (76).

52. Bijsterveld, "Diabolical Symphony," 46.

53. Bijsterveld, *Mechanical Sound*, 170.

54. Ibid., 166–67.

55. Lessing quoted in Bijsterveld, *Mechanical Sound*, 167. For more on the activities of Lessing and his contemporaries and the rhetoric of the antinoise campaigns, see Lawrence Baron, "Noise and Degeneration: Theodor Lessing's Crusade for Quiet," *Journal of Contemporary History* 17, no. 1 (January 1982): 165–78.

56. Lessing quoted in Bijsterveld, "Diabolical Symphony," 46.

57. Bijsterveld, "Diabolical Symphony," 39.

58. See Richard Sennett, *The Fall of Public Man* (New York: Norton, 1976).

59. Ibid., 213.

60. Ibid., 215.

61. Burton J. Bledstein, *The Culture of Professionalism: The Middle Class and the Development of Higher Education in America* (New York: Norton, 1976).

62. Jonathan Crary: *Suspensions of Perception: Attention, Spectacle, and Modern Culture* (Cambridge, MA: MIT Press, 1999), 63.

63. Thomas Hamilton, *Men and Manners in America* (1833; repr., New York: Russell and Russell, 1968), 150. See also Thomas A. Foster, "John Adams and the Choice of Hercules: Manliness and Sexual Virtue in Eighteenth-Century British America," in *New Men: Manliness in Early America*, ed. Thomas A. Foster (New York: New York University Press, 2011), 217–35; E. Anthony Rotundo, *American Manhood: Transformations in Masculinity from the Revolution to the Modern Era* (New York: Basic Books, 1993), 10–31; and Sarah A. Kaiksow, "'Manners' Make the Man: Politeness, Chivalry, and the Construction of Masculinity, 1750–1830," *Journal of British Studies* 44, no. 2 (April 2005): 312–29.

64. Gwendolyn Foster, *Troping the Body*, 30, 2, 10. Foster describes this as a program of "aestheticizing the performing body" (4).

65. Kasson, *Rudeness and Civility*, 117, 123–24.

66. "Table of Contents," *Etiquette for Ladies* (Philadelphia: Lea and Blanchard, 1841), 7.

67. Kasson, *Rudeness and Civility*, 117.

68. Mrs. Oliver Bell Bunce, *What to Do: A Companion to Don't* (New York: D. Appleton, 1892), 26.

69. Florence Hartley, *The Ladies' Book of Etiquette and Manual of Politeness: A Complete Handbook for the Use of the Lady in Polite Society* (Boston: G. W. Cottrell, 1860), 113, in the section "Conduct on the Street."

70. Mary Douglas, *Natural Symbols: Explorations in Cosmology* (New York: Random House, 1973), 12.

71. Mary Douglas, *Purity and Danger: An Analysis of the Concepts of Pollution and Taboo*, vol. 2 of *Collected Works* (New York: Routledge, 1966), 144.

72. Kasson, *Rudeness and Civility*, 124.

73. Elias, *History of Manners*, 139. Elias is writing about how a relaxation of norms in the period after World War I was made possible because the internalization of those norms had been secured through an earlier nineteenth-century and early twentieth-century campaign of manners.

74. Gwendolyn Foster, *Troping the Body*, 30. It is significant to note that embarrassment played a large role here. Etiquette advisers and the popular press could not, of course, single-handedly effect change within their aural cultures. They could, however, strive to change the symbolism of sound within their culture. By depicting noise making on city streets and in entertainment venues as shameful, they helped to associate it with shame in the public mind, thereby changing the culture of sound in lasting ways.

75. Ann Carson, *Glass, Irony and God* (New York: New Directions, 1995), 119–42. See Aristotle, *Metaphysics*, quoted in Carson, *Glass, Irony*, 124.

76. Carson, *Glass, Irony*, 126–30. As she notes, Euripides states that "it is woman's inborn pleasure always to have her current emotions coming up to her mouth and out through her tongue" (*Andromache*, lines 94–95, quoted in Carson, *Glass, Irony*, 126).

77. Carson, *Glass, Irony*, 127–30. The lack of self-control manifested in the Greek dialogue was that of speech and the body both. Woman, according to Carson, "is a creature who puts the inside on the outside." "By projections and leakages of all kinds—somatic, vocal, emotional, sexual—females expose or expend what should be kept in." Plutarch states that a woman's body "should not be public property, nor her speech neither, and she should as modestly guard against exposing her voice to outsiders as she would guard against stripping off her clothes. For in her voice," he writes, "as she is blabbering away can be read her emotions, her character and her physical condition." Plutarch, Carson writes, made an explicit connection "between verbal and sexual continence, between mouth and genitals." Ancient physiologists from Aristotle onward claimed that one could tell by "the sound of a woman's voice private data like whether or not she is menstruating, [or] whether or not she has had sexual experience." A woman's noise was explicitly related to her sexuality. Carson states that women's sound "has a totally private interior [i.e., thoughts and feelings,] yet its trajectory is public." As a result, sound has the strange position of being "a piece of inside projected to the outside"—a form of intimacy expressed out loud. Women's sound seems to have had a very strong, socially relevant connection to the body and all that was uncontrolled about it. This became relevant

again in the nineteenth century with what we can call a new *sophrosyne* in middle-class culture.

78. Kasson, *Rudeness and Civility*, 115; see also Sennett, *Fall of Public Man*, 213, 217, 218; E. Anthony Rotundo, "Learning about Manhood: Gender Ideal and the Middle-Class Family in Nineteenth-Century America," in *Manliness and Morality: Middle-Class Masculinity in Britain and America, 1800–1940*, ed. J. A. Mangan and James Walvin (New York: St. Martin's Press, 1987), 35–51.

79. Kasson, *Rudeness and Civility*, 7, 43, 44.

80. Peter George Buckley, "To the Opera House: Culture and Society in New York City, 1920–1860" (PhD diss., State University of New York at Stony Brook, 1984), 118. In the United States, the "performing arts" were neither segmented nor differentiated from each other until the middle of the nineteenth century. As unbelievable as it now sounds to a twenty-first-century observer, prior to the 1840s, all public entertainments, from circus to opera and musical performance, were staged in the same performance spaces. What's more, they catered to the same public and were performed at the same times.

81. Kasson, *Rudeness and Civility*, 221; Lawrence Levine, *Highbrow/Lowbrow: The Emergence of Cultural Hierarchy in America* (Cambridge, MA: Harvard University Press, 1988), 179–84; Richard Butsch, *The Making of American Audiences: From Stage to Television, 1750–1990* (Cambridge: Cambridge University Press, 2000), 36.

82. Butsch, *Making of American Audiences*, 50. They demanded that favorite parts of a performance be performed again and again, resulting in bizarre scenarios in which "Jump Jim Crow" interrupted a Shakespeare soliloquy again and again. The audience exerted its influence audibly to determine the content of the show, its length, and even the actors who appeared.

83. Ibid.

84. Ibid., 3.

85. Ibid.

86. *London Times*, March 22, 1846. Quoted in Buckley, "To the Opera House," 51. See also Levine, *Highbrow/Lowbrow*, 179. Levine notes "the very ethos of the time encouraged active audience participation."

87. Butsch, *Making of American Audiences*, 5. The reasoning behind this general culture movement is complex, but it may suffice to say here that a middle-class aural ethos began to form in the period just discussed. Between elites' self-indulgent behavior at entertainments and in life, marked by their ongoing chatter and social intercourse, and the rough outbursts associated with working-class entertainment culture, controlled and self-imposed silence presented a middle path. The increasingly dominant middle class adopted this as their aural code while attending entertainments. For more on this, see Sennett, *Fall of Public Man*, Kasson, *Rudeness and Civility*, and Levine, *Highbrow/Lowbrow*.

88. Butsch writes that "American theater managers and civil authorities continued to recognize the rights of audience sovereignty until the mid-nineteenth century. They acknowledged audience prerogatives to call for tunes, chastise performers and managers, hiss, shout and throw things at intransigent performers on the stage, even riot to enforce their will" (*Making of American Audiences*, 5). See also 80.

89. Ibid. This change can be attributed to the upper class's reaction to a changing symbolism of sound. With noise being rewritten as cause for embarrassment, the upper and middle classes sought personal silence when out in public.

90. Ibid. Rioters were often described as "rowdies" in the press of the time as well. See also Buckley, "To the Opera House," 7. This can be seen as an attempt to draw a sonic distinction between classes, marking the working class as rough and criminal and the middle and upper classes as refined and silent.

91. Butsch, *Making of American Audiences*, 5.

92. Ibid., 52.

93. Ibid., 44.

94. Ibid., 5, 56. See also Susan G. Davis, *Parades and Power: Street Theatre in Nineteenth-Century Philadelphia* (Berkeley: University of California Press, 1986).

95. Levine, *Highbrow/Lowbrow*, 177; these groups began to "transform public spaces by rules, systems of taste, and canons of behavior."

96. Kasson, *Rudeness and Civility*, 216. In the last half of the nineteenth century, from the Civil War to the turn of the century, most of the major public entertainments emerged from the undifferentiated sphere of "entertainment." Popular entertainments were later hierarchized, creating an arena of "high art" and one of "popular amusement" where previously no such differentiation had been active: hence the separation of the legitimate stage from the popular stage, popular music from "high opera," and popular musical performance from symphonic performance. For more on how similar trends occurred in Europe, see James H. Johnson, *Listening in Paris: A Cultural History* (Berkeley: University of California Press, 1995), chaps. 12 and 13.

97. Kasson, *Rudeness and Civility*, 216. For more on noise and silence among spectators in entertainment culture, see Peter Gay, *The Naked Heart: The Bourgeois Experience*, vol. 4, *Victoria to Freud* (New York: Harper Collins, 1997); William Weber, "Did People Listen in the 18th Century?" *Early Music* 25, no. 4 (November 1997): 678–91.

98. Quoted in Kasson, *Rudeness and Civility*, 240.

99. Carmen Trammell Skaggs, *Overtones of Opera in American Literature from Whitman to Wharton* (Baton Rouge: Louisiana State University Press, 2010), 20. See also Marvin Carlson, *Theatre Semiotics: Signs of Life* (Bloomington: Indiana University Press, 1990), 154.

100. Wolfgang Schivelbusch, *Disenchanted Night: The Industrialization of Light in the Nineteenth Century*, trans. Angela Davies (Berkeley: University of California Press, 1988), 205.

101. Levine, *Highbrow/Lowbrow*, 195. See also Sennett, *Fall of Public Man*, 230; John Henry Mueller, *The American Symphony Orchestra: A Social History of Musical Taste* (Bloomington: Indiana University Press, 1951), 286; and Joseph Hatton, "American Audiences and Actors," *Theatre* 3 (May 1881): 257.

102. Levine, *Highbrow/Lowbrow*, 195. It is well worth noting that this period was marked by antidemocratic sentiment that was connected with such views on popular culture. As a primary example of this strain of cultural criticism that valorized the judgment of the individual over the "brawling" and uncivilized "mass," see the descriptions of the "Hyde Park rough" who inhibits

the spread of culture as "sweetness and light" in Matthew Arnold, *Culture and Anarchy* (1869; repr., Oxford: Oxford University Press, 2009).

103. Levine, *Highbrow/Lowbrow*, 195.

104. Ibid., 195; see also Sennett, *Rudeness and Civility*, 230, 261.

105. Washington Irving, *Letters of Jonathan Oldstyle* (1824; repr., New York: Columbia University Press, 1941), 12–18, quoted in Kasson, *Rudeness and Civility*, 219.

106. Printed request for silence from the New York Philharmonic Society to its members, quoted in Henry Edward Krehbiel, *The Philharmonic Society of New York* (New York: Novello, Ewer, 1892), 64–65.

107. Edwin Milton Royle, "The Vaudeville Theatre," *Scribner's Magazine*, October 1899, 488, quoted in Kasson, *Rudeness and Civility*, 250.

108. Helen L. Roberts, *Putnam's Handbook of Etiquette* (New York: G.P. Putnam's Sons, 1913), 289–90, quoted in Kasson, *Rudeness and Civility*, 243.

109. Royle, "Vaudeville Theatre," 488, quoted in Kasson, *Rudeness and Civility*, 250.

110. Jennifer Hall-Witt, "The Re-fashioning of Fashionable Society: Opera-Going and Sociability in England, 1821–61" (PhD dissertation, Yale University, 1996).

111. Kasson, *Rudeness and Civility*, 221. For greater detail, see Francis Trollope, *Domestic Manners of the Americans* (1839; repr., [United States]: Reprint Service Corp., 1993).

112. See, for example, *Harper's* suggestion that silence should be the audience's guide in *Harper's New Monthly Magazine*, April 1886, 803, quoted in Levine, *Highbrow/Lowbrow*, 188.

113. Kasson, *Rudeness and Civility*, 44.

114. Robert de Valcourt, *The Illustrated Manners Book: A Manual of Good Behavior and Polite Accomplishments* (New York: Leland Clay, 1855), 274.

115. Hartley, *Ladies' Book of Etiquette*, 175.

116. Kasson, *Rudeness and Civility*, 242.

117. Harrison, "Jackass Music."

118. De Valcourt, *Illustrated Manners Book*, 274.

119. Bruce McConachie, "New York Opera-Going, 1825–1850," *American Music* 6, no. 2 (Summer 1988), 186–87.

120. George William Curtis, *Harper's New Monthly Magazine*, April 1886, 802–3, quoted in Levine, *Highbrow/Lowbrow*, 188.

121. Levine, *Highbrow/Lowbrow*, 188; Kasson, *Rudeness and Civility*, 244.

122. McConachie, "New York Opera-Going," 186.

123. Ibid., 187.

124. Levine, *Highbrow/Lowbrow*, 102. See Mathilda Despard, "Music in New York Thirty Years Ago," *Harper's New Monthly Magazine*, June 1878, 115.

125. Levine, *Highbrow/Lowbrow*, 190.

126. Ibid. See Edward Baxter Perry, "Mutual Courtesy between Artist and Audience," *Music* 2 (July 1892): 252–55; Mueller, *American Symphony Orchestra*, 356.

127. Levine, *Highbrow/Lowbrow*, 190.

128. Ibid., 245.

129. Ibid.

130. Charles Edward Russell, *The American Orchestra and Theodore Thomas* (New York: Doubleday, Page, 1927), 83. See also Theodore Thomas, *A Musical Autobiography* (Chicago: A. A. McClurg, 1905), 133–34, 222.

131. Kasson, *Rudeness and Civility*, 237.

132. See Russell, *American Orchestra*, 67–68. See also Lili Lehmann, *My Pathway through Life*, trans. Alice Benedict Seligman (New York: G. P. Putnam's Sons, 1914), 345.

133. Levine, *Highbrow/Lowbrow*, 188. According to Kasson, "The audience reportedly submitted to Thomas' assertion of authority and made no further disturbance" (*Rudeness and Civility*, 237). The *Nation* in New York called him "a born commander," whose work was marked by "his stubborn determination to carry out his plans." Indeed, it asserted, "As a general he would have held Port Arthur as long as Stoessel held it" (Levine, *Highbrow/Lowbrow*, 189). Thomas enforced several other methods of discipline on his spectators as well. First, he requested that appeals to punctuality and silence be sent to regular patrons via disciplinary mailings. Second, he instituted a practice of locking the doors to the symphonic hall so that only those who approached the concert in all seriousness, with punctuality and in the proper mind-set, could attend. Such methods created an expectation of both seriousness and silence for the viewer. For more descriptions of his methods of audience control, see Thomas, *Musical Autobiography*. For more on the change in audiences at the symphony, see Mueller, *American Symphony Orchestra*.

134. Levine, *Highbrow/Lowbrow*, 188.

135. Ibid., 189.

136. Ibid., 188.

137. Samantha Barbas, "The Political Spectator: Censorship, Protest and the Moviegoing Experience, 1912–1922," *Film History* 11, no. 2 (1999): 220. See also Lise Shapiro Sanders, "'Indecent Incentives to Vice': Regulating Films and Audience Behavior from the 1890s to the 1910s," in *Young and Innocent? The Cinema of Britain, 1896–1930*, ed. Andrew Higson (Exeter: University of Exeter Press, 2002), 97–110.

138. Altman writes that "American audiences were slow to adopt new standards of silent spectatorship" (*Silent Film Sound*, 277).

139. Barbas, "Political Spectator," 219, 220.

140. *New York Mirror*, December 29, 1832, 206; Butsch, *Making of American Audiences*, 3, 44; Barbas, "Political Spectator," 220.

141. Ibid.

142. Kathy Peiss, *Cheap Amusements: Working Women and Leisure in Turn-of-the-Century New York* (Philadelphia: Temple University Press, 1986), 141. See also Garth Jowett, *Film: The Democratic Art* (Boston: Little, Brown, 1976), 41–42, and Barbas, "Political Spectator," 220.

143. Barbas, "Political Spectator," 220.

144. Peiss, *Cheap Amusements*, 141; Jowett, *Film*, 41–42; Barbas, "Political Spectator," 220.

145. Altman, *Silent Film Sound*, 277, 285. He writes that noise, "once the desired outcome of any public performance" for exhibitors and press alike, was "now evaluated in entirely new," and negative, terms.

146. W. Stephen Bush, "The Human Voice as a Factor in the Moving Picture Show," *Moving Picture World,* January 23, 1909, 446–47.

147. Maxim Gorky, "Fleeting Notes," in *Kino: A History of the Russian and Soviet Film,* 3rd ed., ed. Jay Leyda (Princeton, NJ: Princeton University Press, 1983), 407. Originally published in *Nizhny Novgorod Newsletter,* July 7, 1896.

148. Ibid., 407–8.

149. Ibid.

150. Richard Taylor and Ian Christie, "1896–1921: Introduction," *The Film Factory: Russian and Soviet Cinema in Documents* (New York: Routledge, 1994), 19.

151. Gorky, "Fleeting Notes," 408.

152. Yuri Tsivian, *Early Cinema in Russia and its Cultural Reception,* trans. Alan Bodger (New York: Routledge, 1994), 36.

153. See Jacob Smith, *Vocal Tracks: Performance and Sound Media* (Berkeley: University of California Press, 2008), 20. Smith makes the valuable assertion that such interpretations of sounds are bound tightly within their moments in cultural history, complete with the politics of power as played out in debates over gender, class, and race. Here, I agree wholeheartedly with his gendering of the topic, and it serves as a useful model for me in approaching the sounds of female sexuality in this chapter.

154. Ibid., 52.

155. Tsivian, *Early Cinema in Russia,* 36.

156. Ibid., 35.

157. In a short story entitled "Revenge" that he published in the same newspaper as "Lumière" just a week later, Gorky's main character is a fictional girl of the café chantant who, after viewing the Lumière film *Baby's Breakfast,* kills herself from shame.

158. *Harmony* was a word closely associated with the earlier noise debates. Henry Higginson, founder of the Boston Symphony Orchestra, had announced to his musicians, "Our task is to make harmony above all things—harmony even in the most modern music. I expect only harmony." Harmony was the stated goal of many of the practitioners in opera, theater, and symphonic music. H. Earle Johnson, *Symphony Hall, Boston* (Boston: Little, Brown, 1950), 66–67.

159. Attali, *Noise,* 7.

160. Gorky, "Fleeting Notes," 408.

161. See Altman, *Silent Film Sound.*

162. *Oxford English Online Dictionary,* 2007, s.v. "promiscuous: 1a," www.oed.com.

163. "Plucky (Akron) Exhibitor Wins His Case: Ch. 1: To Prison in Wagon," *Moving Picture World* 1, no. 9 (April 6, 1907). The front of the nickelodeon was often termed a "Coney Island front," marking its status as both cheap and tawdry. See F.C. Koening, "The Moving Picture Theater," *Moving Picture World* 8, no. 13 (April 8, 1911): 762.

164. Such ads were commonplace up until 1910. One example from December 3, 1910, shows these devices with a mention of a larger catalog of "All Moving Picture Show Effects" (*Moving Picture World* 7, no. 25).

165. Cartoon by E. H. Hoffman, "What They Want for Christmas," *Moving Picture World* 7, no. 26 (December 24, 1910): 1482. The activity produced with this arsenal of sound effects toys resulted in "intermittent jangles, squeaks, bangs, clangs, groans and toots," which were inflicted upon the audience without any claim to discretion. Silence, the staff writer argues, "is an absolute prerequisite to a full understanding and appreciation of a photoplay," adding, "[or] at least the absence of any noises which specifically and sharply attract the attention." To play such noises "which are entirely out of harmony with the theme of the play," was, "to a real picture lover, little short of criminal."

166. An extreme example of this scenario can be found in Mary Carbine's excellent article on sound accompaniment in south side Chicago movie theaters, "The Finest outside the Loop: Motion Picture Exhibition in Chicago's Black Metropolis, 1905–1928," *Camera Obscura* 23 (May 1990): 8–41.

167. *Oxford English Online Dictionary*, 2007, s.v. "promiscuous: b," www .oed.com.

168. Clyde Martin, "Working the Sound Effects," *Moving Picture World* 9, no. 11 (September 23, 1911): 873.

169. "At Coney Island," *Moving Picture World* 8, no. 27 (July 8, 1911): 1571.

170. "Chicago Houses in Review: The Harmony Theater," *Moving Picture World* 8, no. 22 (June 3, 1911): 1248.

171. *Oxford English Dictionary*, 2007, s.v. "promiscuous: c," www.oed .com.

172. Peiss, *Cheap Amusements*, 186. See also Lauren Rabinovitz, *For the Love of Pleasure: Women, Movies, and Culture in Turn-of-the-Century Chicago* (New Brunswick, NJ: Rutgers University Press, 1998), 15–30, 127–46.

173. Peiss, *Cheap Amusements*, 10.

174. Shelley Stamp, *Movie-Struck Girls: Women and Motion Picture Culture after the Nickelodeon* (Princeton, NJ: Princeton University Press, 2000), 50.

175. Stamp, *Movie-Struck Girls*, 50; Peiss, *Cheap Amusements*, 52. While women of the nineteenth century were advised never to go out to any public amusement without "a relative" or "your fiancé" or some other chaperon, young, working-class women by the turn of the century had quite a different means of operating within the social scene. Working women, Peiss states, earned below a living wage; in practice, this meant that working girls in 1910 were able to bring home less than nine or ten dollars per week. When a ride on the trolley car entailed skipping a meal during the week, they could seldom finance their own evening of entertainment.

176. Linder's study is cited in Stamp, *Movie-Struck Girls*, 49.

177. Stamp, *Movie-Struck Girls*, 49.

178. Quoted in ibid., 49. Even the prudish *Moving Picture World* told of the "effort to save girls" that reformers had to undertake when "a girl in a store, or in an office, may supplement her income by occasional wrong-doing." "The Lay Press and the Picture," *Moving Picture World* 8, no. 2 (January 14, 1911): 70.

179. Jas. A McQuade, "Chicago Letter," *Moving Picture World* 11, no. 12 (March 23, 1912): 1056.

180. Ibid. Peterson added: "When I was an officer of the Juvenile Court I found that most of the delinquent young girls attributed their fall to nickelodeons. Many of these girls, mere children, told me that the wickedness practiced in such places was almost unbelievable." She concluded by saying, "Innumerable young girls have told me that they learned their first lessons of vice in such places." Jane Addams similarly remarked of cinema houses that "the very darkness of the room . . . is an added attraction to many young people, for whom the space is filled with the glamour of love making." Quoted in Hansen, *Babel and Babylon*, 65.

181. McQuade, "Chicago Letter."

182. Robert A. Woods and Albert J. Kennedy's *Young Working Girls* (1913), which describes itself as "a summary of evidence from two thousand social workers," is quoted in Peiss, *Cheap Amusements*, 151.

183. Hansen, *Babel and Babylon*, 63. See also John Collier, "Cheap Amusements," *Charities and the Commons* 20 (April 1908): 74; Lary L. May, *Screening Out the Past: The Birth of Mass Culture and the Motion Picture Industry* (New York: Oxford University Press, 1980), chaps. 2–3; Jowett, *Film*, chaps. 4–5.

184. "Lay Press," 70. The trade paper made an attempt to exhort exhibitors to clean up their hiring practices and, in so doing, cleanse their cinemas. *Moving Picture World*'s "Man about Town" warned against hiring men of no character as theater employees and specifically mentioned the dangers of hiring a "volunteer usher," an unpaid gentleman who attempted to bring young ladies to their seats (or potentially, elsewhere). He concluded that "too often rowdies are clothed in uniforms. Picture houses, like other places of amusement, are sought as sources of employment by many of the worst characters at liberty, and if the greater percentage of them are not crooks or rowdies, they are libertines." "Observations by Our Man about Town," *Moving Picture World* 8, no. 12 (March 25, 1911): 643. The movie theater, then, served as a sort of meat market, with employees behaving in untoward ways with customers, women meeting men they had only just met hours before by prearrangement, and young women and men meeting each other for the very first time as they sat in the dark. The chitchat that accompanied working-class practices of watching a film carried with it the knowledge that new erotic connections were being forged. Frank H. Madison, "Springfield, Ill. Picture Shows," *Moving Picture World* 7, no. 25 (December 17, 1910): 1420.

185. See Madison, "Springfield, Ill. Picture Shows," 1420.

186. Stephen Bottomore, "The Story of Percy Peashaker: Debates about Sound Effects in the Early Cinema," in Abel and Altman, *Sounds of Early Cinema*, 134–42.

187. "Hazel B,'" "Music for the Picture," letter to Clarence E. Sinn, the "Cue Music Man," *Moving Picture World* 8, no. 7 (February 18, 1911): 353.

188. Harrison, "Jackass Music."

189. Bijsterveld, *Mechanical Sound*, 40.

190. "The Stage," *New York Mirror,* October 1, 1831, 100.

191. *New York Evening Post,* June 17, 1826, quoted in Buckley, "To the Opera House," 151.

192. Claudia D. Johnson, "That Guilty Third Tier: Prostitution in Nineteenth-Century American Theaters," *American Quarterly* 27 no. 5 (December 1975): 575–84.

193. Ibid.; see also John Murtaugh and Sarah Harris's account of the Bowery Theatre in *Cast the First Stone* (New York: McGraw-Hill, 1957), 204–5.

194. Statistics originally appear in Timothy J. Gilfoyle, "City of Eros: New York City, Prostitution, and the Commercialization of Sex, 1790–1920" (PhD diss., University of California, Berkeley, 2006), 22–23, cited in Rosemarie K. Bank, *Theatre Culture in America, 1825–1860* (Cambridge: Cambridge University Press, 1997), 136.

195. C. Johnson, "That Guilty Third Tier," 581.

196. Ibid.; see also Irving, *Letters of Jonathan Oldstyle*, 114.

197. Butsch, *Making of American Audiences*, 69.

198. Buckley, "To the Opera House," 110.

199. David H. Agnew, *Theatrical Amusements* (Philadelphia, 1857), 8, 20.

200. Thomas DeWitt Talmadge, *Sports That Kill* (New York: Funk and Wagnall, 1875), 21.

201. George Foster, *New York by Gas-Light and Other Urban Sketches*, ed. Stuart M. Blumin (Berkeley: University of California Press, 1990), 155.

202. Letter writer to the *New York Herald*, November 1842.

203. Richard Grant White, "Opera in New York," *Century* 23 (1882): 869.

204. *Commercial Advertiser*, March 15, 1833, quoted in Bank, *Theatre Culture in America*, 241.

205. Ibid.

206. *Hopkinsian* 3 (February 9, 1829): 327. Tickets, the *Hopkinsian* claims, were handed out to prostitutes "free of all expense." And they added: "The *freedom of the theatre* has been confirmed upon them in consideration of their important and highly acceptable services!" The Hopkinsian sect was evidently disgusted at the immorality of the theater space.

207. C. Johnson, "That Guilty Third Tier," 583.

208. Reverend Robert Turnbull, *The Theatre, in Its Influence upon Literature, Morals, and Religion*, in *The Christian Review, vol. II*, ed. James D. Knowles (Boston: Gould, Kendall, and Lincoln, 1837), 82–87.

209. Johnson, "That Guilty Third Tier," 583.

210. "The Theater 'Gods,'" *Moving Picture World* 8, no. 26 (July 1, 1911): 1498.

211. "The Lost Gallery," *Moving Picture World* 9, no. 3 (July 29, 1911): 397.

212. Tim Anderson, "Reforming 'Jackass Music': The Problematic Aesthetics of Early American Film Music Accompaniment," *Cinema Journal*, 37, no. 1 (Autumn 1997): 3–22.

213. Ibid., 10.

214. Ibid. See also various issues of *Moving Picture World*, 1910–13.

215. Anderson, "Reforming 'Jackass Music,'" 10.

216. Hanford C. Judson, "The Lyric Photoplay," *Moving Picture World* 8, no. 18 (May 6, 1911): 997.

217. As Rick Altman has noted in *Silent Film Sound*, the institution of "appropriate" musical accompaniment, while in one sense increasing "harmony,"

actually decreased the sense of aural community within the theater. Whereas first-period cinema (i.e., before 1908) freely used popular music, the accompaniment suggested by Clarence Sinn and Clyde Martin was generally anonymous and continuous. This made singing along, whistling, or humming, and the sense of fellow-feeling in the audience that this activity had created, nearly impossible (284).

218. "The Variety of Moving Picture Audiences," *Moving Picture World* 13, no. 5 (September 25, 1909): 406.

219. Hansen, *Babel and Babylon*, 65, 106. "Newly founded trade periodicals," Hansen writes, "became a nationwide forum for ... [expressing] ambitions" about garnering a new audience. I would add that this happened with an aural etiquette specifically.

220. Hall-Witt, in "Re-fashioning of Fashionable Society," describes these accounts of audiences as misleading fantasies.

221. "World Reviewer," "The Picture the Audience Likes," *Moving Picture World* 8, no. 6 (February 11, 1911): 310. Hansen, in *Babel and Babylon*, describes similarly how the press would "acknowledge the presence of so-called 'plain people,' but ... emphasize how well-behaved, how spellbound, how eager they were to be impressed by the events on screen" (66).

222. "World Reviewer," "Picture the Audience Likes," 310.

223. Anonymous article in *Film Index*, quoted in Altman, *Silent Film Sound*, 281.

224. W. Stephen Bush, "Facing an Audience," *Moving Picture World* 9, no. 10 (September 16, 1911): 771.

225. Ibid.

226. Michael Fried, *Absorption and Theatricality: Painting and Beholder in the Age of Diderot* (Berkeley: University of California Press, 1980), 31.

227. Ibid., 115.

228. Denis Diderot, *Salons*, vol. 3, ed. Jean Seznec and Jean Adhemar (Oxford: Oxford University Press, 1963), is quoted in Fried, *Absorption and Theatricality*, 130.

229. Louis Reeves Harrison, "Managerial Stupidity," *Moving Picture World*, December 1910.

230. Ibid. See also Lee Grieveson, *Policing Cinema: Movies and Censorship in Early Twentieth-Century America* (Berkeley: University of California Press, 2004); Levine, *Highbrow/Lowbrow*; and Hansen, *Babel and Babylon*. *Moving Picture World* actively encouraged exhibitors to advertise for the "New Patrons" who met the criteria of silence and appropriate behavior; Epes Winthrop Sargent, "Advertising for Exhibitors," *Moving Picture World* 9, no. 11 (September 23, 1911): 876.

231. Peter Kobel, *Silent Movies: The Birth of Film and the Triumph of Movie Culture* (Washington, DC: Library of Congress, 2007), 6. See also Altman, *Silent Film Sound*, 185.

232. Altman, *Silent Film Sound*, 185.

233. Barbas, "Political Spectator," 218.

234. Altman, *Silent Film Sound*, 185.

235. Kasson, *Rudeness and Civility*, 250. See also Altman, *Silent Film Sound*, 185.

236. "Loud Talking or Whistling Not Allowed," etiquette slide, Library of Congress, copyrighted in 1912 by Scott and Van Altena, in "Positive paper prints from lantern slides used in motion picture theaters as announcements," LC Control No. 2005684157, Lot 3040, Library of Congress Prints and Photographs Division, Washington, DC.

237. Barbas, "Political Spectator," 218–21.

238. Altman, *Silent Film Sound*, 185.

239. Ibid., 182.

240. Barbas, "Political Spectator," 218.

CHAPTER 2. THE FILM INDUSTRY LAYS THE GOLDEN EGG

1. Crafton, *Talkies*, 129–31.

2. AMPAS, Minutes of Meeting of the Technicians Branch, October 9, 1928, p. 13, Research Council Papers, Margaret Herrick Library special collections, AMPAS; hereafter RCP.

3. Producers-Technicians Joint Committee of AMPAS, memo, 1929 (no exact date), p. 2, Box 45, RCP.

4. The standardization project was announced in 1929 at a Joint Meeting of the Technicians Branch of AMPAS, the Society of Motion Picture Engineers, Pacific Coast Section, the American Projection Society, California Chapter No. 7, and the American Society of Cinematographers. "August 15, 1919, Academy Lounge, Roosevelt Hotel," transcript, p. 14, RCP.

5. Frank Woods, speech presented at the All Industry Conference, sponsored by the Art and Technique Program Committee of AMPAS, May 2, 1932, Beverly Hills, CA. Irving Thalberg presided, and speakers included Sidney R. Kent, president of the Fox Film Corporation; M.A. Lightman, president of MPP Theater Owners of America; and Conrad Nagel, AMPAS vice president, "who has been meeting with representatives groups throughout the country." Cecil B. DeMille served as chairman.

6. Producers-Technicians Joint Committee, untitled and undated memo, Box 45, RCP.

7. Lastra, *Sound Technology*, 162–65. Lastra argues that "the legendary conflicts between sound engineers and virtually every other worker on the set bear witness to struggles over professional identity and responsibility and over the representational standards developed over time within the competing technical and industrial models" of the labs and the studio system (163). He claims that tensions arose from differences in practice as well as sonic philosophy, and draws on the work of Pierre Bourdieu to show how early film sound recording practice was a site of conflict over "ways of doing" that spoke to different visions of the transition to sound in films (155–57).

8. For more on this tension, see ibid., 171–72. Sound engineers were seen as "experts," and their expertise often threatened the dominance of film studio staff on their own sets. Lastra notes that this perceived dominance was perhaps motivated more by fear than by reality, as sound engineers often felt themselves to be at a disadvantage (171–72).

9. Ibid., 170.

10. Secretary Frank Woods, Memorandum G, "Academy Sound Production Problems Survey," June 21, 1929, RCP.

11. As AMPAS Secretary Frank Woods quipped: "The 'big secret' now is that so few people are acquainted with making talking pictures. And the sooner it is disseminated the better it will be for the entire industry." Meeting Minutes, Technicians Branch of AMPAS, November 14, 1928, p. 23, RCP.

12. Lastra, *Sound Technology*, 160–61.

13. Thompson, *Soundscape of Modernity*, 90.

14. See Luci Marzola, "A Society Apart: The Early Years of the Society of Motion Picture Engineers," *Film History* 28, no. 4 (2016): 11; David F. Noble, *America by Design: Science, Technology, and the Rise of Corporate Capitalism* (New York: Knopf, 1977), 113.

15. Noble, *America by Design*, 113. See also Marzola, "Society Apart," 11.

16. See Noble, *America by Design*; Marzola, "Society Apart."

17. Noble describes how industries during this period strove to rationalize the technologies on which they depended through initiatives aiming at "the standardization of scientific technology and methods, the regularization of patent procedures, the efficient organization of scientific research, and the systematic production of technical manpower" (*America by Design*, 55). All of these initiatives would be taken up by the film industry. See also Marzola, "Society Apart," 3–8.

18. Marzola, "Society Apart," 2. Marzola notes: "Film scholarship, at least since Bordwell, Thompson, and Staiger's *Classical Hollywood Cinema*, has brought to light the role that the SMPE has played in the motion-picture industry through its standardization of the tools of the trade."

19. Ibid., 20.

20. Ibid., 3.

21. Ibid., 20.

22. Secretary Lester Cowan, "Coordination East and West," speech presented to the Producers Branch of AMPAS, n.d., p. 2, RCP.

23. Resources I have drawn upon for the work at hand include the industrial history by S. Millman, ed., *A History of Science and Engineering in the Bell System* (New York: Bell Laboratories, 1983), as well as issues of the *Bell System Technical Journal* from 1926 through 1932 and selected issues of the *Bell Labs Record*, Bell's "house organ." While these documents are rarely cited in this chapter, this is not because they are not relevant but simply because they give more context than text to the specific subjects dealt with here. More theoretical texts on noise that have equally informed this work include Mara Mills, "Deafening: Noise and the Engineering of Communication in the Telephone System," *Grey Room* 43 (Spring 2001): 118–43, and Helge Krage, "Styles of Science and Engineering: The Case of Early Long-Distance Telephony," *Centaurus* 51, no. 3 (August 2009): 175–88. Also helpful for personal anecdotes is Frank Massa, "Some Personal Recollections of Early Experiences on the New Frontier of Electroacoustics during the Late 1920s and Early 1930s," *Journal of the Acoustical Society of America* 77, no. 4 (April 1965): 1296–1302. I used multiple more basic primers to refresh my own understanding of physics and electroacoustics.

24. See Dana Polan, *Scenes of Instruction: The Beginnings of the U.S. Study of Film* (Berkeley: University of California Press, 2007), 194. See also Pierre Sands, *Historical Study of the Academy of Motion Picture Arts and Sciences* (Manchester, NH: Ayer, 1972).

25. See Sands, *Historical Study*.

26. Sidney Kent, speech delivered at the All Industry Conference sponsored by AMPAS, May 2, 1932, RCP.

27. For more on the history of Bell Labs, see Leonard S. Reich, *Radio Electronics and the Development of Industrial Research in the Bell System* (Baltimore: Johns Hopkins University Press, 1977), and *The Making of American Industrial Research: Science and Business at GE and Bell, 1876–1926* (Cambridge: Cambridge University Press, 2002). See also Marc de Vries, "The History of Industrial Research Laboratories as a Resource for Teaching about Science-Technology Relationships," *Research in Science Education* 31 (2001): 15–28.

28. Reich, *Making of American Industrial Research*, 252–53.

29. "Fundamental" research is done for the extension of knowledge, rather than the solution of a particular practical problem. Fundamental research at Bell occurred in chemistry, material science, and physics. The results of such research could later be applied to products, but the research itself stood relatively independent from them.

30. M. D. Fagen, ed., *A History of Science and Engineering in the Bell System: The Early Years, 1875–1925* (New York: Bell Telephone Laboratories, Inc., 1975), 25, 28.

31. Ibid., 911.

32. Reich, *Making of American Industrial Research*, 137–40.

33. William Jacques, one of the nation's first physics PhDs, arrived at Bell in 1881 and soon became the head of the company's first laboratory, the Electrical and Patent Department. He focused on eliminating interference and "crosstalk." In 1883, the Experimental Shop was created to support research. In 1884, its name was changed to the Mechanical Department. It immediately began work designing better receivers and wires. See ibid., 143.

34. Ibid., 159. See also Chen-Pang Yeang, "Tubes, Randomness, and Brownian Motions: Or, How Engineers Learned to Start Worrying about Electronic Noise," *Archive for History of Exact Sciences* 65 (2011): 438–40.

35. Reich, *Making of American Industrial Research*, 159, 910.

36. Yeang, "Tubes, Randomness," 438.

37. Reich, *Making of American Industrial Research*, 144.

38. Yeang, "Tubes, Randomness," 439. For the sake of clarity and space, I am focusing on the Bell model rather than the General Electric model here, as telephony and radio taught different lessons regarding noise.

39. Ibid., 469.

40. For more on these two influential early categorizations of noise, see Fagen, *Engineering and Science*, 910–12. See also Walter Schottky, "Small-Shot Effect and Flicker Effect," *Physical Review* 28 (1926): 74–103, and John B. Johnson, "Thermal Agitation of Electricity in Conductors," *Physical Review* 32 (1928): 97–109. For a more definitive study of these two types of noise, see also

Gunter Dorfel and Dieter Hoffman, "From Albert Einstein to Norbert Weiner: Early Views and Insights on the Phenomenon of Electronic Noise," Preprint 301 (Berlin: Max Planck Institute for the History of Science, 2005).

41. Yeang, "Tubes, Randomness," 439.

42. Reich, *Making of American Industrial Research*, 188.

43. See *Bell System Technical Journal* archives online, accessed May 1, 2014, http://www3.alcatel-lucent.com/bstj/.

44. See Lewis M. Branscomb and Paul C. Gilmore, "Education in Private Industry," *Daedalus* 104, no. 1 (Winter 1975): 222–23, and Stan Luxenberg, "Education at AT&T," *Change* 10, no. 11 (December 1978): 26–35.

45. Fagen, *History and Science*, 44.

46. Technical Bureau Report No. 16, September 15, 1930, RCP. See also *AMPAS Bulletin*, no. 25, September 25, 1929, RCP.

47. Cowan, "Coordination East and West," 2.

48. Ibid.

49. Ibid.

50. "Testimony [*sic*] between Producers and Technicians Branch," July 19, 1927, transcript, p. 62, RCP.

51. See *AMPAS Bulletin*, no. 28, January 29, 1930, RCP.

52. *AMPAS Bulletin*, no. 25, September 25, 1929, RCP.

53. Notes taken at a meeting of the Technicians Branch of AMPAS, July 11, 1926, p. 1, RCP.

54. Fred Pelton, handwritten memo, n.d., RCP; Irving Thalberg, speech presented at a meeting of the Producers-Technicians Joint Committee, May 14, 1930, p. 3, RCP.

55. Notes taken at a meeting of the Technicians Branch of AMPAS, May 9, 1928, p. 13, RCP.

56. Thalberg, speech, 2.

57. Ibid., 3.

58. "Testimony," p. 7.

59. Ibid.

60. Secretary of the Academy to Frederick N. Sammis of the RCA Photophone Corporation, November 19, 1929, RCP.

61. AMPAS, memo describing the transfer of the Technical Bureau from the Association of Motion Picture Producers and future plans regarding this institution, n.d., p. 4, RCP.

62. It is worth noting that the AMPAS documents' assertion of chaos should be considered as just one perspective on the issue. As we know from the evolving film scholarship on the sound transition, the period has been variously described as utterly chaotic and rather well planned. For the latter perspective, see Gomery's *Coming of Sound*; its first chapter is actually entitled "Order and Profit Not Chaos."

63. Technicians Meeting of AMPAS, August 8, 1928, 2, RCP.

64. "Testimony," p. 68.

65. Meeting of Producers-Technicians Joint Committee, July 19, 1927, transcript, p. 57, RCP.

66. "Testimony," p. 61.

67. For instance, Lester Cowan, Assistant Secretary of AMPAS, wrote to John Mills, Director of Publications, Bell Telephone Laboratories, on December 6, 1928, that "the importance of communication and understanding between those who make and those who use talking picture equipment cannot be over-estimated. The Academy stands as the medium through which such communication may be carried on" (p. 1, RCP).

68. Frank Woods, "Improvement of Equipment," memo, n.d., pp. 1–2, RCP. Woods writes: "The necessity of understanding and respecting each other if there is to be an harmonious cooperation is well demonstrated by actual events. The equipment now in use was developed in the Bell Labs and Bell Lab. [Technicians] accompanied it to Hollywood. . . . Their purpose was to acquaint the studios so as to get [the] best efficiency." That efficacy, however, was diminished by the interpersonal conflict between members of the two warring factions (1).

69. These memos and speeches constitute a body of evidence on the sound shift that has never previously been analyzed by film historians.

70. Producers-Technicians Joint Committee, untitled and undated memo, p. 2, Box 45, RCP.

71. The earlier copy of the same memo is not dated but is marked up with penciled comments that show up in type in the memo from above).

72. Woods, "Improvement of Equipment."

73. Lightman is quoted in the transcript of a meeting of the Members of the Art and Technique Committee on April 30, 1932, RCP.

74. Producers-Technicians Joint Committee, untitled and undated memo, p. 2, Box 45, RCP.

75. B.P. Schulberg at the Meeting of the Producers' Branch of AMPAS with Sound Engineers, July 31, 1929, RCP. This meeting is described in an August 1, 1929, memo by Frank Woods, p. 1, and in a letter from Frank Woods to the Executive Committee of the Technicians Branch, dated August 2, 1929, both RCP.

76. Ibid.

77. Schulberg is quoted in a memo from Secretary Frank Woods dated August 1, 1929, p. 2, RCP.

78. Office of Secretary Frank Woods, Memorandum G, "Academy Sound Production Problems Survey," June 21, 1929, RCP.

79. This research was in the spirit of the Academy's ongoing efforts. Frank Woods, "The Academy of Motion Picture Arts and Sciences and its Service as a Forum for the Industry," first draft of a paper for the SMPE Convention in Toronto, October 7–10, 1930, n.d., p. 1, RCP.

80. Quote from Crafton, *Talkies*, 129.

81. J.T. Reed, statement read aloud in Minutes of the Meeting of the Technicians Branch of AMPAS, November 14, 1929, p. 9, RCP.

82. "Testimony," p. 64.

83. B.P. Schulberg at Meeting of Producers Branch of AMPAS with Sound Engineers, July 31, 1929, p. 1, RCP.

84. "Testimony," p. 67.

85. Minutes of Meeting of the Technicians Branch of AMPAS, November 14, 1929, transcript, p. 7, RCP.

86. AMPAS announced the research plan via a memo, stating: "Systematic technical research with a view to preparing for developments in the motion picture industry during the next two to five years will be undertaken cooperatively by producers and technicians under the sponsorship of the Academy of Motion Picture Arts and Sciences, it was announced today." Secretary Frank Woods, Memorandum G, "Academy Sound Production Problems Survey," n.d., RCP. In a 1929 progress report, AMPAS reported that "seven engineers are now in the field making a complete survey of all studios. The large amount of data already collected by these engineers is in preparation for quantitative laboratory tests as completed in the plan." AMPAS Progress Report No. 1, Producers-Technicians Joint Committee, December 23, 1929, p. 1, RCP. The results were published in January 1930.

87. AMPAS Progress Report No. 1, p. 1.

88. AMPAS Progress Report No. 2, on the subject of set materials, January 4, 1930, RCP.

89. See, for example, Crafton, *Talkies,* 231.

90. Preliminary Report of a Study of Methods of Camera Silencing and A Measure of Their Effectiveness, from the Sub-committee on Camera Silencing Methods, Progress Report No. 7, Producers-Technicians Joint Committee, February 6, 1930, pp. 3–5, RCP.

91. L. E. Clark, "The Nature of Sound," in *Motion Picture Sound Engineering* (New York: D. Van Nostrand, 1938), 81–87.

92. As Fred Pelton of the Academy put it, "If one is going to develop the best method and doesn't tell the other studios, there are going to be worse pictures because the best method is hidden." Notes taken at a meeting of the Technicians Branch of AMPAS, July 11, 1928, RCP.

93. Frank Woods, memos, August 27, 1929, and December 23, 1929, RCP.

94. Articles and papers included Harvey Fletcher, "The Nature of Speech and Its Interpretation," *Journal of the Franklin Institute,* June 1922; Donald MacKenzie, "The Relative Sensitivity of the Ear," *Physics Review* October 1922; Harvey Fletcher, "Physical Properties of Speech, Music, and Noise," paper presented at the Joint Meeting of the New York Electrical Society and New York Telephone Society New York City, February 1924; J. P. Maxfield and H. C. Harrison, "High Quality Recording and Reproducing of Music and Speech," Bell System, July 1926; and W. H. Martin and Harvey Fletcher, "High-Quality Transmission and Reproduction of Speech and Music," *A.I.W.W. Journal,* March 1924. See RCP.

95. In a letter to Irving Thalberg on December 30, 1930, Lester Cowan outlines AMPAS's plan of hosting technical talks on noise recording, p. 1, RCP.

96. In a "Confidential Memorandum in Relation to AMPAS," n.d., p. 1, RCP, Frank Woods claims that "book publication is a legitimate function of the Academy in connection with the university cultural courses and the subject of sound fundamentals."

97. "Sound School for Studios Planned," AMPAS Progress Report supplement to *AMPAS Bulletin,* August 6, 1929, RCP.

98. Experts' lectures would acquaint the "artistic workers" of Hollywood with the "possibilities and limitations of sound equipment." "Minutes of Conference of Academy Members and Sound Engineers," July 27, 1929, RCP.

99. Meeting of the Producers Branch of AMPAS, July 31, 1929, transcript, p. 8, RCP.

100. AMPAS Progress Report, supplement to *AMPAS Bulletin*, August 6, 1929, p. 2, RCP.

101. Meeting of the Producers Branch of AMPAS, July 31, 1929, transcript, p. 29, RCP.

102. AMPAS, "Progress Report," Supplement to *AMPAS Bulletin*, August 6, 1929, RCP.

103. Schulberg is quoted in a memo by Secretary Frank Woods, August 1, 1929, p. 2, RCP.

104. Meeting of the Producers Branch of AMPAS, July 31, 1929, transcript, p. 12, RCP.

105. "Report on Survey of Sound Problems," July 31, 1929, p. 2, RCP. This was a report of a meeting of the Producers Branch of AMPAS with sound engineers. Ten producing companies were represented, and according to the accompanying letter by Secretary Frank Woods, forty sound engineers were present.

106. "Testimony," p. 71.

107. "Academy of Motion Picture Arts and Sciences: Second Symposium on Sound Picture Art and Technique," n.d., p. 38, RCP.

108. Meeting of the Producers Branch of AMPAS, July 31, 1929, transcript, RCP.

109. Woods, "Academy," p. 2.

110. *AMPAS Bulletin*, No. 30, April 18, 1930, "Sound School Success," p. 5, RCP.

111. Lester Cowan to Peter Mole, Mole-Richardson Company, October 1, 1929, p. 1, RCP.

112. J. I. Crabtree of Eastman Kodak to Julia B. Johnson of AMPAS, January 29, 1929, RCP.

113. J. I. Crabtree to Julia B. Johnson, January 1929, RCP.

114. Producers Branch meeting with Sound Engineers, July 31, 1929, transcript, p. 2, RCP. The anonymous engineer's assertion directly contradicted an earlier memo claiming that the sound man was the "dictator" of the set; see Producers-Technicians Joint Committee, untitled and undated memo, p. 2, Box 45, RCP.

115. Producers-Technicians Joint Committee, untitled and undated memo, p. 2, Box 45, RCP. See also meeting, August 15, 1929, Academy Lounge, Roosevelt Hotel, transcript, p. 2, RCP.

116. The Technical Bureau's memo of January 2, 1931, states: "For the Glossary to fulfill these purposes effectively, it has been necessary to include many of the slang terms which have been established in everyday use in the studios. Definitions of 'audio frequency' and 'vacuum tube' might be of much less practical use if the Glossary did not also explain that to the sound engineer an 'apple' means an audio-frequency vacuum tube" (p. 1, RCP). Wesley C. Miller's "Basis of Motion Picture Sound," in *Motion Picture Sound Engineering* (New York: D. Van Nostrand, 1938), refers to sound technicians' language as "that of decibels, gammas and equalizers which are entire strangers to the rest of the motion picture world" (6). Miller's book and Cowan's *Recording Sound* both included glossaries.

117. AMPAS, "Problems Developing [on] Account of Sound Pictures," re: General Academy Meetings, memo, August 1929 (no exact date given), p. 2, RCP.

118. Producers Branch, transcript, p. 14, RCP.

119. Carl Dreher, foreword to Cowan, *Recording Sound*, xiii.

120. "Report on Survey of Sound Problems," July 31, 1929, p. 3, RCP.

121. The Academy of Motion Picture Arts and Sciences and Its Service as a Forum for the Industry," first draft of a paper for SMPE Convention in Toronto, October 7–10, 1929, believed to have been given by Frank Woods, p. 2, RCP.

122. Summary of Meeting of Producers' Branch of AMPAS with Sound Engineers, July 31, 1929, p. 2, RCP.

123. AMPAS Secretary, "Improvement of Equipment," memo, n.d., p. 2, RCP.

124. Ibid. See also AMPAS Secretary, "Re: Art and Technique Program," memo, December 18, 1930, RCP: "The value of art appreciation on the part of sound engineers should not be overlooked" (4).

125. *AMPAS Bulletin*, September 12, 1930, p. 5, RCP.

126. Minutes of Meeting of the Technicians Branch of AMPAS, November 14, 1929, p. 14, RCP.

127. "Memorandum to Secretary Describing Contemplated Course for Studio Employees in Fundamentals of Sound Recording and Reproduction," n.d., p. 1, RCP.

128. Producers Branch, transcript, p. 15, RCP.

129. "Producers Branch Meeting with Sound Engineers," n.d., RCP.

130. This argument has been well addressed by Lastra in *Sound Technology*, in his section on AMPAS and the engineers (176–77). See also Crafton, *Talkies*, 235–38.

131. AMPAS, "About the Science and Technology Council," AMPAS website, n.d., accessed June 10, 2014, www.oscars.org/science-technology/council/.

132. Ibid.

133. Ibid.

CHAPTER 3. "MACHINES FOR LISTENING"

1. Sky Sitney, "The Search for the Invisible Cinema," *Grey Room* 19 (2005): 102–13. In this article, Sky Sitney interviews her father, P. F. Sitney, and other members of Anthology Archives.

2. Quoted in ibid., 110.

3. Based on a quote from Kubelka speaking about the theater in ibid., 106.

4. Quoted in ibid., 108.

5. Kubelka quoted in ibid., 111.

6. Kubelka quoted in ibid., 103.

7. Kelman and Kubelka both quoted in ibid., 105.

8. Architectural acoustics is the study of how a space's architectural design affects the quality of the sound produced within the space. It includes the performance of acoustical analysis of spaces, acoustical design for optimal sound,

noise control, and acoustical treatment for minimizing undesirable reverbera-
tion. This is done in both new and preexisting buildings. See Madan Mehta,
James Johnson, and Jorge Rocafort, *Architectural Acoustics: Principles and
Design* (New York: Prentice Hall, 1999).

9. Much has been written about cinema's tendency to enable the spectator's
narrative immersion. See, for example, psychoanalytic/structuralist accounts,
such as Kaja Silverman's on "suture," that situate the question in terms of spectators' placement within the text; Kaja Silverman, *The Subject of Semiotics*
(New York: Oxford University Press, 1983). A similar perspective may be found
in Heath, "Narrative Space," and Browne, "Spectator-in-the-Text." Apparatus
theories such as Jean-Louis Baudry and Jean-Louis Comolli's trace out how the
structure of the apparatus suggests the spectator's absence; see Baudry, "Ideological Effects" and "The Apparatus: Metapsychological Approaches to the
Impression of Reality in Cinema," both in Rosen, *Narrative, Apparatus, Ideology,* 286–98 and 299–318 respectively; and Comolli, "Technique and Ideology." Historical accounts such as Tom Gunning's "Cinema of Attractions" are
highly influential in examining the creation of an expectation of immersion in
cinema culture (see 52–62). One may find a similar discourse on distraction in
the trade press of the time. My argument applies the discourse consistently
present in the visual to the case of cinema's aural culture.

10. Such a model of attentiveness, Fried asserts, played "an increasingly
important role" in French painting and art criticism in the eighteenth century,
showcasing that absorption was a veritable desideratum in the artistic culture of
the time. See Fried, *Absorption and Theatricality,* 10.

11. Abbé Marc-Antoine Laugier, *Jugement d'un amateur sur l'exposition des
tableaux. Lettre à M le marquis de V___ [Vence]* (1753), 42–43, on the painter
Jean-Baptiste-Siméon Chardin's *Un philosophe occupe de la lecture,* quoted in
Fried, *Absorption and Theatricality,* 11.

12. Laugier, *Jugement d'un amateur,* quoted in Fried, *Absorption and Theatricality,* 13.

13. Fried, *Absorption and Theatricality,* 30.

14. Diderot speaking on the experience of viewing paintings by Claude
Joseph Vernet in the Salon of 1767, in *Salons,* ed. Seznec and Adhemar, vol. 3,
139, quoted in Fried, *Absorption and Theatricality,* 126.

15. Fried, *Absorption and Theatricality,* 115.

16. As Anthony Barlow writes, "All present could be performer or audience,
their roles shifting and changing within the total event." In such an environment, the audiences would "enrich [the performance] by their own impromptu
performances, their asides, their gossip, their interruptions or applause, their
involvement or detachment"—indeed, by "their very presence." Anthony D.
Barlow, "Lighting Control and Concepts of Theatre Activity," *Educational
Theatre Journal* 25, no. 2 (May 1973): 137, 140.

17. Beat Wyss, "*Ragnarök* of Illusion: Richard Wagner's 'Mystical Abyss' at
Bayreuth," trans. Denise Bratton, *October* 54 (Autumn 1990): 74.

18. Barlow, "Lighting Control," 143.

19. Ibid., 139.

20. Schivelbusch, *Disenchanted Night,* 204.

21. See Anne Leonard, "Picturing Listening in the Late Nineteenth Century," *Art Bulletin* 89, no. 2 (June 2007): 269; Weber, "Did People Listen"; Gay, *Naked Heart*, 15.

22. This rhetoric emerged in musical aesthetics but also in art and literature. Leonard provides examples in "Picturing Listening," 270.

23. Crary, *Suspensions of Perception*, 2, 74–75. Cinema was one of a host of technologies (although Crary seldom mentions it) that enacted a separation between participants. Cinema houses focus on "techniques of isolation" between subjects in their very design and are intent on "cellularization, and above all separation" of bodies in physical space. Crary says very little about sound, but his thoughts on spectacle are easily applied to sonic situations, and his formulations allow room for such an interpretation.

24. Lewis Kaye, "The Silenced Listener: Architectural Acoustics, the Concert Hall and the Conditions of Audience," *Leonardo Music Journal* 22 (December 2012): 63.

25. Ibid. "The modern concert hall, as an exemplar of acoustically architected space, physically frames a persistent, idealized and hegemonic practice of listening by the way it organizes sound as spectacle."

26. Crary, *Suspensions of Perception*, 74–75. He focuses on how strategies of spectacle form "in which individuals are isolated, separated, and *inhabit time as disempowered*" (3). This will happen in the context of certain art cinemas I will describe throughout this chapter. The entire sensorium, including, especially, the ear, is engaged (and subdued) as a means of expressing a culture intent on subduing the sounds of the body. This is "an *effect* of other kinds of forces and relations of power" (2).

27. Crary, *Suspensions of Perception*, 2, 10, 229. As Wilhelm Wundt postulated, concentration required "inhibition" of other stimuli in order to produce focus. Wilhelm Wundt, *Principles of Physiological Psychology*, trans. Edward Bradford Titchener (New York: Macmillan, 1904).

28. Wilhelm Wundt, *Outlines of Psychology*, trans. Charles Hubbard Judd (New York: G. E. Stechert, 1907), 238.

29. Angelo Mosso, *Fatigue*, trans. Margaret Drummond and William Blackley Drummond (New York: S. Sonnenschein, 1906), 183–84. As William James argues, "A little introspective observation will show any one that voluntary attention cannot be continuously sustained—that it comes in beats." William James, *Talks to Teachers on Psychology and Students on Some of Life's Ideals* (Rockville, MD: Arc Manor Classic Reprints, 2008), 60. See also James, *Principles of Psychology*, vol. 1 (1890; repr., New York: Dover, 1950), 403–4.

30. Thaddeus Bolton, "Rhythm," *American Journal of Psychology* 6, no. 2 (January 1894): 145–238. As Crary argues, these studies of attention resonate also with Hegel's description of "'sense-certainty' as a self-canceling form of apprehension, as a rhythm of 'appearing' and 'melting away.'" See G. W. F. Hegel, *The Phenomenology of Mind*, trans. J. B. Baillie (New York: Harper and Row, 1967), 149–61, quoted in Crary, *Suspensions of Perception*, 64.

31. See also Theodule Ribot, *Diseases of the Will*, trans. Merwin-Marie Snell (Chicago: Open Court, 1894), 72–76, and James, *Principles of Psychology*, vol. 1, 414–25.

32. Weber, "Did People Listen," 690. Hector Berlioz's description of listening to Franz Liszt playing Beethoven's "Moonlight Sonata" reinforces such an impression of the necessity of silence, as well as its conflict with the reality of the physical bodies of the listeners: "It was the shade of Beethoven, conjured up by the virtuoso to whose voice we were listening. We all trembled in silence, and when the last chord had sounded no one spoke—we were in tears." Quoted in Gay, *Naked Heart*, 28.

33. Leonard, "Picturing Listening," 270.

34. Emile Verhaeren, *Quelques notes sur l'ouevre de Fernand Khnopff* (Brussels: Madame Veuve Monnom, 1887), 261, quoted in Leonard, "Picturing Listening," 275. Verhaeren adds: "The effect of art, of our art, is an influence of vague attraction toward a sad and solemn ideal."

35. Gay, *Naked Heart*, 19.

36. Grevel Lindop, *The Opium Eater: A Life of Thomas De Quincey* (London: Dent, 1981), quoted in Gay, *Naked Heart*, 12.

37. Ibid., 15–16. This was quite a new assertion spurred by the attitude taken by the Romantics; in *Allegemeine Theorie der schonen Kunste* (1774), Johann Georg Sulzer wrote that music should be considered "a lively and not unpleasant noise, or a civil and entertaining chatter, but not one that engages the heart" (quoted in Gay, *Naked Heart*, 16). By the late nineteenth century, the "theology of music" made musical listening a much more exalted art.

38. Gay, *Naked Heart*, 22.

39. Ibid., 12, 34.

40. Stephen Downes, "Musical Pleasures and Amorous Passions: Stendhal, the Crystallization Process, and Listening to Rossini and Beethoven," *19th Century Music* 26, no. 3 (Spring 2003): 236.

41. Ibid., 239.

42. Veit Erlmann, *Reason and Resonance: A History of Modern Aurality* (Cambridge, MA: Zone Books, 2010), 162. See also Weber, "Did People Listen," 690. He notes that the discourse on the nature of listening was "closely linked to issues of sexual mores" and often dealt with how to avoid impropriety in one's act of listening.

43. Ibid., 162.

44. Quoted in Downes, "Musical Pleasures," 239.

45. Gay, *Naked Heart*, 12. Scholars including Leonard and Weber also postulate that a form of listening emerged that was caught in a tension between a state of "pure listening, oblivious of the visible," and an awareness of the collective. Leonard writes in "Picturing Listening" that depictions of listening tended to represent an experience that was both "collective and interiorized." Listening posed the problem of a tension between "the public and the private." A listener, music critics articulated, could "oscillate between participation" and what cinema theory would call primary "identification" (270–71).

46. Ned A. Bowman, "Investing a Theatrical Ideal: Wagner's Bayreuth *Festspielhaus*," *Educational Theatre Journal* 18, no. 4 (December 1966): 429.

47. Ibid., 430.

48. Arnold Aronson, "Theatres of the Future," *Theater Journal* 33, no. 4 (December 1981): 492.

49. For more on Wagner and cinematic listening, see Lastra, "Film and the Wagnerian Aspiration: Thoughts on Sound Design and the History of the Senses," in *Lowering the Boom: Critical Studies in Film Sound*, ed. Jay Beck and Tony Grajeda (Urbana: University of Illinois Press, 2008), 123–40. Lastra's analysis of *Apocalypse Now* identifies a Wagnerian tendency in the effect of cinema surround sound. Viewing this through the *Gesamtkunstwerk*, he identifies a late nineteenth- and early twentieth-century "mechanization of the human" through the manipulation of hearing. What he misses, however, is the body of literature this chapter deals with, which would undercut the totalizing force that he identifies in the prosthesis. Studies of noise indicate that there has *always* been a conflict between the totalizing effects of these apparatuses encouraging attention and the nature of distraction in noise.

50. Stendhal's *Life of Rossini* is quoted in Downes, "Musical Pleasures," 236.

51. Downes, "Musical Pleasures," 236.

52. Gay, *Naked Heart*, 22.

53. Leonard, "Picturing Listening," 276.

54. Schopenhauer, *Studies in Pessimism*, 76–77.

55. Ibid., 77.

56. Ibid., 77, 78.

57. For descriptions of Bayreuth's architecture, one can go directly to Wagner. For the multiple arguments that connect Wagner's opera house with the idea of a cinema theater, see also Aronson, "Theatres of the Future"; Marvin Carlson, *Places of Performance: The Semiotics of Theatre Architecture* (Ithaca, NY: Cornell University Press, 1989), 43; Wyss, "Ragnarök of Illusion."

58. Schivelbusch writes about this transition from a lighted auditorium, with an active and audible audience, to a silent auditorium that was darkened, in *Disenchanted Night*, as do Richard Sennett in *The Fall of Public Man* and Wyss in "Ragnarök of Illusion."

59. Richard Wagner, *Art, Life, and Theories of Richard Wagner, Selected from His Writings*, trans. Edward L. Burlingame (New York: Henry Holt, 1904).

60. Wyss, "Ragnarök of Illusion," 77.

61. Nietzsche is quoted in Kärsten Harries, *The Ethical Function of Architecture* (Cambridge, MA: MIT Press, 1998), 316. In "Film and the Wagnerian Aspiration," Lastra has argued that the feelings of anesthesia posited by these thinkers serve as a sort of neutralizing force for the pangs of a jolting urban existence.

62. Gay, *Naked Heart*, 35.

63. Ibid., 31.

64. Crary, *Suspensions of Perception*, 249.

65. Ibid., 247. See also Theodor Adorno, *In Search of Wagner*, trans. Rodney Livingstone (London: Verso Press, 1981). See also Andreas Huyssen, "Adorno in Reverse: From Hollywood to Richard Wagner," in *After the Great Divide: Modernism, Mass Culture, Postmodernism* (Bloomington: Indiana University Press, 1986), 16–43. Crary has posited that such listening is present in other scenarios depicted by nineteenth-century art. In specific, he writes: "Seurat's

paintings, too, use the notion of theater as a figure that can describe both collective public experiences, such as ones literally depicted in his paintings, and also individuated experiences, produced by the management of perception in terms of a solitary subject" (247). The theater was a place where a collective aspect and an individual and highly sensory vision were both active. We can trace how this corresponds with levels of higher and lower forms of listening in what we discuss here. Crary notes that much modernist art and music theory has been based on such "dualistic systems of perception in which a rapt, timeless presence of perception is contrasted with lower, mundane or quotidian forms of seeing or listening" (46). See also Konrad Fiedler, *On Judging Works of Visual Art* (1876), trans. Henry Schaefer-Simmern (Berkeley: University of California Press, 1949).

66. Jonathan Sterne, *The Audible Past: The Cultural Origins of Sound Reproduction* (Durham, NC: Duke University Press, 2003), 62.

67. Jonathan Crary, *Techniques of the Observer: On Vision and Modernity in the Nineteenth Century* (Cambridge, MA: MIT Press, 1990), 19.

68. Ibid., 82.

69. Ibid., 81.

70. Robert Jütte, *A History of the Senses: From Antiquity to Cyberspace*, trans. James Lynn (Cambridge: Polity Press, 2005), 218.

71. Ibid.

72. Ibid., 227.

73. Ibid., 228–29.

74. For more on this, see Hermann von Helmholtz, *On the Sensations of Tone as a Physiological Basis for a Theory of Music* (London: Longmans Green, 1885).

75. See William J. Cavanaugh and Joseph A. Wilkes, *Architectural Acoustics: Principles and Practice* (New York: John Wiley and Sons, 1999). See also Mehta, Johnson, and Rocafort, *Architectural Acoustics*. For more on architectural acoustics and how they work in musical auditoriums, see also Leo Beranek, "Concert Hall Acoustics," *Journal of the Audio Engineering Society* 64, no. 7 (2008): 1–39, and Michael Barron, *Auditorium Acoustics and Architectural Design* (New York: Spon Press, 2009).

76. See G. Millington, "A Modified Formula for Reverberation," *Journal of the Acoustical Society of America* 4, no. 1 (1932): 69–82. See also Leo L. Beranek, "Analysis of Sabine and Eyring Equations and Their Application to Concert Hall Audience and Chair Absorption," *Journal of the Acoustical Society of America* 120, no. 3 (2006): 1399–1410; and Carl F. Eyring, "Reverberation Time in 'Dead' Rooms," *Journal of the Acoustical Society of America* 1, no. 2 (1930): 168.

77. Charles Garnier is quoted in Leo Beranek, *Concert Halls and Opera Houses: Music, Acoustics, and Architecture* (New York: Springer Science and Business Media, 2012), 267.

78. C. A. Mason and J. Moir, "Acoustics of Cinema Auditoria," *Journal of the Institution of Electrical Engineers* 88, no. 2 (February 1941): 93–96. See also C. C. Potwin and J. P. Maxfield, "A Modern Concept of Acoustical Design," *Journal of the Acoustical Society of America* 11 (July 1939): 48–55; C. C.

Potwin and Ben Schlanger, "Coordinating Acoustics and Architecture in the Design of the Motion Picture Theater," *Journal of the Society of Motion Picture Engineers* 32 (February 1939): 156–67; and Ben Schlanger, "Advancement of Motion Picture Theater Design," *Journal of the Society of Motion Picture Engineers* 50 (1948): 303–13.

79. N. Fleming, "Acoustics in the Motion Picture Theatre and Studio," *Journal of the British Kinematograph Society* 6, no. 2 (April 1943): 49–50. According to Fleming, acoustical engineers found that the most likely sources of undesirable echoes lay along the ceiling and the back wall. Ceilings therefore needed to be kept from rising too high in designs, as the path difference between sound arriving directly from the loudspeakers and that reflecting off the ceiling itself needed to be kept small. The rear wall presented its own challenges with regard to the cinema's reflective surfaces. Although a concave back wall was often preserved to maximize sight lines and "preserve seating area," such a plan had the side effect of producing severe echoes. To combat this concern, acoustical engineers broke up the single concave arc into a small number of large convex surfaces.

80. C. C. Potwin, "The Control of Sound in Theaters and Preview Rooms," *Journal of the Society of Motion Picture Engineers* 35, no. 8 (August 1940): 111–25.

81. Acoustical materials such as draping and acoustical matting fronted by corrugated metal were available but were expensive and were therefore considered a last resort. Auditorium shape and materials were carefully planned to prevent any reliance upon such materials. See Potwin and Maxfield, "Modern Concept," for additional information.

82. Fleming, "Acoustics," 48. Echoes and loudness, Fleming notes, are "mainly bound up with the size and shape of the auditorium." The degree of reverberation depends a great deal on the walls and furnishings, and, significantly, "freedom from extraneous noise" is based upon "insulation against external sources of noise" outside the auditorium, as well as "avoidance of internal sources."

83. Ibid., 53. The only noise-producing element of the soundscape that could not be controlled effectively was, he states, the audience.

84. According to Fleming, "The main requirements for good hearing in an auditorium" are (1) the absence of echoes; (2) adequate and uniform loudness; (3) a suitable degree of reverberation; and (4) the absence of extraneous noise. Ibid., 48.

85. Ibid., 50–51.

86. Ibid., 49.

87. S. K. Wolf, "Theatre Acoustics for Reproduced Sound, Also: Reproduction in the Theatre," reprint no. 6 from AMPAS's Academy Technical Digest (Los Angeles, 1929), 82.

88. Ibid., 81.

89. Fleming, "Acoustics," 50.

90. Louis E. Bisch, "How the Screen Hypnotizes You: The Doctor Explains Why the Movies Exert an Uncanny Influence on Audiences," *Photoplay Magazine*, February 1928, 40–41. Bisch, a medical doctor and PhD in psychology, was brought in on multiple occasions to educate *Photoplay* readers on how the movies interacted in one way or another with the mind. Another entry in this

ongoing series was "Are We Morons? The Scientific Answer to Those Who Belittle the Intelligence of Movie Audiences," *Photoplay Magazine*, February 1929, 50–51. The answer was, of course, "No, we aren't."

91. Bisch, "How the Screen Hypnotizes."

92. Ibid.

93. In fact, the only light Kubelka intended to be included in the cinema was that reflected off the screen. Prior to screenings, a spotlight was to be shone on the screen to illuminate the space as much as was deemed necessary for safety. For more on this, see Peter Kubelka, "The Invisible Cinema," *Design Quarterly* 93 (1974): 32–36.

94. See ibid., as well as Rob White, "Velvet Boxes and Reliquaries," *Film Quarterly* 61, no. 1 (Fall 2007): 92–93.

95. Kubelka, "Invisible Cinema," 32. The fabric partitions, Kubelka boasted, "made it impossible to see one's neighbors." See also Peter Decherney, *Hollywood and the Culture Elite: How the Movies Became American* (New York: Columbia University Press, 2006), 199.

96. Rose is quoted in Kubelka, "Invisible Cinema," 32.

97. Kubelka, "Invisible Cinema," 35.

98. Kubelka does not call it this, but a possible interpretation of this kind is evident in his statements about the Cinema's sound.

99. These devices are discussed at some length in military and popular science articles, particularly in Frank Parker Stockbridge, "How Far Off Is That German Gun? How Sixty-Three German Guns Were Located by Sound Waves Alone in a Single Day," *Popular Science*, December 1930, 39. For more on the interesting history of the widespread military use of acoustical location, see Judd A. Case, "Logistical Media: Fragments from Radar's Prehistory," *Canadian Journal of Communication* 38, no. 3 (2013): 379–95.

100. Kubelka, "Invisible Cinema," 32.

101. "When the lights are turned up you may see that they are thinking about what they have just seen, for the intensity of expression, so plainly visible in their faces, relaxes but slowly, showing how deeply they have been impressed with what their eyes have seen." W. Stephen Bush, "Facing an Audience," *Moving Picture World* 9, no. 10 (September 16, 1911).

102. Kubelka, "Invisible Cinema," 34. Kubelka was actually surprisingly interested in the concept of community and brought it up several times during this interview. He was oriented toward creating "a community in which people liked each other." This, he argued, they could do only if they could not clearly hear one another.

103. Quoted in Sitney, "Search," 107.

104. For more on how the Cinema blended public and private realms, see Juliet Koss, "On the Limits of Empathy," *Art Bulletin* 88, no. 1 (March 2006): 139–57, who writes that "it combined the private activity of individual spectatorship with the communal activity of movie-going" (153).

105. Brakhage quoted in Sitney, "Search," 108.

106. See Annette Michelson, "Gnosis and Iconoclasm: A Case Study in Cinephilia," *October* 83 (1998): 3–18.

107. Baudry, "Ideological Effects," 295.

108. See Silverman on suture in *Subject of Semiotics*; she draws on Jean-Pierre Oudart, "Cinema and Suture," *Screen* 18, no. 4 (1977–78): 35–47, originally published in *Cahiers du Cinema* (April and May 1969), nos. 211 and 212.

109. Stephen Heath, "Narrative Space," 386, 391.

110. Ibid. Silverman writes: "For both Metz and Baudry, there is a certain inevitability about this identification. Thus, Metz writes that, 'the spectator can do no other than identify with the camera . . . which has looked before him at what he is now looking at and whose stationing . . . determines the vanishing point.'" Kaja Silverman quoting Christian Metz's *The Imaginary Signifier*, in *The Threshold of the Visible World* (New York: Routledge, 1996), 126.

111. Metz, *Imaginary Signifier*, 49; Jay Beck, "The Sounds of 'Silence': Dolby Stereo, Sound Design, and *The Silence of the Lambs*," in Beck and Grajeda, *Lowering the Boom*, 76; Michel Chion, *Audio-vision: Son et image au cinema* (Paris: Armand Colin, 2013), 69–71.

112. Beck, "Sounds of 'Silence,'" 77. This is an example of manipulation of what Rick Altman has elsewhere called the perceived "point of audition." See Altman, "Sound Space," in *Sound Theory/Sound Practice*, ed. Rick Altman (New York: Routledge, 1992), 58–64.

113. Metz, *Imaginary Signifier*, 253.

114. To ensure a high-quality sound system, one must control the accidental sounds of the theater environment. THX was originally designed to make more of a soundscape audible. Following the release of *Star Wars*, George Lucas was troubled to find that some theaters' sound systems were so poorly designed that many elements of the soundscape were lost. James Cameron is quoted in TAP publicity material, "Aligned Success" (Lucasfilm, 1992), available from LucasArts Entertainment Company, THX Division, PO Box 2009, San Rafael, CA 94912.

115. THX, "THX Certified Cinemas," n.d., accessed August 15, 2013, www.thx.com/professional/cinema-certification/.

116. THX, "THX Certified Cinemas: Speaker Layout and Baffle Wall," n.d., accessed August 15, 2013, www.thx.com/professional/cinema-certification /speaker-layout-and-baffle-wall/.

117. THX, "THX Certified Cinemas: Auditorium Isolation," n.d., accessed August 15, 2013, www.thx.com/professional/cinema-certification/thx-auditorium-isolation/.

118. THX, "Reverberation Control," n.d., accessed August 15, 2013, www .thx.com/professional/cinema-certification/thx-certified-cinema-reverberation-control/.

119. Many of the tactics employed by THX were actually suggested decades earlier, presumably motivated by acoustical engineers' same desire for aural immersion. N. Fleming's speech in 1943 mentions many of them.

120. Nick Watson, "Twelve Years of Digital Cinema," part 2 of "The Evolution of Cinema Sound: From Film to Digital Cinema and Beyond," by Julian Pinn and Nick Watson, *Cinema Technology* 25, no. 2 (2012): 54–59. Watson quotes Ioan Allen at Dolby Atmos: "Suddenly I can put a sound anywhere I like. In fact, not just on the horizontal plane but in the vertical plane as well. Dolby Atmos creates a totally symmetrical hemisphere in terms of the playback" (59). This has also been compared with a form of aural 3-D in terms of

its complete immersion. For more on this perspective on Dolby Atmos, see Tim Carroll, "3D: The Audio Part," *IBE: International Broadcast Engineer* (July/August 2012): 12–13.

121. Peter Parnham, "Surrounded by Sound," *Onfilm* 29, no. 6 (June 2012): 20–22. See also Bill Mead, "A New Way to Listen," *Film Journal International* 115, no. 9 (September 2012): 56–58. For more on the setup of Atmos-equipped theaters, see Kris Sangani, "The Vastness of Sound," *Engineering and Technology* 8, no. 6 (July 2013): 78–79; "Tech Specs and Tips," *Film Journal International* 116, no. 5 (May 2013): 66–67. For more on the use of Dolby surround sound, see Mark Kerins, *Beyond Dolby (Stereo): Cinema in the Digital Sound Age* (Bloomington: Indiana University Press, 2010). See also Gianluca Sergi, *The Dolby Era: Film Sound in Contemporary Hollywood* (Manchester, UK: Manchester University Press, 2005) and "The Sonic Playground: Hollywood Cinema and Its Listeners," in *Hollywood Spectatorship: Changing Perceptions of Cinema Audiences*, ed. Richard Maltby and Melvyn Stokes (London: British Film Institute, 2001), 121–51. For a history of surround sound formats in cinema, see Jay Shields Beck in his *A Quiet Revolution: Changes in American Film Sound Practices, 1967–1979* (Iowa City, IA: University of Iowa Press, 2003).

122. Dolby Atmos advertisement, "Dolby Atmos for Dramatic Cinema Sound Experiences," Dolby Atmos, n.d., accessed June 3, 2014, www.dolby.com/us/en/consumer/technology/movie/dolby-atmos.html.

123. There is no established number or arrangement prescribed by Atmos—the system is entirely flexible to number of output speakers, and it is symmetry alone that matters. "The industry appears to agree that there is not an ideal number or placement of channels. As a result, Dolby Atmos is adaptable and able to play back accurately in a variety of auditoria, whether they have a limited number of playback channels or many channels with highly flexible configurations" (Watson, "Twelve Years," 58). For more on the possibilities of sound speaker placement, see "Dolby Bows Revolutionary New Platform," *Mix* 36, no. 5 (May 2012): 8. See also Geoffrey Morrison, "The Future of Surround Sound," *Sound and Vision* 77, no. 6 (October 2012): 20–25.

124. Watson, "Twelve Years," 56, 58.

125. Ibid., 55.

126. Rudyard Coltman is quoted in "Exhibitors Sound Off on Dolby Atmos," *Film Journal International* 116, no. 5 (May 2013): 67.

127. Benjamin Dauhrer, technical manager at CineCitta theaters, is quoted in "Exhibitors Sound Off," 68.

128. Carolyn Giardina, "Dolby Breaks a Sound Barrier," *Hollywood Reporter*, July 20, 2012, 58. See also Andreas Fuchs, "Brave New Worlds," *Film Journal International* 115, no. 9 (September 2012): 60–64.

129. "Introduction to Atmos" video, Dolby, n.d., accessed October 15, 2013, www.dolby.com.

130. Watson, "Twelve Years," 55: "Atmos supports multiple screen channels, resulting in increased definition and improved audio-visual coherence for on-screen sounds or dialogue. The ability to position sources anywhere in the surround zones also improves the audio-visual transition of screen to room. An example is if a character on screen looks inside the room towards a source of

sound, the mixer has the ability to precisely position the sound so that it matches the character's line of sight, and the effect will be consistent."

131. Heath, "Narrative Space," 387. Atmos's promotional posters feature a movie theater seat, complete with concessions, but empty (as if to invite the "Absent One" as an auditor) sitting in numerous narrative film locations.

132. Steve Martz, Senior Design Engineer, THX, "THX Certified Cinemas" (video), THX vids (THX official YouTube channel), n.d., accessed August 21, 2013, https://www.youtube.com/watch?v=JAvdCkR2vZA.

133. Silverman, *Subject of Semiotics*, 139.

134. Heath, "Narrative Space," 389.

135. Silverman, *Subject of Semiotics*, 141. Heath's *Questions of Cinema* is quoted in Silverman, *Subject of Semiotics*, 147.

136. Janet Cardiff and George Bures Miller, *The Paradise Institute* (2001), installation. Cardiff and Miller previously became famous for their "site-specific 'artwalks'" that led participants through urban spaces as they listened to a Foley-laden voice-over narration performed by Cardiff. This voice-over was intended to narrate the listener's journey as she walked through urban space by virtue of creating an artificial sense of the space through aural techniques. See *Janet Cardiff & George Bures Miller, Works from the Goetz Collection*, exhibition program, Haus der Kunst, Munich, April 13, 2012–July 8, 2012, https://hausderkunst.de /en/exhibitions/janet-cardiff-george-bures-miller-werke-aus-der-sammlung-goetz.

137. Janet Cardiff and George Bures Miller, "*Paradise Institute*: 2001," n.d., accessed February 10, 2012,www.cardiffmiller.com/artworks/inst/paradise_ institute.html.

138. For more on binaural recording, see Robert Gilkey and Timothy R. Anderson, eds., *Binaural and Spatial Hearing in Real and Virtual Environments* (New York: Psychology Press, 2014). See also Steve La Cerra, "Advanced Stereo Miking Techniques," *Electronic Musician* 29, no. 7 (July 2013): 56–64.

139. Janet Cardiff, interview by Atom Egoyan, *Bomb* 79 (Spring 2002): 64.

140. Ibid., 63.

141. *Janet Cardiff & George Bures Miller*, exhibition program.

142. Cardiff, interview by Egoyan, 69.

143. Ibid., 65.

144. "Spatial Articulation of Sounds and Voices," video interview transcript, *Meet the Artist*, National Gallery of Canada, n.d., accessed February 10, 2012, www.cybermuse.gallery.ca/showcases/meet/artist, no longer available online.

145. Cardiff, interview by Egoyan, 66.

146. *Janet Cardiff & George Bures Miller*, exhibition program.

147. "Spatial Articulation of Sounds and Voices."

CHAPTER 4. CINEMA THEATERS AS ANTIQUATED AS "EDISON AND HIS WAX CYLINDERS"

1. All quotations in this paragraph are from respondents to my *Static in the System* Mobile Listening Survey, 2018.

2. Andrew O'Hehir, "Beyond the Multiplex: Steve Buscemi and Sienna Miller Team Up for a Trashy Take on Celebrity Culture. Plus: Mind-Blowing

Apocalyptic Anime and Kim Ki-duk's Fun with Monsters," *Salon*, July 12, 2007, www.salon.com/2007/07/12/btm_115/.

3. See Ben Child, "North American Cinema Attendance Drops to Lowest Level in Two Decades," *Guardian*, January 2, 2015, www.theguardian.com /film/2015/jan/02/north-american-box-office-takings-drop. See also Pamela McClintock, "Box Office 104: Moviegoing Hits Two Decade Low," *Hollywood Reporter*, December 31, 2014, www.hollywoodreporter.com/news/box-office-2014-moviegoing-hits-760766; Jack Coyle, "With Digital Forces at the Gate, a Down Year for Hollywood," *Advocate,* January 8, 2015, http://theadvocate.com /entertainment/red/11222195–31/with-digital-forces-at-the.

4. Child, "North America Cinema Attendance." A record low of 1.26 billion bought tickets to see a movie at the theater in 2014, which was the lowest number since 1995. Overall revenue finished at approximately $10.36 billion, which was down 5 percent over 2013. This marks the biggest year-over-year decline in almost ten years.

5. Kevin Murnane, "Nielsen Reports that TV Crushes Mobile for Time Spent Watching Video," *Forbes*, May 29, 2017, https://www.forbes.com/sites /kevinmurnane/2017/05/29/nielsen-reports-that-tv-crushes-mobile-for-time-spent-watching-video/#1918d0f40b15.

6. See Brian Stelter, "Netflix Hits Milestone and Raises Its Sights," *New York Times,* October 21, 2013, www.nytimes.com/2013/10/22/business/media /netflix-hits-subscriber-milestone-as-shares-soar.html?_r=0.

7. "The Digital Age: Young Adults Gravitate toward Digital Devices," Nielsen.com, October 10, 2016, www.nielsen.com/us/en/insights/news/2016 /the-digital-age-young-adults-gravitate-toward-digital-devices.html.

8. O'Hehir, "Beyond the Multiplex."

9. Yaz Holloway, comment on my post "Re: Update! I Asked You This Question Three Years Ago," Facebook, May 3, 2017, https://www.facebook .com/meredith.c.ward.

10. Kate Ewald, comment on my post "Re: Update! I Asked You This Question Three Years Ago," Facebook, May 3, 2017, https://www.facebook.com /meredith.c.ward.

11. David Beer, "Tune Out: Music, Soundscapes and the Urban Mise-en-Scene," *Information, Communication and Society* 10, no. 6 (2007): 861.

12. In his essay "Upon Leaving the Movie Theater" (in *The Rustle of Language,* trans. Richard Howard [New York: Hill and Wang, 1986]), Barthes specifically contrasts this with the home environment, stating, in a subsection entitled "Difference from Home," "In this darkness of the cinema . . . lies the very fascination of the film (any film). Think of the contrary experience: on television, where films are also shown, no fascination; here darkness is erased, anonymity repressed; space is familiar, articulated (by furniture, known objects), tamed. . . . The eroticization of the place is foreclosed: television *doomed* us to the Family, whose household instrument it has become—what the hearth used to be, flanked by its communal kettle" (346). This experience is something I will draw in contrast to the mobile phone experience, which takes place not in private but in public space, and in which one's anonymity is incredibly effectively preserved. The mobile phone experience, as I will argue, is in this way unlike the

home viewing experience and has the possibility of retaining a bit more of the public/private tension that the moviegoing experience also contained.

13. See Bisch, "How the Screen Hypnotizes You."

14. Brian Stelter, "Youths Are Watching, But Less Often on TV," *New York Times*, February 8, 2012, www.nytimes.com/2012/02/09/business/media/young-people-are-watching-but-less-often-on-tv.html?pagewanted=all.

15. Cited in ibid. For the study, which was not yet released at the time of Stelter's article, see Nielsen Company, "State of the Media: Cross-Platform Report, Q1 2012," September 11, 2012, www.nielsen.com/us/en/insights/reports.html?start=130.

16. Billie Gold, the director of programming research for Carat USA, an agency that sells advertising space, is the interviewee being quoted in Stelter, "Youths Are Watching."

17. Ryan Bushey, "The 11 Best Streaming Apps to Turn Your Tablet and Smartphone into a TV," *Business Insider*, December 4, 2013.

18. See Colin Dixon, "Millennial Migration to Online Video to Accelerate in 2017," Nscreenmedia.com, December 20, 2016, www.nscreenmedia.com/millennial-online-video-usage-accelerate-2017; Matthew Ingram, "The Smartphone Is Eating the Television, Nielsen Admits," *Fortune*, December 7, 2015, http://fortune.com/2015/12/07/smartphone-tv-report/.

19. Taylor Soper, "Netflix Still King of Streaming Video, but Amazon Gaining Market Share," *Geekwire*, March 12, 2015, www.geekwire.com/2015/netflix-still-king-of-streaming-video-but-amazon-gaining-market-share/.

20. Nielsen Company, "U.S. Digital Consumer Report," February 10, 2014, www.nielsen.com/us/en/insights/reports/2014/the-us-digital-consumer-report.html.

21. MWW Group, "Smartphone vs. Tablet: What the Research Says," Summer 2012, https://www.slideshare.net/mwwgroupNY/2014-smartphone-vstablet, also available at https://issuu.com/mwwgroup/docs/messaging-smartphone-vs-tablet-based-vide/7.

22. The ultimate stated goal of MWW's plan of research was not commercial or academic; it was to "determine the optimal context, situations, activities and words to associate with long-form video on smartphone and tablet devices" (as many other media research companies are doing right now).

23. MWW Group, "Smartphone versus Tablet."

24. Respondent to my *Static in the System* Mobile Listening Survey, 2018.

25. MWW Group, "Smartphone versus Tablet."

26. See Dixon, "Millennial Migration."

27. Ibid.

28. Richard Iurilli, "How Do People View Video on Their Smart Phones?" *Wainscot Media Blog*, May 2, 2016, http://wainscotmedia.com/blog/people-view-videos-smartphones.

29. Greg Jarboe, "Millennials Ensure 46% of Video Is Consumed Via Mobile," Tubular Insights Video Marketing Insights, March 21, 2016, http://tubularinsights.com/millennials-ensure-46-percent-video-consumed-via-mobile/.

30. Todd Spangler, "Americans Are Watching Less Traditional TV as Smartphone Media Usage Booms," *Variety*, June 27, 2016, http://variety.com/2016/digital/news/live-tv-declining-smartphone-boom-nielsen-1201804202/.

31. Ibid.

32. Nielsen Company, "U.S. Digital Consumer Report."

33. "Nielsen Launched New Performance Testing Solution for Mobile Video," press release, December 7, 2017, www.nielsen.com/us/en/press-room/2017/nielsen-launches-new-performance-testing-solution-for-mobile-video.html, and Nielsen Company, "The Nielsen Total Audience Q1 Report," 2017, www.nielsen.com/content/dam/corporate/us/en/reports-downloads/2017-reports/total-audience-report-q1-2017.pdf.

34. According to Heather Kelly of CNN.com, recent data makes it clear that the larger the smartphone screen, the more likely the user is to watch movies and to use it for other media viewing. She writes that "people in the United States with smartphones that have screens 4.5 inches and larger use 44% more data than those tapping away on smaller phones," according to recent research by the NDP Group. Wider-screened smartphones ate up 7.2 gigabytes per month, as opposed to a mere 5 gigabytes for smaller phones. After social media (which remains a giant in media use), video was the second largest sector, along with navigation, music, and, at times, retail. But the evidence is in that viewing on mobile phones is certainly on the rise. Such a strong and noticeable trend is apparent in the Nielsen Company's 2014 Digital Consumer Report, where such moves are accounted for. See Heather Kelly, "Side Effect of Larger Smartphones: More Data Usage," CNN.com, November 19, 2013, www.cnn.com/2013/11/18/tech/mobile/phone-size-data-usage/index.html.

35. Giselle Abramovich, "Move Over, Tablet—Smartphone Is Now No. 1 Mobile-Video Viewing Device: ADI," CMO.com, December 11, 2015, www.cmo.com/adobe-digital-insights/articles/2015/12/4/adi-q3–2015-digital-video-report.html#gs.TUizZgQ.

36. Ibid.

37. Spangler, "Americans Are Watching."

38. "Video Consumption on Mobile Devices Stabilizes in Q1 2018 Nearly Three of Every Five Videos Watched," Ooyala press release, June 19, 2018, https://www.ooyala.com/resources/news/press-releases/video-consumption-mobile-devices-stabilizes-q1-2018-nearly-three-every.

39. Hendrik Haandrikman, "5 Reasons Mobile Video Streaming Will Rule 2017," Knect365.com, January 6, 2017, https://knect365.com/media-networks/article/1567b64d-7643-45c5-804d-b0e363cc7359/5-reasons-mobile-video-streaming-will-rule-2017..

40. Respondents to my *Static in the System* Mobile Listening Survey, 2018.

41. Respondents to my *Static in the System* Mobile Listening Survey, 2018.

42. For more on this, see Richard Berry, "A Golden Age of Podcasting? Evaluating Serial in the Context of Podcast Histories," *Journal of Radio and Audio Media* 22, no. 2 (2015): 170–78. See also Sirena Bergman, "I Listen to 35 Hours of Podcasts Every Week. Is That . . . Bad?," *Cut*, October 27, 2017, https://www.thecut.com/2017/10/what-is-listening-to-podcasts-all-day-doing-to-my-brain

.html; Henry Bodkin, "'New Golden Age' of Digital Radio Heralds Review That Could End FM," *Telegraph*, April 13, 2017, https://www.telegraph.co.uk /news/2017/04/13/new-golden-age-digital-radio-heralds-review-could-end-fm/. For just one of a whole host of articles advising readers of blogs and magazines what podcasts they should listen to while running, walking, taking public transportation, listening at home, or at work, see also Madeleine Burry, "12 Must-Listen Podcasts that Will Make You Want to Go for a Longer Walk," *Prevention*, August 4, 2017, https://www.prevention.com/fitness/odcasts-that-will-make-you-want-to-go-for-a-longer-walk.

43. For more on how podcast listening is formulated with respect to radio, see, for example, Richard Berry, "Will the iPod Kill the Radio Star? Profiling Podcasting as Radio," *Convergence* 12, no. 2 (2006): 143–62.

44. Tom Webster, VP Strategy and Marketing, Edison Research, "The Podcast Consumer 2016," Edison Research/Triton Digital, May 2016, www .edisonresearch.com/wp-content/uploads/2016/05/The-Podcast-Consumer-2016.pdf.

45. Bergman, "I Listen."

46. Francesco Casetti and Sara Sampietro, "With Eyes, with Hands: The Relocation of Cinema into the iPhone," in *Moving Data: The iPhone and the Future of Media*, ed. Pelle Snickars and Peter Vonderau (New York: Columbia University Press, 2012), 19–32.

47. See ibid., 23.

48. Casetti and Sampietro, however, articulate that this is, in fact, not so different from the traditional cinema-going environment; in the movie theater environment, also, we felt ourselves to be simultaneously publicly on view and privately engaged with a text. As they write, "When using a medium in public situations, one often surrounds oneself with invisible barriers that offer refuge, even though one continues to feel open to the gazes of others. This situation is not dissimilar from that of the traditional movie theater, in which one slips from a collective encounter to individual attention to the film." In fact, "In the first moment one confronts the surrounding public; in the second moment one enters into intimacy with what is represented on the screen." Ibid., 21.

49. Sarah Atkinson, *Beyond the Screen: Emerging Cinema and Engaging Audiences* (New York: Bloomsbury Academic, 2014), 6.

50. See their debates on the notion of the photogenic that emerged out of these contexts, collected in *French Theory and Criticism A History/Anthology, 1907–1939*, ed. Richard Abel (Princeton, NJ: Princeton University Press, 1993).

51. For more on the practice of moviegoing and the Cinémathèque Française during the period of the French New Wave, see Richard Roud, *A Passion for Cinema: Henri Langlois and the Cinémathèque Francaise* (New York: Viking Press, 1983). See also Georges Patrick Langlois and Glenn Myrent, *Henri Langlois: First Citizen of the Cinema* (New York: Prentice Hall International, 1995). For more on the screenings of the early film societies, or *cine-clubs*, see Ben Davis, "Beginnings of the Film Society Movement in the U.S.," *Film and History* 3, no. 4 (1994): 6–26. See also Scott MacDonald, *Cinema 16: Documents toward a History of the Film Society* (Philadelphia: Temple University

Press, 2003) and *Art in Cinema: Documents toward a History of the Film Society* (Philadelphia: Temple University Press, 2006).

52. See Robert Sklar, "A Passion for Films: Henri Langlois and the Cinematheque Française," *Cineaste* 14, no. 2 (1985): 52. See also Julia Lesage, "Godard and Gorin's Left Politics, 1967–1972," *Jump Cut: A Review of Contemporary Media* 28 (1983): 51–58.

53. Haidee Wasson, *Museum Movies: The Museum of Modern Art and the Birth of Cinema* (Berkeley: University of California Press, 2005).

54. Girish Shambu, "Taken Up by Waves: The Experience of New Cinephilia," Project: New Cinephilia, May 23, 2011, http://projectcinephilia.mubi.com/2011/05/23/taken-up-by-waves-the-experience-of-new-cinephilia/. For more along these lines, see Shambu, *The New Cinephilia* (Montreal: Caboose Books, 2014).

55. See Shambu, "Taken Up by Waves."

56. See ibid.

57. See ibid.

58. Susan Sontag, "The Decay of Cinema," *New York Times Magazine,* February 25, 1996, https://www.nytimes.com/books/00/03/12/specials/sontag-cinema.html.

59. See ibid.

60. See Jacques Richard, dir., *Henri Langlois: Phantom of the Cinémathèque,* DVD (New York: Kino Video, 2006).

61. See, among other sources, Wasson, *Museum Movies*; Charles Acland and Haidee Wasson, eds., *Useful Cinema* (Durham, NC: Duke University Press, 2011); Scott MacDonald, *Canyon Cinema: The Life and Times of an Independent Film Distributor* (Berkeley: University of California Press, 2008).

62. See Devin Orgeron and Marsha Orgeron, *Learning with the Lights Off: Educational Film in the United States* (New York: Oxford University Press, 2012). See also Jennifer Lynn Peterson, *Education in the School of Dreams: Travelogues and Early Nonfiction Film* (Durham, NC: Duke University Press, 2013).

63. The first commercially available transistor radio was released in November 1954 by a company named I.D.E.A. They continued to be produced, in larger numbers, throughout the 1960s and 1970s. See Michael F. Wolff, "The Secret Six-Month Project: Why Texas Instruments Decided to Put the First Transistor Radio on the Market by Christmas 1954 and How It Was Accomplished," *IEEE Spectrum,* December 1985, 64–69. See also Brian Schiffer, *The Portable Radio in American Life* (Tucson: University of Arizona Press, 1991).

64. See David L. Morton Jr., *Sound Recording: The Life Story of a Technology* (Baltimore: Johns Hopkins University Press, 2004), 169.

65. See Joseph Schloss and Bill Bahng Boyer, "Urban Echoes: The Boombox and Sonic Mobility in the 1980s," in *The Oxford Handbook of Mobile Music Studies,* vol. 1, ed. Sumanth Gopinath and Jason Stanyek (New York: Oxford University Press, 2014), 399–412.

66. For a basic introduction to the notion of "sodcasting," see Dan Hancox, "Mobile Disco: How Phones Make Music Inescapable," *Guardian,* August 12, 2010, www.theguardian.com/music/2010/aug/12/sodcasting-music-in-public-mobile-phones. See also Alex Hudson, "Why Do People Play Music in Public

through a Phone?" BBC.com, June 14, 2011, www.bbc.co.uk/news/magazine-13749313. For a scholarly take on how "sodcasting" may be seen as a site of noise as well as social conflict, see Anneli B. Haake, "Sodcasting: Music as Antisocial Behaviour?," *Music at Work* (blog), June 14, 2011, http://musicatwork .net/sodcasting-music-as-anti-social-behaviour/.

67. Wayne Marshall, "Treble Culture," in *The Oxford Handbook of Mobile Music Studies*, vol. 2, ed. Sumanth Gopinath and Jason Stanyek (New York: Oxford University Press, 2014), 45–46.

68. Ibid., 46.

69. Ibid., 46, 50.

70. See Hancox, "Mobile Disco," and Marshall, "Treble Culture," 46. *Musicking* is a term coined by ethnomusicologist Christopher Small to denote the communal making of music as being, in itself, an act of community. For more on this, see Christopher Small, *Musicking: The Meanings of Performing and Listening* (Middletown, CT: Wesleyan University Press, 2011).

71. See Hancox, "Mobile Disco"; Owen Hatherley, "In (Partial) Defence of 'Sodcasting,'" *Sit Down, Man; You're a Bloody Tragedy* (blog), February 6, 2008, http://nastybrutalistandshort.blogspot.com/2008/02/in-partial-defence-of-sodcasting.html.

72. See Shuhei Hosokawa, "The Walkman Effect," in *The Sound Studies Reader*, ed. Jonathan Sterne (New York: Routledge, 2012), 104–16.

73. Ibid., 105.

74. Ibid.

75. See Phil Patton, "Humming Off Key for Two Decades," *New York Times*, July 29, 1999, http://partners.nytimes.com/library/tech/99/07/circuits /articles/29walk.html. See also Michael Bull, *Sounding Out the City: Personal Stereos and the Management of Everyday Life* (New York: Bloomsbury Academic Press, 2000).

76. Kenneth Gergen, "The Challenge of Absent Presence," in *Perpetual Contact: Mobile Communication, Private Talk, Public Performance*, ed. James E. Katz and Mark Aakhus (Cambridge: Cambridge University Press, 2002), 227–41.

77. Rainer Schönhammer, "The Walkman and the Primary World of the Senses," *Phenomenology + Pedagogy* 7 (1989): 130, 133.

78. He writes that "absence does not mean that the world is no longer worth attention. On the contrary, the subject's disengagement sets him free to enjoy the world attentively as a colorful and rich spectacle." Ibid., 134.

79. Ibid., 136.

80. Beer, "Tune Out," 846.

81. Ibid., 848–49.

82. Hosokawa, "Walkman Effect," 115.

83. Drew Hemment, "The Mobile Effect," *Convergence: The Journal of Research into New Media Technologies* 11, no. 2 (2005): 32–40.

84. Ibid., 35.

85. Michael Bull, *Sound Moves: iPod Culture and Urban Experience* (New York: Routledge, 2008), 34. For more on listening and urban experience, see also Bull, *Sounding Out the City*.

86. Michael Bull, "No Dead Air! The iPod and the Culture of Mobile Listening," *Leisure Studies* 24, no. 4 (2005): 343. See also multiple essays in James E. Katz and Mark Aakhus, eds., *Perpetual Contact: Mobile Communication, Private Talk, Public Performance* (Cambridge: Cambridge University Press, 2002), especially Gergen's "Challenge of Absent Presence," 227–41.

87. Bull, *Sound Moves*, 345.

88. See Sterne, *Audible Past*, 24.

89. Gergen, "Challenge of Absent Presence," 235, 240.

90. Bull, "No Dead Air!," 354.

91. Beer, "Tune Out," 858.

92. Ibid., 859.

93. Gergen, "Challenge of Absent Presence," 233.

94. See Carolyn Marvin, *When Old Technologies Were New: Thinking about Electric Communication in the Late Nineteenth Century* (Oxford: Oxford University Press, 1988), and Max Dawson, "Little Players, Big Shows: Format, Narration, and Style on Television's New Smaller Screens," *Convergence* 13, no. 3 (August 2007): 231–50.

95. See Dawson, "Little Players," 240.

96. Barbara Klinger, *Beyond the Multiplex: Cinema, New Technologies, and the Home* (Berkeley: University of California Press, 2006), 7. See also Barbara Klinger, "The New Media Aristocrats: Home Theater and the Domestic Film Experience," *Velvet Light Trap* 42 (1998): 4–19.

97. See Shambu, *New Cinephilia*. See also Stephen Harrington, Tim Highfield, and Axel Bruns, "More Than a Backchannel: Twitter and Television," *Participations: Journal of Audience and Reception Studies* 10, no. 1 (May 2013): 405–9; Mark Lochrie and Paul Coulton, "Mobile Phones as Second Screen for TV, Enabling Inter-Audience Interaction," paper presented at the Proceedings of the 8th International Conference on Advances in Computer Entertainment Technology, 2011, Lisbon, Portugal; Cedric Courtois and Evelien D'heer, "Second Screen Applications and Tablet Users: Constellation, Awareness, Experience, and Interest," paper presented at the Proceedings of the 10th European Conference on Interactive TV and Video, 2012, New York. The subject is also the topic of conversation in the American popular press, including the *New York Times*. See Annie Lowrey, "Advertisers Seek a 'Second Screen' Connection with Viewers," *New York Times,* May 4, 2014, www.nytimes.com/2014/05/05/business/media/advertisers-seek-a-second-screen-connection-with-viewers.html?_r=0. See also Vindu Goel and Brian Stelter, "Social Networks in a Battle for the Second Screen," *New York Times,* October 2, 2013, www.nytimes.com/2013/10/03/technology/social-networks-in-a-battle-for-the-second-screen.html. For a video essay on the "second screen" experience, see Fritzie Andrade, Emily B. Hager, Zena Barakat, Samantha Stark, and Pedro Rafael Rosado, "The Impact of Second Screen TV Viewing," *New York Times,* January 7, 2013, www.nytimes.com/video/business/100000001990834/the-impact-of-second-screen-tv-viewing.html.

98. Beer, "Tune Out," 860.

99. William J. Mitchell, *Placing Words: Symbols, Space, and the City* (Cambridge, MA: MIT University Press, 2005), 8.

100. Max Dawson, review of *Beyond the Multiplex: Cinema, New Technologies, and the Home*, by Barbara Klinger, *Technology and Culture* 48, no. 2 (2007): 436–38.

101. Klinger, *Beyond the Multiplex*, 3.

102. See, for example, "David Lynch for iPhone," *Funny or Die*, February 19, 2008, www.funnyordie.com/videos/5fcae148b7/david-lynch-for-iphone-from-that-happened.

103. David Lynch, "Waxing Lyrical: David Lynch on His New Passion—and Why He May Never Make Another Movie," interview by Tim Walker, *Independent*, June 23, 2013, https://www.independent.co.uk/arts-entertainment/music/features/waxing-lyrical-david-lynch-on-his-new-passion-and-why-he-may-never-make-another-movie-8665457.html.

104. See Nick Douglas, "David Lynch Hates Your iPhone," *Gawker.com*, January 4, 2008, comments section, http://gawker.com/340930/david-lynch-hates-your-iphone.

105. Ibid.

106. See Roland Barthes, "The Death of the Author," in *Image-Music-Text* (New York: Macmillan, 1978), 142–48. For more on the power of readers /users, see also Michel de Certeau, *The Practice of Everyday Life* (Berkeley: University of California Press, 2011).

107. David Lynch's personal high investment in film sound may go a long way to explaining his particular dissatisfaction with viewers experiencing film texts in this manner. See, for example, his thoughts on sound design in David Lynch, *Catching the Big Fish* (New York: Penguin, 2016).

108. Dolby Corporation, "Smart Phones with Dolby Audio," Dolby.com, n.d., accessed January 5, 2015, www.dolby.com/us/en/categories/smartphone .html.

109. As of 2016, Dolby Atmos is oriented toward four markets: the cinema theater market, the music venue market, the home market, and the mobile market. See "Dolby on Mobile Devices," n.d., accessed March 18, 2018, https://www.dolby.com/us/en/mobile/index.html, for more on the mobile listening experience as it is conceived by Dolby.

110. This innovation harks back to similar priorities among sound engineers for the elucidation of the dialogue track in the mix of the early talkies.

111. Dolby Corporation, "Smart Phones."

112. Several studies are beginning to address this, at least in part, but much more work needs to be done. A Korean study published in 2014 notices the dearth of material (either scholarly or popular) on whether, and how much, users *like* watching on their smartphones. Kim, Park, and Yang conclude from their study of 160 smartphone media users that there is, among users in Korea, a notably high level of satisfaction. The content that users viewed took a significant backseat to these other factors in determining the user's satisfaction, according to Kim, Park, and Yang's data. Along all of the axes tested by the survey—these being instant connectivity, personalization, and personal convenience—users rated their mobile phone streaming experience of films very highly. A smartphone user survey conducted by the Korea Internet Agency and the Korea Communications Commission revealed that 43.7 percent of all Koreans use their

smartphones more than their televisions and "mostly watch video and VOD via smart phones." For this reason, they write, "it is necessary to examine the users who watch movies via smart phones." See Hyungjoon Kim, Seongwon Park, and Hyelin Yang, "A Study on Satisfaction of Movie Viewers Watching Movies on Smartphones," *Advanced Society and Technology Letters* 67 (2014): 78.

113. Yue is Assistant Professor of Culture and Media at the New School, in addition to being a participant in Project: New Cinephilia. See Genevieve Yue, "Cinephilia, Love, and Being Caught Off-Guard," Project: New Cinephilia Online Roundtable Two, August 6, 2011, http://projectcinephilia.mubi.com /category/online-roundtable-2/. For the entire discussion, see the collection of posts for "Online Roundtable Two," at http://projectcinephilia.mubi.com /category/online-roundtable-2/.

114. Yue, "Cinephilia." For an earlier and more comprehensive assertion of this conception, see Charles Musser, "Toward a History of Screen Practice," *Quarterly Review of Film Studies* 9, no. 1 (1984): 59–69, and Musser, *The Emergence of Cinema: The American Screen to 1907* (Berkeley: University of California Press, 1994).

115. See Richard Linklater, dir., *Before Sunset*, DVD (Los Angeles: Warner Independent Pictures, 2004). See also Charles Laughton, dir., *The Night of the Hunter* (Los Angeles: United Artists, 1955).

116. Christian Keathley, *Cinephilia and History, or the Wind in the Trees* (Bloomington: Indiana University Press, 2005), 31, 33.

117. Respondent to my *Static in the System* Mobile Listening Survey, 2018.

118. Samuel Clawson-Simons, "Re: Hello, Students!" Facebook, April 10, 2015, https://www.facebook.com/meredith.c.ward.

119. Douglas Ross, "Re: Hello, Students!" Facebook, April 10, 2015, https:// www.facebook.com/meredith.c.ward.

CONCLUSION

1. See Ed Key, *Proteus*, created by Ed Key and David Kanaga (Asheville, NC: Curve Studios, 2013), video game for the Sony Playstation 3.

2. In making these assertions, I am touching only very briefly on an area of research that is well established and lies outside the boundaries of this work. I do so in hopes of pointing out how an aural culture perspective would be a welcome addition to the ongoing dialogue on our changing modes of media consumption with digital technologies. Two schools of research already address this rather well, however. These are from the perspective of aural culture studies and of media studies. For some sense of the debates from the side of aural culture, see Jonathan Sterne, *MP3: The Meaning of a Format* (Durham, NC: Duke University Press, 2012) and Bull, *Sound Moves*. For vital information on the television age and its role in the domestic sphere, see the essential work of Lynn Spigel, particularly *Make Room for TV: Television and the Family Ideal in Postwar America* (Chicago: University of Chicago Press, 1992), "Yesterday's Future, Tomorrow's Home," *Emergences: Journal for the Study of Media and Composite Cultures* 11, no. 1 (May 2001): 29–49, "Designing the Smart House: Posthuman Domesticity and Conspicuous Production," *European Journal of Cultural*

Studies 8, no. 4 (November 2005): 403–26, and more recently "Object Lessons for the Media Home: From Storagewall to Invisible Design," *Public Culture* 24, no. 3 (2012): 535–76. For necessary history on the shift to the home theater, see Klinger, *Beyond the Multiplex*. For much more current discussions of streaming media's effect on our modes of engagement with both the visual and the sonic, see the many works of Max Dawson, including "Little Players"; "Home Video and the 'TV Problem': Cultural Critics and Technological Change," *Technology and Culture: The International Quarterly of the Society for the History of Technology* 48, no. 3 (July 2007): 524–49; "Defining Mobile Television: The Social Construction and Deconstruction of Old and New Media," *Popular Communication: The International Journal of Media and Culture* 10, no. 4 (October 2012): 253–68; and "Rationalizing Television in the USA: Neoliberalism, the Attention Economy and the Digital Video Recorder," *Screen* 55, no. 2 (Summer 2014): 221–37.

3. See, for example, the work of Bull and Sterne, as well as Mark Katz, *Capturing Sound: How Technology Has Changed Music* (Berkeley: University of California Press, 2010). See also David Beer, "Mobile Music, Coded Objects and Everyday Spaces," *Mobilities* 5, no. 4 (2010): 469–84, and Andrew Scott and Ian Woodward, "Living with Design Objects: A Qualitative Study of iPod Relationships," *Design Principles and Practice: An International Journal* 5, no. 6 (2011): 499–508.

References

Abel, Richard, ed. *French Theory and Criticism: A History/Anthology, 1907–1939*. Princeton, NJ: Princeton University Press, 1993.

Abel, Richard, and Rick Altman, eds. *The Sounds of Early Cinema*. Bloomington: Indiana University Press, 2001.

Abramovich, Giselle. "Move Over, Tablet—Smartphone Is Now No. 1 Mobile-Video Viewing Device: ADI." CMO.com, December 11, 2015. www.cmo.com /adobe-digital-insights/articles/2015/12/4/adi-q3-2015-digital-video-report .html#gs.TUizZgQ.

Academy of Motion Picture Arts and Sciences. *Motion Picture Sound Engineering*. New York: D. Van Nostrand, 1938.

———. "Science and Technology Committee." AMPAS website, n.d., accessed June 10, 2014. www.oscars.org/science-technology/council/.

Acland, Charles, and Haideee Wasson, eds. *Useful Cinema*. Durham, NC: Duke University Press, 2011.

Adorno, Theodor. *In Search of Wagner*. Translated by Rodney Livingstone. London: Verso Press, 1981.

Agnew, David H. *Theatrical Amusements*. Philadelphia, 1857.

Allen, Robert C. "Manhattan Myopia; or Oh! Iowa! Robert C. Allen on Ben Singer's 'Manhattan Nickelodeons: New Data on Audiences and Exhibitors.'" *Cinema Journal* 34, no. 3 (Spring 1996): 75–103.

Altman, Rick. "The Material Heterogeneity of Recorded Sound." In Altman, *Sound Theory/Sound Practice*, 15–34.

———. *Silent Film Sound*. New York: Columbia University Press, 2004.

———. "The Sound Space." In Altman, *Sound Theory/Sound Practice*, 46–64.

———, ed. *Sound Theory/Sound Practice*. New York: Routledge, 1992.

Ameri, Amir. "Imaginary Placements: The Other Space of Cinema." *Journal of Aesthetics and Art Criticism* 69, no. 1 (Winter 2011): 81–91.

Anderson, Tim. "Reforming 'Jackass Music': The Problematic Aesthetics of Early American Film Music Accompaniment." *Cinema Journal,* 37, no. 1 (Autumn 1997): 3–22.

Andrade, Fritzie, Emily B. Hager, Zena Barakat, Samantha Stark, and Pedro Rafael Rosado. "The Impact of Second Screen TV Viewing." *New York Times,* January 7, 2013. www.nytimes.com/video/business/100000001990834 /the-impact-of-second-screen-tv-viewing.html.

Archer, Melanie, and Judith R. Blau. "Class Formation in Nineteenth-Century America: The Case of the Middle Class." *Annual Review of Sociology* 19 (1993): 17–41.

Arnold, Matthew. *Culture and Anarchy.* 1869. Reprint, Oxford: Oxford University Press, 2009.

Aronson, Arnold. "Theatres of the Future." *Theater Journal* 33, no. 4 (December 1981): 489–503.

"At Coney Island." *Moving Picture World* 8, no. 27 (July 8, 1911): 1571.

Atkinson, Sarah. *Beyond the Screen: Emerging Cinema and Engaging Audiences.* New York: Bloomsbury Academic, 2014.

Attali, Jacques. *Noise: The Political Economy of Music.* Minneapolis: University of Minnesota Press, 1985.

B., Hazel. "Music for the Picture." Letter to Clarence E. Sinn, the "Cue Music Man." *Moving Picture World* 8, no. 7 (February 18, 1911): 353.

Balazs, Bela. *Theory of the Film: Character and Growth of a New Art.* Translated by Edith Bone. London: Dennis Dobson, 1952.

Bank, Rosemarie K. *Theatre Culture in America, 1825–1860.* Cambridge: Cambridge University Press, 1997.

Barbas, Samantha. "The Political Spectator: Censorship, Protest and the Moviegoing Experience, 1912–1922." *Film History* 11, no. 2 (1999): 217–29.

Barlow, Anthony D. "Lighting Control and Concepts of Theatre Activity." *Educational Theatre Journal* 25, no. 2 (May 1973): 135–46.

Baron, Lawrence. "Noise and Degeneration: Theodor Lessing's Crusade for Quiet." *Journal of Contemporary History* 17, no. 1 (January 1982): 165–78.

Barron, Michael. *Auditorium Acoustics and Architectural Design.* New York: Spon Press, 2009.

Barthes, Roland. "The Death of the Author." In *Image-Music-Text,* edited by Stephen Heath, 142–48. New York: Macmillan, 1978.

———. "Upon Leaving the Movie Theater." In *The Rustle of Language,* trans. Richard Howard, 345–49. New York: Hill and Wang, 1986.

Baudry, Jean-Louis. "The Apparatus: Metapsychological Approaches to the Impression of Reality in Cinema." In Rosen, *Narrative, Apparatus, Ideology,* 299–318.

———. "Ideological Effects of the Basic Cinema Apparatus." In Rosen, *Narrative, Apparatus, Ideology,* 286–98.

Beck, Jay Shields. *A Quiet Revolution: Changes in American Film Sound Practices, 1967–1979.* Iowa City: University of Iowa Press, 2003.

———. "The Sounds of 'Silence': Dolby Stereo, Sound Design, and *The Silence of the Lambs.*" In Beck and Grajeda, *Lowering the Boom,* 68–85.

Beck, Jay Shields, and Tony Grajeda, eds. *Lowering the Boom: Critical Studies in Film Sound*. Urbana: University of Illinois Press, 2008.
Beer, David. "Mobile Music, Coded Objects and Everyday Spaces." *Mobilities* 5, no. 4 (2010): 469–84.
———. "Tune Out: Music, Soundscapes and the Urban Mise-en-Scene." *Information, Communication and Society* 10, no. 6 (2007): 846–66.
Belam, Martin. "The Second Screen Experience: Mobiles, Tablets, and TVs." Guardian.com, *Media Network Blog*, September 10, 2012. www.theguardian.com/media-network/media-network-blog/2012/sep/10/second-screen-experience-mobile-tablet-tv.
Bellour, Raymond. "The Cinema Spectator: A Special Memory." In *Audiences: Defining and Researching Screen Entertainment Reception,* edited by Ian Christie, 206–18. Amsterdam: Amsterdam University Press, 2012.
Belton, John. *Widescreen Cinema*. Cambridge, MA: Harvard University Press, 1992.
Benjamin, Walter. "The Work of Art in the Age of Its Technological Reproducibility (Second Version)." In *Critical Visions in Film Theory,* edited by Timothy Corrigan, Patricia White, and Meta Mazaj, 229–51. New York: Bedford /St. Martins, 2011.
Beranek, Leo. "Analysis of Sabine and Eyring Equations and Their Application to Concert Hall Audience and Chair Absorption." *Journal of the Acoustical Society of America* 120, no. 3 (2006): 1399–1410.
———. "Concert Hall Acoustics." *Journal of the Audio Engineering Society* 64, no. 7 (2008): 1–39.
———. *Concert Halls and Opera Houses: Music, Acoustics, and Architecture.* New York: Springer Science and Business Media, 2012.
Bergman, Sirena. "I Listen to 35 Hours of Podcasts Every Week. Is That . . . Bad?" *Cut,* October 27, 2017. https://www.thecut.com/2017/10/what-is-listening-to-podcasts-all-day-doing-to-my-brain.html.
Berry, Richard. "A Golden Age of Podcasting? Evaluating *Serial* in the Context of Podcast Histories." *Journal of Radio and Audio Media* 22, no. 2 (2015): 170–78.
———. "Will the iPod Kill the Radio Star? Profiling Podcasting as Radio." *Convergence* 12, no. 2 (2006): 143–62.
Bijsterveld, Karin. "The Diabolical Symphony of the Mechanical Age: Technology and Symbolism of Sound in European and North American Noise Abatement Campaigns, 1900–40." *Social Studies of Science* 31, no. 1 (February 2001): 37–70.
———. *Mechanical Sound: Technology, Culture, and the Public Problems of Noise in the Twentieth Century.* Cambridge, MA: MIT Press, 2008.
Bisch, Louis E. "Are We Morons? The Scientific Answer to Those Who Belittle the Intelligence of Movie Audiences." *Photoplay Magazine,* February 1929, 50–51.
———. "How the Screen Hypnotizes You: The Doctor Explains Why the Movies Exert an Uncanny Influence on Audiences." *Photoplay Magazine* 33, no. 3 (February 1928): 40–41.

Bledstein, Burton J. *The Culture of Professionalism: The Middle Class and the Development of Higher Education in America.* New York: Norton, 1976.

Blumin, Stuart. *The Emergence of the Middle Class: Social Experience in the American City, 1760–1900.* New York: Cambridge University Press, 1989.

Bodkin, Henry. "'New Golden Age' of Digital Radio Heralds Review That Could End FM." *Telegraph,* April 13, 2017. https://www.telegraph.co.uk/news/2017/04/13/new-golden-age-digital-radio-heralds-review-could-end-fm/.

Bolton, Thaddeus. "Rhythm." *American Journal of Psychology* 6, no. 2 (January 1894): 145–238.

Bonitzer, Pascal. "The Silences of the Voice." In Rosen, *Narrative, Apparatus, Ideology,* 319–34.

Bordwell, David. *Narration in the Fiction Film.* Madison: University of Wisconsin Press, 1985.

Bottomore, Stephen. "The Story of Percy Peashaker: Debates about Sound Effects in the Early Cinema." In Abel and Altman, *Sounds of Early Cinema,* 134–42.

Bowman, Ned A. "Investing a Theatrical Ideal: Wagner's Bayreuth *Festspielhaus.*" *Educational Theatre Journal* 18, no. 4 (December 1966): 429–38.

Branscomb, Lewis M., and Paul C. Gilmore. "Education in Private Industry." *Daedalus* 104, no. 1 (Winter 1975): 222–23.

Browne, Nick. "The Spectator-in-the-Text: The Rhetoric of *Stagecoach.*" In Rosen, *Narrative, Apparatus, Ideology,* 102–19.

Buckley, Peter George. "To the Opera House: Culture and Society in New York City, 1920–1860." PhD diss., State University of New York at Stony Brook, 1984.

Bull, Michael. "No Dead Air! The iPod and the Culture of Mobile Listening." *Leisure Studies* 24, no. 4 (2005): 343–55.

———. *Sounding Out the City: Personal Stereos and the Management of Everyday Life.* New York: Bloomsbury Academic Press, 2000.

———. *Sound Moves: iPod Culture and Urban Experience.* New York: Routledge, 2008.

Burry, Madeleine. "12 Must-Listen Podcasts That Will Make You Want to Go for a Longer Walk." *Prevention,* August 4, 2017. https://www.prevention.com/fitness/podcasts-that-will-make-you-want-to-go-for-a-longer-walk.

Bush, W. Stephen. "Facing an Audience." *Moving Picture World* 9, no. 10 (September 16, 1911): 771.

———. "The Human Voice as a Factor in the Moving Picture Show." *Moving Picture World* 4 (January 23, 1909): 446–47.

Bushey, Ryan. "The 11 Best Streaming Apps to Turn Your Tablet and Smartphone into a TV." *Business Insider,* December 4, 2013. https://www.businessinsider.com/best-streaming-apps-2013-12.

Butsch, Richard. *The Making of American Audiences: From Stage to Television, 1750–1990.* Cambridge: Cambridge University Press, 2000.

Carbine, Mary. "The Finest outside the Loop: Motion Picture Exhibition in Chicago's Black Metropolis, 1905–1928." *Camera Obscura* 23 (May 1990): 8–41.

Cardiff, Janet. Interview by Atom Egoyan. *Bomb* 79 (Spring 2002): 60–67.

——. "Spatial Articulation of Sounds and Voices." Video interview transcript. *Meet the Artist*. National Gallery of Canada. N.d. www.cybermuse.gallery.ca/showcases/meet/artist. Accessed February 10, 2012. No longer available online.

Cardiff, Janet, and George Bures-Miller. "*Paradise Institute*: 2001." N.d., accessed February 10, 2012.www.cardiffmiller.com/artworks/inst/paradise_institute.html.

Carlson, Marvin. *Places of Performance: The Semiotics of Theatre Architecture*. Ithaca, NY: Cornell University Press, 1989.

——. *Theatre Semiotics: Signs of Life*. Bloomington: Indiana University Press, 1990.

Carroll, Tim. "3D: The Audio Part." *IBE: International Broadcast Engineer*, July/August 2012, 12–13.

Carson, Ann. *Glass, Irony and God*. New York: New Directions, 1995.

Carter, Stephen. *Civility, Manners, Morals, and the Etiquette of Democracy*. New York: Basic Books, 1998.

Case, Judd A. "Logistical Media: Fragments from Radar's Prehistory." *Canadian Journal of Communication* 38, no. 3 (2013): 379–95.

Casetti, Francesco, and Sara Sampietro. "With Eyes, with Hands: The Relocation of Cinema into the iPhone." In *Moving Data: The iPhone and the Future of Media*, edited by Pelle Snickars and Peter Vonderau, 19–32. New York: Columbia University Press, 2012.

Cavanaugh, William J., and Joseph A. Wilkes. *Architectural Acoustics: Principles and Practice*. New York: John Wiley and Sons, 1999.

Cawelti, Andrea. "The Stage as a Well-Designed House: Frederick Kiesler's Ideal Theatre." *Biblion* 3, no. 1 (Fall 1994): 111–39.

Chateauvert, Jean, and Andre Gaudreault. "The Noises of Spectators, or the Spectator as Additive to the Spectacle." In Abel and Altman, *Sounds of Early Cinema*, 183–92.

"Chicago Houses in Review: Harmony Theater." *Moving Picture World* 8, no. 22 (June 3, 1911): 1248.

Child, Ben. "North American Cinema Attendance Drops to Lowest Level in Two Decades." *Guardian*, January 2, 2015. www.theguardian.com/film/2015/jan/02/north-american-box-office-takings-drop.

Chion, Michel. *Audio-vision: Son et image au cinema*. Paris: Armand Colin, 2013.

——. "The Silence of the Loudspeakers, or Why with Dolby Sound It Is the Film That Listens to Us." In *Soundscape: The School of Sound Lectures, 1998–2001*, edited by Larry Sider and Diane Freeman, 150–54. London: Wallflower Press, 2003.

——. "Wasted Words." In Altman, *Sound Theory/Sound Practice*, 104–13.

Clark, L.E. "The Nature of Sound." In *Motion Picture Sound Engineering*, 81–87. New York: D. Van Nostrand, 1938.

Cohen, Leon. "The History of Noise (on the 100th Anniversary of Its Birth)." *IEEE Signal Processing Magazine*, November 2005, 85–129.

Collier, John. "Cheap Amusements." *Charities and the Commons* 20 (April 1908): 73–78.

Comolli, Jean-Louis. "Machines of the Visible." In *The Cinematographic Apparatus,* edited by Teresa de Lauretis and Stephen Heath, 121–50. New York: St. Martin's Press, 1980.

———. "Technique and Ideology: Camera, Perspective, Depth of Field (Parts 3 and 4)." In Rosen, *Narrative, Apparatus, Ideology,* 421–43.

Corbella, Maurizio, and Anna Katharin Windisch. "Sound Synthesis, Representation and Narrative Cinema in the Transition to Sound." *Cinemas* 24, no. 1 (Fall 2013): 59–81.

Cossar, Harper. *Letterboxed: The Evolution of Widescreen Cinema.* Lexington: University of Kentucky Press, 2010.

Courtois, Cedric, and Evelien D'heer. "Second Screen Applications and Tablet Users: Constellation, Awareness, Experience, and Interest." Paper presented at the Proceedings of the 10th European Conference on Interactive TV and Video, New York, NY, 2012.

Cowan, Lester, ed. *Recording Sound for Motion Pictures.* AMPAS. New York: McGraw-Hill, 1931.

Coyle, Jack. "With Digital Forces at the Gate, a Down Year for Hollywood," *Advocate,* January 8, 2015. http://theadvocate.com/entertainment/red/11222195-31 /with-digital-forces-at-the.

Crafton, Donald. *The Talkies: American Cinema's Transition to Sound, 1926–1931.* Berkeley: University of California Press, 1997.

Crary, Jonathan. *Suspensions of Perception: Attention, Spectacle, and Modern Culture.* Cambridge, MA: MIT Press, 2001.

———. *Techniques of the Observer: On Vision and Modernity in the Nineteenth Century.* Cambridge, MA: MIT Press, 1990.

Curtin, Michael. *Propriety and Position: A Study of Victorian Manners.* New York: Garland, 1987.

Curtis, Scott. "The Taste of a Nation: Training the Senses and Sensibility of Cinema Audiences in Imperial Germany." *Film History* 6, no. 4 (1994): 445–69.

Davis, Ben. "Beginnings of the Film Society Movement in the U.S." *Film and History* 3, no. 4 (1994): 6–26.

Davis, Nicola. "Whisper It—Greek Theatre's Legendary Acoustics Are a Myth." *Guardian,* October 16, 2018. https://www.theguardian.com/science/2017 /oct/16/whisper-it-greek-amphiteatre-legendary-acoustics-myth-epidaurus.

Davis, Susan G. *Parades and Power: Street Theatre in Nineteenth-Century Philadelphia.* Berkeley: University of California Press, 1986.

Dawson, Max. "Defining Mobile Television: The Social Construction and Deconstruction of Old and New Media." *Popular Communication: The International Journal of Media and Culture* 10, no. 4 (October 2012): 253–68.

———. "Home Video and the 'TV Problem': Cultural Critics and Technological Change." *Technology and Culture: The International Quarterly of the Society for the History of Technology* 48, no. 3 (July 2007): 524–49.

———. "Little Players, Big Shows: Format, Narration, and Style on Television's New Smaller Screens." *Convergence: The Journal of Research into New Media Technologies* 13, no. 3 (August 2007): 231–50.

———. "Rationalizing Television in the USA: Neoliberalism, the Attention Economy and the Digital Video Recorder." *Screen* 55, no. 2 (Summer 2014): 221–37.

———. Review of *Beyond the Multiplex: Cinema, New Technologies, and the Home*, by Barbara Klinger. *Technology and Culture* 48, no. 2 (2007): 436–38.

de Certeau, Michel. *The Practice of Everyday Life*. Berkeley: University of California Press, 2011.

Decherney, Peter. *Hollywood and the Culture Elite: How the Movies Became American*. New York: Columbia University Press, 2006.

Demers, Joanna. *Listening through the Noise: The Aesthetics of Experimental Electronic Music*. New York: Oxford University Press, 2010.

Despard, Mathilda. "Music in New York Thirty Years Ago." *Harper's New Monthly Magazine*, June 1878, 102.

de Valcourt, Robert. *The Illustrated Manners Book: A Manual of Good Behavior and Polite Accomplishments*. New York: Leland Clay, 1855.

de Vries, Marc. "The History of Industrial Research Laboratories as a Resource for Teaching about Science-Technology Relationships." *Research in Science Education* 31 (2001): 15–28.

"The Digital Age: Young Adults Gravitate toward Digital Devices." Nielsen. com, October 10, 2016. www.nielsen.com/us/en/insights/news/2016/the-digital-age-young-adults-gravitate-toward-digital-devices.html.

Dixon, Colin. "Millennial Migration to Online Video to Accelerate in 2017." Nscreenmedia.com, December 20, 2016. www.nscreenmedia.com/millennial-online-video-usage-accelerate-2017/.

Doane, Mary Ann. "The Voice in the Cinema: The Articulation of Body and Space." In Rosen, *Narrative, Apparatus, Ideology*, 335–48.

———. "'When the Direction of the Force Acting on the Body Is Changed': The Moving Image." *Wide Angle* 7, no. 1 (1985): 44.

"Dolby Bows Revolutionary New Platform." *Mix* 36, no. 5 (May 2012): 8.

Dolby Corporation. "Smart Phones with Dolby Audio," Dolby.com, n.d., accessed January 5, 2015. www.dolby.com/us/en/categories/smartphone.html.

Dorfel, Gunter, and Dieter Hoffman. "From Albert Einstein to Norbert Weiner: Early Views and Insights on the Phenomenon of Electronic Noise." Preprint 301. Berlin: Max Planck Institute for the History of Science, 2005.

Douchet, Jean. *The French New Wave*. New York: Distributed Art Publishers, 1999.

Douglas, Mary. *Natural Symbols: Explorations in Cosmology*. New York: Random House, 1973.

———. *Purity and Danger: An Analysis of the Concepts of Pollution and Taboo*. Vol. 2 of *Collected Works*. New York: Routledge, 1966.

Douglas, Nick. "David Lynch Hates Your iPhone." Comments section, *Gawker. com*, January 4, 2008. http://gawker.com/340930/david-lynch-hates-your-iphone.

Downes, Stephen. "Musical Pleasures and Amorous Passions: Stendhal, the Crystallization Process, and Listening to Rossini and Beethoven." *19th Century Music* 26, no. 3 (Spring 2003): 235–57.

Dreher, Carl. Foreword to *Recording Sound for Motion Pictures*, edited by Lester Cowan, xiii–xvii. New York: McGraw-Hill, 1931.

Dyson, Tony. "Shot Noise." Physics lecture, University of California, Davis. N.d., accessed December 30, 2013. http://123.physics.ucdavis.edu/shot_files/ShotNoise.pdf.

Eichold, Alice. "Frederick Kiesler: Curved Objects of Desire." London: *Designweek*, November 24, 1989.

Elias, Norbert. *The History of Manners*. Vol. 1 of *The Civilizing Process*. New York: Pantheon, 1982.

Erlmann, Veit. *Reason and Resonance: A History of Modern Aurality*. Cambridge, MA: Zone Books, 2010.

Etiquette for Ladies. Philadelphia: Lea and Blanchard, 1841.

"Exhibitors Sound Off on Dolby Atmos." *Film Journal International* 116, no. 5 (May 2013): 66–68.

Eyring, Carl F. "Reverberation Time in 'Dead' Rooms." *Journal of the Acoustical Society of America* 1, no. 2 (1930): 168.

Fagen, M.D., ed. *A History of Science and Engineering in the Bell System: The Early Years, 1875–1925*. New York: Bell Telephone Laboratories, 1975.

Fiedler, Konrad. *On Judging Works of Visual Art*. Translated by Henry Schaefer-Simmern. 1876. Reprint, Berkeley: University of California Press, 1949.

Fitch, Walter M. "The Motion Picture Story Considered as a New Literary Form." *Moving Picture World* 6, no. 7 (February 19, 1910).

Fleming, N. "Acoustics in the Motion Picture Theatre and Studio." *Journal of the British Kinematograph Society* 6, no. 2 (April 1943): 48–62.

Foster, George. *New York by Gas-Light and Other Urban Sketches*. Edited by Stuart M. Blumin. Berkeley: University of California Press, 1990.

Foster, Gwendolyn Audrey. *Troping the Body: Gender, Etiquette, and Performance*. Carbondale: Southern Illinois University Press, 2000.

Foster, Thomas A. "John Adams and the Choice of Hercules: Manliness and Sexual Virtue in Eighteenth-Century British America." In *New Men: Manliness in Early America*, edited by Thomas A. Foster, 217–35. New York: New York University Press, 2011.

Fried, Michael. *Absorption and Theatricality: Painting and Beholder in the Age of Diderot*. Berkeley: University of California Press, 1980.

Fuchs, Andreas. "Brave New Worlds." *Film Journal International* 115, no. 9 (September 2012): 60–64.

———. "Soundsational!" *Film Journal International* 115, no. 5 (May 2012): 66.

Funny or Die. "David Lynch for iPhone." *Funny or Die*, February 19, 2008. www.funnyordie.com/videos/5fcae148b7/david-lynch-for-iphone-from-that-happened.

Gay, Peter. *The Naked Heart: The Bourgeois Experience*. Vol. 4. *Victoria to Freud*. New York: Norton, 1996.

Gergen, Kenneth. "The Challenge of Absent Presence." In *Perpetual Contact: Mobile Communication, Private Talk, Public Performance*, edited by James E. Katz and Mark Aakhus, 227–41. Cambridge: Cambridge University Press, 2002.

Giardina, Carolyn. "Dolby Breaks a Sound Barrier." *Hollywood Reporter*, July 20, 2012, 58.

Gilfoyle, Timothy J. "City of Eros: New York City, Prostitution, and the Commercialization of Sex, 1790–1920." PhD diss., University of California, Berkeley, 2006.

Gilkey, Robert, and Timothy R. Anderson, eds. *Binaural and Spatial Hearing in Real and Virtual Environments*. New York: Psychology Press, 2014.

Goehr, Lydia. "Schopenhauer and the Musicians: An Inquiry into the Sounds of Silence and the Limits of Philosophizing about Music." In *Schopenhauer, Philosophy, and the Arts*, edited by Dale Jacquette, 200–228. Cambridge: Cambridge University Press, 1996.

Goel, Vindu, and Brian Stelter. "Social Networks in a Battle for the Second Screen," *New York Times*, October 2, 2013. www.nytimes.com/2013/10/03/technology/social-networks-in-a-battle-for-the-second-screen.html.

Goffman, Erving. "Embarrassment and Social Organization." In *Interaction Ritual: Essays in Face-to-Face Behavior*, 97–112. Garden City, NY: Doubleday/Anchor Books, 1967.

Gomery, Douglas. *The Coming of Sound: A History*. New York: Psychology Press, 2005.

Goodman, Steve. *Sonic Warfare: Sound, Affect, and the Ecology of Fear*. Cambridge, MA: MIT Press, 2010.

Gorky, Maxim. "Fleeting Notes." In *Kino: A History of the Russian and Soviet Film*, 3rd ed., edited by Jay Leyda, 407–8. Princeton, NJ: Princeton University Press, 1983. Originally published in *Nizhny Novgorod Newsletter*, July 7, 1896.

Grieveson, Lee. *Policing Cinema: Movies and Censorship in Early Twentieth-Century America*. Berkeley: University of California Press, 2004.

Gross, Edward, and Gregory P. Stone. "Embarrassment and the Analysis of Role Requirements." *American Journal of Sociology* 70 (July 1964): 1–15.

Gunning, Tom. "The Cinema of Attractions: Early Film, Its Spectator and the Avant-Garde." In *Early Cinema: Space, Frame, Narrative*, edited by Thomas Elsaesser and Adam Barker, 52–62. London: British Film Institute, 1990.

Guzzy, Marina. "The Sound of Life: What Is a Soundscape?" *Smithsonian Center for Folklife and Cultural Heritage Magazine*, May 4, 2017. https://folklife.si.edu/talkstory/the-sound-of-life-what-is-a-soundscape.

Haake, Anneli B. "Sodcasting: Music as Anti-social Behaviour?" *Music at Work* (blog), June 14, 2011. http://musicatwork.net/sodcasting-music-as-anti-social-behaviour/.

Haandrikman, Hendrik. "5 Reasons Mobile Video Streaming Will Rule 2017." Knect365.com, January 6, 2017. https://knect365.com/media-networks/article/1567b64d-7643-45c5-804d-b0e363cc7359/5-reasons-mobile-video-streaming-will-rule-2017.

Hall, Sheldon, and Stephen Neale. *Epics, Spectacles, and Blockbusters: A Hollywood History*. Detroit, MI: Wayne State University Press, 2010.

Hall-Witt, Jennifer. "The Re-fashioning of Fashionable Society: Opera-Going and Sociability in England, 1821–61." PhD diss., Yale University, 1996.

Halttunen, Karen. *Confidence Men and Painted Women: A Study of Middle-Class Culture in America, 1830–1870.* New Haven, CT: Yale University Press, 1982.

Hamilton, Thomas. *Men and Manners in America.* 1833. Reprint, New York: Russell and Russell, 1968.

Hancox, Dan. "Mobile Disco: How Phones Make Music Inescapable." *Guardian*, August 12, 2010. www.theguardian.com/music/2010/aug/12/sodcasting-music-in-public-mobile-phones.

Hansen, Miriam. *Babel and Babylon: Spectatorship in American Silent Film.* Cambridge, MA: Harvard University Press, 1991.

Harries, Kärsten. *The Ethical Function of Architecture.* Cambridge, MA: MIT Press, 1998.

Harrington, Stephen, Tim Highfield, and Axel Bruns. "More Than a Backchannel: Twitter and Television." *Participations: Journal of Audience and Reception Studies* 10, no. 1 (May 2013): 405–9.

Harrison, Louis Reeves. "Jackass Music." With sketches by H. F. Hoffman. *Moving Picture World* 8, no. 3 (January 21, 1911): 125.

———. "Managerial Stupidity." *Moving Picture World*, December 1910.

Hart, Rollin Lynde. *The People at Play.* Boston: Houghton Mifflin, 1909.

Hartley, Florence. *The Ladies' Book of Etiquette and Manual of Politeness: A Complete Handbook for the Use of the Lady in Polite Society.* Boston: G. W. Cottrell, 1860.

Hatherley, Owen. "In (Partial) Defence of 'Sodcasting.'" *Sit Down, Man; You're a Bloody Tragedy* (blog), February 6, 2008. http://nastybrutalistandshort.blogspot.com/2008/02/in-partial-defence-of-sodcasting.html.

Hatton, Joseph. "American Audiences and Actors." *Theatre* 3 (May 1881): 257.

Heath, Stephen. "Narrative Space." In Rosen, *Narrative, Apparatus, Ideology,* 379–420.

Hegarty, Paul. *Noise/Music: A History.* New York: Bloomsbury Academic, 2007.

Held, Roger L. *Endless Innovations: Frederick Kiesler's Theory and Scenic Design.* Ann Arbor, MI: UMI Research Press, 1982.

Helmholtz, Hermann von. *On the Sensations of Tone as a Physiological Basis for a Theory of Music.* London: Longmans Green, 1885.

Hemment, Drew. "The Mobile Effect." *Convergence: The Journal of Research into New Media Technologies* 11, no. 2 (2005): 32–40.

Hillier, Jim, ed. *Cahiers du Cinema: The 1950s.* Cambridge, MA: Harvard University Press, 1985.

———, ed. *Cahiers du Cinema: The 1960s.* Cambridge, MA: Harvard University Press, 1992.

Hilmes, Michele. "Review: Is There a Field Called Sound Culture Studies? And Does It Matter?" *American Quarterly* 57, no. 1 (2005): 249–59.

Hosokawa, Shuhei. "The Walkman Effect." In *The Sound Studies Reader,* edited by Jonathan Sterne, 104–16. New York: Routledge, 2012. Originally published in *Popular Music* 4 (1984): 165–80.

Hudson, Alex. "Why Do People Play Music in Public through a Phone?" BBC.com, June 14, 2011. www.bbc.co.uk/news/magazine-13749313.

Huyssen, Andreas. *After the Great Divide: Modernism, Mass Culture, Postmodernism.* Bloomington: Indiana University Press, 1986.

Ingram, Matthew. "The Smartphone Is Eating the Television, Nielsen Admits." *Fortune,* December 7, 2015. http://fortune.com/2015/12/07/smartphone-tv-report/.

Irving, Washington. *Letters of Jonathan Oldstyle.* 1824. Reprint, New York: Columbia University Press, 1941.

Iurilli, Richard. "How Do People View Video on Their Smart Phones?" *Wainscot Media Blog,* May 2, 2016. http://wainscotmedia.com/blog/people-view-videos-smartphones.

Jacobs, Lea. "The Innovation of Re-recording in the Hollywood Studios." *Film History* 24, no. 1 (March 2012): 5–34.

Jacobs, Lewis. *The Rise of the American Film.* New York: Harcourt Brace, 1939.

James, William. *Principles of Psychology.* Vol. 1. 1890. Reprint, New York: Dover, 1950.

———. *Talks to Teachers on Psychology and Students on Some of Life's Ideals.* Rockville, MD: Arc Manor Classic Reprints, 2008.

Janet Cardiff & George Bures Miller: Works from the Goetz Collection. Exhibition program. Haus der Kunst, Munich, April 13, 2012–July 8, 2012. https://hausderkunst.de/en/exhibitions/janet-cardiff-george-bures-miller-werke-aus-der-sammlung-goetz.

Jarboe, Greg. "Millennials Ensure 46% of Video Is Consumed Via Mobile." Tubular Insights, March 21, 2016, accessed May 1, 2017. http://tubularinsights.com/millennials-ensure-46-percent-video-consumed-via-mobile/.

Johnson, Claudia D. "That Guilty Third Tier: Prostitution in Nineteenth-Century American Theaters." *American Quarterly* 27, no. 5 (December 1975): 575–84.

Johnson, H. Earle. *Symphony Hall, Boston.* Boston: Little, Brown, 1950.

Johnson, James H. *Listening in Paris: A Cultural History.* Berkeley: University of California Press, 1995.

Johnson, John B. "Thermal Agitation of Electricity in Conductors." *Physical Review* 32 (1928): 97–109.

Johnson, Martin L. "The Well-Lighted Theater or the Semi-darkened Room? Transparency, Opacity and Participation in the Institution of Cinema." *Early Popular Visual Culture* 12, no. 2 (2014): 199–212.

Jowett, Garth. *Film: The Democratic Art.* Boston: Little, Brown, 1976.

Judson, Hanford C. "The Lyric Photoplay." *Moving Picture World* 8, no. 18 (May 6, 1911): 997.

Jütte, Robert. *A History of the Senses: From Antiquity to Cyberspace.* Translated by James Lynn. Cambridge: Polity Press, 2005.

Kahn, Douglas. *Noise, Water, Meat: A History of Voice, Aurality, and Sound in the Arts.* Cambridge, MA: MIT Press, 2001.

Kaiksow, Sarah A. "'Manners' Make the Man: Politeness, Chivalry, and the Construction of Masculinity, 1750–1830." *Journal of British Studies* 44, no. 2 (April 2005): 312–29.

Kasson, John. *Rudeness and Civility: Manners in 19th Century Urban America.* New York: Hill and Wang, 1990.

Katz, James E., and Mark Aakhus, eds. *Perpetual Contact: Mobile Communication, Private Talk, Public Performance*. Cambridge: Cambridge University Press, 2002.

Katz, Mark. *Capturing Sound: How Technology Has Changed Music*. Berkeley: University of California Press, 2010.

Kaye, Lewis. "The Silenced Listener: Architectural Acoustics, the Concert Hall and the Conditions of Audience." *Leonardo Music Journal* 22 (December 2012): 63–65.

Keathley, Christian. *Cinephilia and History, or the Wind in the Trees*. Bloomington: Indiana University Press, 2005.

Kelly, Caleb. *Cracked Media: The Sound of Malfunction*. Cambridge, MA: MIT Press, 2009.

———. *Sound*. Cambridge, MA: MIT Press, 2011.

Kelly, Heather. "Side Effect of Larger Smartphones: More Data Usage." CNN.com, November 19, 2013. www.cnn.com/2013/11/18/tech/mobile/phone-size-data-usage/index.html.

Kerins, Mark. *Beyond Dolby (Stereo): Cinema in the Digital Sound Age*. Bloomington: Indiana University Press, 2010.

Kim, Hyungjoon, Seongwon Park, and Hyelin Yang. "A Study on Satisfaction of Movie Viewers Watching Movies on Smartphones." *Advanced Society and Technology Letters* 67 (2014): 78–83.

Klinger, Barbara. *Beyond the Multiplex: Cinema, New Technologies, and the Home*. Berkeley: University of California Press, 2006.

———. "The New Media Aristocrats: Home Theater and the Domestic Film Experience." *Velvet Light Trap* 42 (1998): 4–19.

Kobel, Peter. *Silent Movies: The Birth of Film and the Triumph of Movie Culture*. Washington, DC: Library of Congress, 2007.

Koening, F. C. "The Moving Picture Theater." *Moving Picture World* 8, no. 13 (April 8, 1911): 762.

Koss, Juliet. "On the Limits of Empathy." *Art Bulletin* 88, no. 1 (March 2006): 139–57.

Krage, Helge. "Styles of Science and Engineering: The Case of Early Long-Distance Telephony." *Centaurus* 51, no. 3 (August 2009): 175–88.

Krehbiel, Henry Edward. *The Philharmonic Society of New York*. New York: Novello, Ewer, 1892.

Kubelka, Peter. "The Invisible Cinema." *Design Quarterly* 93 (1974): 32–36.

La Cerra, Steve. "Advanced Stereo Miking Techniques." *Electronic Musician* 29, no. 7 (July 2013): 56–64.

Langlois, Georges Patrick, and Glenn Myrent. *Henri Langlois: First Citizen of the Cinema*. New York: Prentice Hall International, 1995.

Lastra, James. "Film and the Wagnerian Aspiration: Thoughts on Sound Design and the History of the Senses." In Beck and Grajeda, *Lowering the Boom*, 123–40.

———. *Sound Technology and the American Cinema: Perception, Representation, Modernity*. New York: Columbia University Press, 2000.

"The Lay Press and the Picture." *Moving Picture World* 8, no. 2 (January 14, 1911): 70.

Lehmann, Lili. *My Pathway through Life*. Translated by Alice Benedict Seligman. New York: G. P. Putnam's Sons, 1914.

Leonard, Anne. "Picturing Listening in the Late Nineteenth Century." *Art Bulletin* 89, no. 2 (June 2007): 266–86.

Lesage, Julia. "Godard and Gorin's Left Politics, 1967–1972." *Jump Cut: A Review of Contemporary Media* 28 (1983): 51–58.

Levine, Lawrence. *Highbrow/Lowbrow: The Emergence of Cultural Hierarchy in America*. Cambridge, MA: Harvard University Press, 1988.

LoBrutto, Vincent. *Sound on Film: Interviews with Creators of Film Sound*. Westport, CT: Praeger, 1994.

Lochrie, Mark, and Paul Coulton. "Mobile Phones as Second Screen for TV, Enabling Inter-audience Interaction." Paper presented at Proceedings of the 8th International Conference on Advances in Computer Entertainment Technology, Lisbon, Portugal, 2011.

"The Lost Gallery." *Moving Picture World* 9, no. 3 (July 29, 1911): 397.

Lowrey, Annie. "Advertisers Seek a 'Second Screen' Connection with Viewers." *New York Times*, May 4, 2014. www.nytimes.com/2014/05/05/business/media/advertisers-seek-a-second-screen-connection-with-viewers.html?_r=0.

Luxenberg, Stan. "Education at AT&T." *Change* 10, no. 11 (December 1978): 26–35.

Lynch, David. *Catching the Big Fish*. New York: Penguin, 2016.

———. "Waxing Lyrical: David Lynch on His New Passion—and Why He May Never Make Another Movie." Interview by Tim Walker, *Independent*, June 23, 2013. https://www.independent.co.uk/arts-entertainment/music/features/waxing-lyrical-david-lynch-on-his-new-passion-and-why-he-may-never-make-another-movie-8665457.html.

MacDonald, Scott. *Art in Cinema: Documents toward a History of the Film Society*. Philadelphia: Temple University Press, 2006.

———. *Canyon Cinema: The Life and Times of an Independent Film Distributor*. Berkeley: University of California Press, 2008.

———. *Cinema 16: Documents toward a History of the Film Society*. Philadelphia: Temple University Press, 2003.

Madison, Frank H. "Springfield, Ill. Picture Shows." *Moving Picture World* 7, no. 25 (December 17, 1910): 1420.

Magee, Bryan. *Wagner and Philosophy*. New York: Penguin Books, 2001.

Marshall, Wayne. "Treble Culture." In *The Oxford Handbook of Mobile Music Studies*, vol. 2, edited by Sumanth Gopinath and Jason Stanyek, 43–76. New York: Oxford University Press, 2014.

Martin, Clyde. "Working the Sound Effects." *Moving Picture World* 9, no. 11 (September 23, 1911): 873.

Marvin, Carolyn. *When Old Technologies Were New: Thinking about Electric Communication in the Late Nineteenth Century*. Oxford: Oxford University Press, 1988.

Marzola, Luci. "A Society Apart: The Early Years of the Society of Motion Picture Engineers." *Film History* 28, no. 4 (2016): 1–28.

Mason, C. A., and J. Moir. "Acoustics of Cinema Auditoria." *Journal of the Institution of Electrical Engineers* 88, no. 2 (February 1941): 93–96.

Massa, Frank. "Some Personal Recollections of Early Experiences on the New Frontier of Electroacoustics during the Late 1920s and Early 1930s." *Journal of the Acoustical Society of America* 77, no. 4 (April 1965): 1296–1302.

May, Lary L. *Screening Out the Past: The Birth of Mass Culture and the Motion Picture Industry*. New York: Oxford University Press, 1980.

McCarthy, Anna. *Ambient Television: Visual Culture and Public Space*. Durham, NC: Duke University Press, 2001.

McClintock, Pamela. "Box Office 104: Moviegoing Hits Two Decade Low." *Hollywood Reporter*, December 31, 2014. www.hollywoodreporter.com /news/box-office-2014-moviegoing-hits-760766.

McConachie, Bruce. "New York Opera-Going, 1825–1850." *American Music* 6, no. 2 (Summer 1988): 181–93.

McGuire, Laura M. "A Movie House in Space and Time: Frederick Kiesler's Film Arts Guild Cinema, New York, 1929." *Studies in the Decorative Arts* 14, no. 2 (Spring 2007): 45–78.

McQuade, Jas. A. "Chicago Letter." *Moving Picture World* 11, no. 12 (March 23, 1912): 1056.

Mead, Bill. "A New Way to Listen." *Film Journal International* 115, no. 9 (September 2012): 56–58.

Mehta, Madan, James Johnson, and Jorge Rocafort. *Architectural Acoustics: Principles and Design*. New York: Prentice Hall, 1999.

Metz, Christian. *The Imaginary Signifier: Psychoanalysis and the Cinema*. Bloomington: Indiana University Press, 1986.

Michelson, Annette. "Gnosis and Iconoclasm: A Case Study in Cinephilia." *October* 83 (Winter 1998): 3–18.

Miller, Wesley C. "Basis of Motion Picture Sound." In *Motion Picture Sound Engineering*, edited by AMPAS Research Council, 1–10. New York: D. Van Nostrand, 1938.

Millington, G. "A Modified Formula for Reverberation." *Journal of the Acoustical Society of America* 4, no. 1 (1932): 69–82.

Millman, S., ed. *A History of Science and Engineering in the Bell System*. New York: Bell Laboratories, 1983.

Mills, Mara. "Deafening: Noise and the Engineering of Communication in the Telephone System." *Grey Room* 43 (Spring 2001): 118–43.

Mitchell, William J. *Placing Words: Symbols, Space, and the City*. Cambridge, MA: MIT University Press, 2005.

Modigliani, Andre. "Embarrassment and Embarrassibility." *Sociometry* 31 (1968): 313–26.

Morgan, Marjorie. *Manners, Morals and Class in England*. New York: St. Martin's Press, 1994.

Morrison, Geoffrey. "The Future of Surround Sound." *Sound and Vision* 77, no. 6 (October 2012): 20–25.

Morton, David L., Jr. *Sound Recording: The Life Story of a Technology*. Baltimore: Johns Hopkins University Press, 2004.

Mosso, Angelo. *Fatigue*. Translated by Margaret Drummond and William Blackley Drummond. New York: S. Sonnenschein, 1906.

Mueller, John Henry. *The American Symphony Orchestra: A Social History of Musical Taste*. Bloomington: Indiana University Press, 1951.

Murtaugh, John, and Sarah Harris. *Cast the First Stone*. New York: McGraw-Hill, 1957.

Musser, Charles. *The Emergence of Cinema: The American Screen to 1907*. Berkeley: University of California Press, 1994.

———. "Toward a History of Screen Practice." *Quarterly Review of Film Studies* 9, no. 1 (1984): 59–69.

MWW Group. "Smartphone vs. Tablet: What the Research Says." Summer 2012. https://www.slideshare.net/mwwgroupNY/2014-smartphone-vstablet. Also available at https://issuu.com/mwwgroup/docs/messaging-smartphone-vs-tablet-based-vide/7.

Nasaw, David. *Going Out*. New York: Basic Books, 1992.

Nielsen Company. "The Nielsen Total Audience Q1 Report." 2017. www.nielsen.com/content/dam/corporate/us/en/reports-downloads/2017-reports/total-audience-report-q1-2017.pdf.

———. "State of the Media: Cross-Platform Report, Q1 2012." September 11, 2012. www.nielsen.com/us/en/insights/reports/2012/state-of-the-media--cross-platform-report-q1-2012.html.

———. "The U.S. Digital Consumer Report." February 10, 2014. www.nielsen.com/us/en/insights/reports/2014/the-us-digital-consumer-report.html.

Noble, David F. *America by Design: Science, Technology, and the Rise of Corporate Capitalism*. New York: Knopf, 1977.

"Observations by Our Man about Town." *Moving Picture World* 8, no. 12 (March 25, 1911): 643.

O'Hehir, Andrew. "Beyond the Multiplex: Steve Buscemi and Sienna Miller Team Up for a Trashy Take on Celebrity Culture. Plus: Mind-Blowing Apocalyptic Anime and Kim Ki-duk's Fun with Monsters." Salon.com, July 12, 2007. www.salon.com/2007/07/12/btm_115/.

Olsson, Jan. *Los Angeles before Hollywood: Journalism and American Film Culture, 1905 to 1915*. New York: Columbia University Press, 2009.

Orgeron, Devin, and Marsha Orgeron. *Learning with the Lights Off: Educational Film in the United States*. New York: Oxford University Press, 2012.

Oudart, Jean-Pierre. "Cinema and Suture." *Screen* 18, no. 4 (1977–78): 35–47. Originally published in *Cahiers du Cinema* (April and May 1969), nos. 211 and 212.

Parnham, Peter. "Surrounded by Sound." *Onfilm* 29, no. 6 (June 2012): 20–22.

Patterson, Joseph Medill. "The Nickelodeons: The Poor Man's Elementary Course in the Drama." In *Spellbound in Darkness*, edited by George Pratt, 46–52. Greenwich, CT: New York Graphic Society, 1973. Originally published in *Saturday Evening Post*, November 23, 1907.

Patton, Phil. "Humming Off Key for Two Decades." *New York Times,* July 29, 1999. http://partners.nytimes.com/library/tech/99/07/circuits/articles/29walk.html.

Peiss, Kathy. *Cheap Amusements: Working Women and Leisure in Turn-of-the-Century New York*. Philadelphia: Temple University Press, 1986.

Peterson, Jennifer Lynn. *Education in the School of Dreams: Travelogues and Early Nonfiction Film*. Durham, NC: Duke University Press, 2013.

Philips, Stephen. "Introjection and Projection: Frederick Kiesler and His Dream Machine." In *Surrealism and Architecture*, edited by Thomas Mical, 140–55. New York: Routledge, 2005.

"Plucky (Akron) Exhibitor Wins His Case: Ch. 1: To Prison in Wagon." *Moving Picture World* 1, no. 9 (April 6, 1907).

Polan, Dana. *Scenes of Instruction: The Beginnings of the U.S. Study of Film*. Berkeley: University of California Press, 2007.

Potwin, C. C. "The Control of Sound in Theaters and Preview Rooms." *Journal of the Society of Motion Picture Engineers* 35, no. 8 (August 1940): 111–25.

Potwin, C. C., and J. P. Maxfield. "A Modern Concept of Acoustical Design." *Journal of the Acoustical Society of America* 11 (July 1939): 48–55.

Potwin, C. C., and Ben Schlanger. "Coordinating Acoustics and Architecture in the Design of the Motion Picture Theater." *Journal of the Society of Motion Picture Engineers* 32 (February 1939): 156–67.

Rabinovitz, Lauren. *For the Love of Pleasure: Women, Movies, and Culture in Turn-of-the-Century Chicago*. New Brunswick, NJ: Rutgers University Press, 1998.

Reich, Leonard S. *The Making of American Industrial Research: Science and Business at GE and Bell, 1876–1926*. Cambridge: Cambridge University Press, 2002.

———. *Radio Electronics and the Development of Industrial Research in the Bell System*. Baltimore: Johns Hopkins University Press, 1977.

Research Council Papers. Margaret Herrick Library Special Collections, Academy of Motion Picture Arts and Sciences, Beverly Hills, CA.

Ribot, Theodule. *Diseases of the Will*. Translated by Merwin-Marie Snell. Chicago: Open Court, 1894.

Richard, Jacques. *Henri Langlois: Phantom of the Cinémathèque*. Directed by Jacques Richard. DVD. New York: Kino Video, 2006.

Roberts, Helen L. *Putnam's Handbook of Etiquette*. New York: G. P. Putnam's Sons, 1913.

Roberts, Jason. "The Awkward Ages: Film Criticism, Technological Change, and Cinephilia." PhD diss., Northwestern University, 2015.

Rosen, Philip, ed. *Narrative, Apparatus, Ideology: A Film Theory Reader*. New York: Columbia University Press, 1986.

Rosenbaum, Jonathan. *Movie Wars: How Hollywood and the Media Limit What Movies We Can See*. Chicago: Chicago Review Press, 2002.

Rotundo, E. Anthony. *American Manhood: Transformations in Masculinity from the Revolution to the Modern Era*. New York: Basic Books, 1993.

———. "Learning about Manhood: Gender Ideal and the Middle-Class Family in Nineteenth-Century America." In *Manliness and Morality: Middle-Class Masculinity in Britain and America, 1800–1940*, edited by J. A. Mangan and James Walvin, 35–51. New York: St. Martin's Press, 1987.

Roud, Richard. *A Passion for Cinema: Henri Langlois and the Cinémathèque Francaise*. New York: Viking Press, 1983.

Royle, Edwin Milton. "The Vaudeville Theatre." *Scribner's Magazine*, October 1899.

Russell, Charles Edward. *The American Orchestra and Theodore Thomas.* New York: Doubleday, Page, 1927.

Salt, Barry. *Film Style and Technology: History and Analysis.* New York: Starword, 1983.

Sanders, Lise Shapiro. "'Indecent Incentives to Vice': Regulating Films and Audience Behavior from the 1890s to the 1910s." In *Young and Innocent? The Cinema in Britain, 1896–1930*, edited by Andrew Higson, 111–27. Exeter: University of Exeter Press, 2002.

Sands, Pierre. *Historical Study of the Academy of Motion Picture Arts and Sciences.* Manchester, NH: Ayer, 1972.

Sangani, Kris. "The Vastness of Sound." *Engineering and Technology* 8, no. 6 (July 2013): 78–79.

Sargent, Epes Winthrop. "Advertising for Exhibitors." *Moving Picture World* 9, no. 11 (September 23, 1911): 876.

Schafer, R. Murray. *The Soundscape: Our Sonic Environment and the Tuning of the World.* Rochester, VT: Destiny Books, 1993.

———. *The Tuning of the World.* New York: Random House, 1977.

Schiffer, Brian. *The Portable Radio in American Life.* Tucson: University of Arizona Press, 1991.

Schivelbusch, Wolfgang. *Disenchanted Night: The Industrialization of Light in the Nineteenth Century.* Translated by Angela Davies. Berkeley: University of California Press, 1988.

Schlanger, Ben. "Advancement of Motion Picture Theater Design." *Journal of the Society of Motion Picture Engineers* 50 (1948): 303–13.

Schlesinger, Arthur M. *Learning How to Behave: A Historical Study of American Etiquette Books.* New York: Macmillan, 1947.

Schloss, Joseph, and Bill Bahng Boyer. "Urban Echoes: The Boombox and Sonic Mobility in the 1980s." In *The Oxford Handbook of Mobile Music Studies*, vol. 1, edited by Sumanth Gopinath and Jason Stanyek, 399–412. New York: Oxford University Press, 2014.

Schönhammer, Rainer. "The Walkman and the Primary World of the Senses." *Phenomenology + Pedagogy* 7 (1989): 127–44.

Schopenhauer, Arthur. *Studies in Pessimism.* Translated by T. Bailey Saunders. New York: Cosimo Classics, 2007.

Schottky, Walter. "Small-Shot Effect and Flicker Effect." *Physical Review* 28 (1926): 74–103.

Schwarzer, Mitchell. "Schopenhauer's Theory of Architecture." In *Schopenhauer, Philosophy, and the Arts*, edited by Dale Jacquette, 277–98. New York: Cambridge University Press, 1996.

Sconce, Jeffrey. "Cult Cinema: A Critical Symposium." *Cineaste* 34, no. 1 (Winter 2008): 48.

Scott, Andrew, and Ian Woodward. "Living with Design Objects: A Qualitative Study of iPod Relationships." *Design Principles and Practice: An International Journal* 5, no. 6 (2011): 499–508.

Sennett, Richard. *Authority*. New York: Knopf, 1980.

———. *The Fall of Public Man*. New York: Norton, 1976.

Sergi, Gianluca. *The Dolby Era: Film Sound in Contemporary Hollywood*. Manchester, UK: Manchester University Press, 2005.

———. "The Sonic Playground: Hollywood Cinema and Its Listeners." In *Hollywood Spectatorship: Changing Perceptions of Cinema Audiences*, edited by Richard Maltby and Melvyn Stokes, 121–51. London: British Film Institute, 2001.

Serres, Michel. "Noise." *Substance* 12, no. 3 (1983): 48–60.

Shambu, Girish. *The New Cinephilia*. Montreal: Caboose Books, 2014.

———. "Taken Up by Waves: The Experience of New Cinephilia." Project: New Cinephilia, May 23, 2011. http://projectcinephilia.mubi.com/2011/05/23/taken-up-by-waves-the-experience-of-new-cinephilia/.

Silverman, Kaja. *The Subject of Semiotics*. New York: Oxford University Press, 1983.

———. *The Threshold of the Visible World*. New York: Routledge, 1996.

Singer, Ben. "Manhattan Nickelodeons: New Data on Audiences and Exhibitors." *Cinema Journal* 34, no. 3 (Spring 1996): 5–35.

Sitney, Sky. "The Search for the Invisible Cinema." *Grey Room* 19 (Spring 2005): 102–13.

Skaggs, Carmen Trammell. *Overtones of Opera in American Literature from Whitman to Wharton*. Baton Rouge: Louisiana State University Press, 2010.

Sklar, Robert. "A Passion for Films: Henri Langlois and the Cinematheque Francaise." *Cineaste* 14, no. 2 (1985): 52.

Small, Christopher. *Musicking: The Meanings of Performing and Listening*. Middletown, CT: Wesleyan University Press, 2011.

Smilor, Raymond. "Cacophony at 34th and 6th: The Noise Problem in America, 1900–1930." *American Studies* 18, no. 1 (1971): 23–28.

———. "Toward an Environmental Perspective: The Anti-noise Campaign, 1893–1932." In *Pollution and Reform in American Cities, 1870–1930*, edited by Martin V. Melosi, 135–51. Austin: University of Texas Press, 1980.

Smith, Jacob. *Spoken Word: Postwar American Phonograph Cultures*. Berkeley: University of California Press, 2011.

———. "Tearing Speech to Pieces: Voice Technologies of the 1940s." *Music, Sound, and the Moving Image* 2, no. 2 (Fall 2008): 183–206.

———. *Vocal Tracks: Performance and Sound Media*. Berkeley: University of California Press, 2008.

Smith, Nick. "The Splinter in Your Ear: Noise as the Semblance of Critique." *Culture, Theory and Critique* 46, no. 1 (2005): 43–59.

Sontag, Susan. "The Decay of Cinema." *New York Times Magazine*, February 25, 1996. https://www.nytimes.com/books/00/03/12/specials/sontag-cinema.html.

Soper, Taylor. "Netflix Still King of Streaming Video, but Amazon Gaining Market Share." *Geekwire*, March 12, 2015. www.geekwire.com/2015/netflix-still-king-of-streaming-video-but-amazon-gaining-market-share/.

Spangler, Todd. "Americans Are Watching Less Traditional TV as Smartphone Media Usage Booms." *Variety*, June 27, 2016. http://variety.com/2016/digital/news/live-tv-declining-smartphone-boom-nielsen-1201804202/.

Spigel, Lynn. "Designing the Smart House: Posthuman Domesticity and Conspicuous Production." *European Journal of Cultural Studies* 8, no. 4 (November 2005): 403–26.

———. *Make Room for TV: Television and the Family Ideal in Postwar America.* Chicago: University of Chicago Press, 1992.

———. "Object Lessons for the Media Home: From Storagewall to Invisible Design." *Public Culture* 24, no. 3 (2012): 535–76.

———. "Yesterday's Future, Tomorrow's Home." *Emergences: Journal for the Study of Media and Composite Cultures* 11, no. 1 (May 2001): 29–49.

"The Stage." *New York Mirror,* October 1, 1831, 100.

Stamp, Shelley. *Movie-Struck Girls: Women and Motion Picture Culture after the Nickelodeon.* Princeton, NJ: Princeton University Press, 2000.

Stelter, Brian. "Netflix Hits Milestone and Raises Its Sights." *New York Times,* October 21, 2013. www.nytimes.com/2013/10/22/business/media/netflix-hits-subscriber-milestone-as-shares-soar.html?_r=0.

———. "Youths Are Watching, but Less Often on TV." *New York Times,* February 8, 2012. www.nytimes.com/2012/02/09/business/media/young-people-are-watching-but-less-often-on-tv.html?pagewanted=all.

Stern, Seymour. "An Aesthetic of the Cinema House: A Statement of the Principles Which Constitute the Philosophy and the Format of the Ideal Film Theatre." *Spectator* 18 (Spring/Summer 1998): 30–31. Originally published in *National Board of Review Magazine* 2, no. 5 (May 1927).

Sterne, Jonathan. *The Audible Past: The Cultural Origins of Sound Reproduction.* Durham, NC: Duke University Press, 2003.

———. *MP3: The Meaning of a Format.* Durham, NC: Duke University Press, 2012.

Stockbridge, Frank Parker. "How Far Off Is That German Gun? How Sixty-Three German Guns Were Located by Sound Waves Alone in a Single Day." *Popular Science,* December 1930, 39.

Szczepaniak-Gillece, Jocelyn. "Machines for Seeing: Cinematic and Architectural Constructions of Mid-century American Spectatorship." PhD diss., Northwestern University, 2013.

Talmadge, Thomas DeWitt. *Sports That Kill.* New York: Funk and Wagnall, 1875.

Taylor, Richard, and Ian Christie. "1896–1921: Introduction." In *The Film Factory: Russian and Soviet Cinema in Documents.* New York: Routledge, 1994.

"Tech Specs and Tips." *Film Journal International* 116, no. 5 (May 2013): 66–67.

"The Theater 'Gods.'" *Moving Picture World* 8, no. 26 (July 1, 1911): 1498.

Thomas, Theodore. *A Musical Autobiography I.* Chicago: A. A. McClurg, 1905.

Thompson, Emily. *The Soundscape of Modernity: Architectural Acoustics and the Culture of Listening in America, 1900–1933.* Cambridge, MA: MIT Press, 2004.

Trollope, Francis. *Domestic Manners of the Americans.* 1839. Reprint, [United States]: Reprint Service Corp., 1993.

Tsivian, Yuri. *Early Cinema in Russia and its Cultural Reception.* Translated by Alan Bodger. New York: Routledge, 1994.

Turnbull, Reverend Robert. "The Theatre, in Its Influence upon Literature, Morals, and Religion." In *The Christian Review, vol. II,* edited by James D. Knowles, 82–87. Boston: Gould, Kendall, and Lincoln, 1837.

"The Variety of Moving Picture Audiences." *Moving Picture World* 13, no. 5 (September 25, 1909): 406.

von Helmholtz, Hermann. *On the Sensations of Tone as a Physiological Basis for a Theory of Music.* London: Longmans Green, 1885.

Wagner, Richard. *Art, Life, and Theories of Richard Wagner, Selected from His Writings.* Translated by Edward L. Burlingame. New York: Henry Holt, 1904.

Warren, Christina. "When Did the 'Second Screen' Become a Thing?" Mashable.com, May 2, 2103. http://mashable.com/2013/05/02/second-screen/.

Wasson, Haidee. *Museum Movies: The Museum of Modern Art and the Birth of Cinema.* Berkeley: University of California Press, 2005.

Watson, Nick. "Twelve Years of Digital Cinema." Part 2 of "The Evolution of Cinema Sound: From Film to Digital Cinema and Beyond." *Cinema Technology* 25, no. 2 (2012): 54–59.

Weber, William. "Did People Listen in the 18th Century?" *Early Music* 25, no. 4 (November 1997): 678–91.

Webster, Tom. "The Podcast Consumer 2016." Edison Research/Triton Digital, May 2016. www.edisonresearch.com/wp-content/uploads/2016/05/The-Podcast-Consumer-2016.pdf.

White, Richard Grant. "Opera in New York." *Century* 23 (1882): 869.

White, Rob. "Velvet Boxes and Reliquaries." *Film Quarterly* 61, no. 1 (Fall 2007): 92–93.

Wilinsky, Barbara. *Sure Seaters: The Emergence of Art House Cinema.* Minneapolis: University of Minnesota Press, 2001.

Wolff, Michael F. "The Secret Six-Month Project: Why Texas Instruments Decided to Put the First Transistor Radio on the Market by Christmas 1954 and How It Was Accomplished." *IEEE Spectrum,* December 1985, 64–69.

"World Reviewer." "The Picture the Audience Likes." *Moving Picture World* 8, no. 6 (February 11, 1911): 310.

Wundt, Wilhelm. *Outlines of Psychology.* Translated by Charles Hubbard Judd. New York: G. E. Stechert, 1907.

———. *Principles of Physiological Psychology.* Translated by Edward Bradford Titchener. New York: Macmillan, 1904.

Wyss, Beat. "Ragnarök of Illusion: Richard Wagner's 'Mystical Abyss' at Bayreuth." Translated by Denise Bratton. *October* 54 (Autumn 1990): 57–78.

Xiao, Zhiwei. "Movie House Etiquette Reform in Early-Twentieth-Century China." *Modern China* 32, no. 4 (October 2006): 513–36.

Yeang, Chen-Pang. "Tubes, Randomness, and Brownian Motions: Or, How Engineers Learned to Start Worrying about Electronic Noise." *Archive for History of Exact Sciences* 65 (2011): 437–70.

Yue, Genevieve. "Cinephilia, Love, and Being Caught Off-Guard." Project: New Cinephilia Online Roundtable Two. August 6, 2011, http://projectcinephilia.mubi.com/category/online-roundtable-2/.

Index

electro-acoustical industry, 63. *See also* Bell
  Labs/AT&T
electro-acoustics industry and AMPAS
  Bell/AT&T, 55–56, 64–65, 68–69,
    187n68
  conflict with, 69
  as danger, 70
  knowledge exchange with, 68
  meetings with, 71
  as models, 55–56, 61, 64–65, 68, 72
  relationships with, 65, 68, 75–76
  research methods, use of, 54
  School of Sound Fundamentals, 78
Elias, Norbert, 28, 173n73
engineers. *See* sound technicians
eroticism, 92
etiquette
  bodily control as, 27–29
  and gender, 29, 173n76–77
  manuals of, 20–21, 26–28
  of mobile listening and viewing,
    157–58
  and noise, 26–27, 29, 50, 173n74
  and public spaces, 27
  as self-effacement, 28, 50
  as social control, 25–26

Festspielhaus. See Bayreuth opera house
figure-ground reversals, 140, 206n78
Five Cornered Agreement, the, 53
Fleming, N., 99–101, 196n79, 196n82–84
Fried, Michael, 49, 87–88, 96, 191n10

gallery gods, 45–47, 50
Garnier, Charles, 89, 98
Gaudreault, Andre, 23–24, 170n34
Gay, Peter, 92–93, 96
gender, 29, 173n76–77, 178n153. *See
  also* dating culture
Gergen, Kenneth, 139, 141–42
goals, author's, 2–4, 6
Gorky, Maxim, 36–39, 178n57
ground noise, 74
Gunning, Tom, 21–24

Hansen, Miriam, 22–24, 42, 48, 169n18
harmony, 38, 178n58
headphones, 139–40, 206n78. *See also*
  earbuds
hearing, studies of, 96–97
Hegarty, Paul, 8–9
Helmholtz, Hermann von, 97
home viewing, 119–20, 142–43, 146–47
Hosokawa, Shuhei, 138, 140

incidental noise, 74
industrial research, 59–60, 184n17
The Invisible Cinema (Kubelka)
  acoustic design of, 85–86, 102–5, 107
  Brakhage on, 85, 107
  goals of, 103–4
  Kelman on, 86, 107
  legacy of, 86
  light in, 197n93
  overviews of, 85–86, 102–3
  photographs of, *103–4*
  scholarship on, 102–3
  and sex, 107
  spectator isolation in, 105, 107
  spectator sounds, presence of, 107

"Jackass Music," 33, 43–44
Jewett, Frank B., 63–64

Kahn, Douglas, 8–9
Kasson, John F., 25–26, 28–29, 31, 33,
  171n42, 175n96, 177n133
Kaye, Lewis, 90–91, 192n25
Kelly, Caleb, 8–9
Kelman, Ken, 86, 107
Klinger, Barbara, 142, 146–47
Kubelka, Peter, 85–86, 102–4, 105, 107. *See
  also* The Invisible Cinema

Langlois, Henri, 133–35
Lasky, Jesse M., 68, 78
Lastra, James, 57–58, 183n7–8, 194n49
laughter, 37
Lessing, Theodor, 27
Levine, Lawrence, 31–32, 34–35
listening. *See also* mobile listening and
  viewing; new listening
  convergence of, 137, 155, 159
  forms of, as shifting, 10
  to music, 157
  as social experience, 89–90, 191n16
Lynch, David, 147–49, 206n107

Marzola, Luci, 58–60, 184n18
Mayer, Louis B., 68
McConachie, Bruce, 33–34
media technologies, 142
methods, author's, 2–6, 60–61, 184n23
Metz, Christian, 108–9, 198n110
middle class, the, 25
middle class etiquette
  bodily control as, 27–29
  and gender, 29, 173n76–77
  manuals for, 20–21, 26–28

Tsivian, Yuri, 37–38
Twitter, 143

video, short-form, 121, 126, 128, 131,
146
video games, 156–57
vision, studies of, 96–97
visual absorption, 87, 191n9–10

Wagner, Richard
and acoustics, architectural, 98
Bayreuth opera house, 92–96, 99
and cinema surround sound, 194n49
and new listening, 90–91

and Schopenhauer, 94
Walkman, the, 122, 138–41
women
and cinema houses, early, 16–17
and dating culture, 41–42, 180n180
Lily Limpwrist, 43–44
and musical accompaniment, 38, 40
prostitution, 37–39, 42, 44–45, 181n206
working, 179n175
Woods, Frank, 55, 68, 71, 187n68
Wundt, Wilhelm, 91, 192n27
Wyss, Beat, 89, 95

Yue, Genevieve, 150–51, 209n113